KICK BACK IN THE KITCHEN
COOKBOOK

A Collection of family recipes
from Sun City Texas

P & P PUBLISHING
temple, texas

First Printing 2005

5,000 copies

Copyright © 2005

ISBN: 0-9760462-1-0

For additional copies, send $19.95 plus $3.50 shipping (Texas residents add $1.93 sales tax) to:

P & P Publishing
3802 Antelope Trail
Temple, TX 76504

Order by phone: 888-458-1229
or on line: www.pandppublishing.com

Cover and book design by Barbara Jezek, Austin

Printed in China

CONTENTS

4

ACKNOWLEDGMENTS

A common bond that brings all people together is FOOD. No matter our heritage, we all bring with us foods that are unique to our culture. This book is a collection of recipes submitted by the residents of Sun City Texas in Georgetown. Some of the recipes were handed down to us by family members and dear friends, and some are personal favorites.

We wish to express our sincere thanks to all who contributed to our cookbook. The response has been heartwarming and overwhelming. We hope you will discover some new favorites here or maybe find an old favorite you may have forgotten.

A special thanks to Bob Lilly for giving us permission to use his beautiful artwork. And our thanks to Sondra Carlton, Rob McDaniel and Jim Romine for their support of this project.

Committee Members:

Lucy Pate

Edie Blood

Zina Graalfs

Carol Ryan

ABOUT THE PHOTOGRAPHER

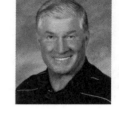

Bob Lilly, one of Texas' most talented football greats, was the first Dallas Cowboy inducted into the Pro Football Hall of Fame in Canton, Ohio. His ability is legendary and he is a greatly respected athlete — who also happens to be a multifaceted photographer. A resident of Sun City Texas, Bob has shared some of his favorite photos with the cookbook committee for inclusion in this salute to easy Texas living and Kickin' Back in the Kitchen. We are privileged to be able to include his photographic interpretation of life in Texas — the way it used to be.

In the foreword to his book, Bob Lilly *Reflections*, Sam Blair, sports writer for the Dallas Morning News and Bob's co-author writes:

"Lilly's career as a photographer began in a wonderfully logical way. As a senior at Texas Christian University in 1960, he was a member of the Kodak All-American team. With the honor came a trip to New York to appear on the Ed Sullivan television show, a round of dinners and parties and a gift, a camera.

Lilly began snapping pictures and soon was hooked. Photography became his special love. The No. 1 draft choice of the year-old Dallas Cowboys, he signed a contract and soon had more money to indulge that love. He bought more cameras and equipment and by the time he reported to his first Cowboy training camp he was shooting pictures wherever he went.

In *Bob Lilly Reflections*, the most honored player in the club's history takes you back to the years when the Cowboys grew from a shaky expansion team to Super Bowl champions. His photos and his words capture that era when watching the Cowboy games first became a national pastime, the beginning of "America's Team."

Bob and his wife Ann have four grown children, and eleven grandchildren. His photographs are available on his website: *www.boblilly.com*

SUN CITY TEXAS

Nestled in the lovely rolling hills of Central Texas, Sun City Texas is one of Del Webb's loveliest communities. It is an active adult community for people 55 and better. Sun City Texas residents take full advantage of the lovely Texas climate, residing in easy to care for, stylish homes nestled among golf courses, walking and jogging trails, club houses and tennis courts.

Discover the many cultural and recreational opportunities at Sun City Texas, where residents can nurture all of their interests and develop totally new ones. A large variety of clubs and activities are always available at the multi-million-dollar Village Center. From gardening and painting to tennis and fishing, there's a special interest club for every enthusiast. Included are a fine art studio and woodshop. Sun City Texas is only a few miles north of Austin.

Visit the 16,000 square foot Recreation Center, which features a 6-lane indoor and resort-style outdoor pool, a state-of-the-art fitness center with classes from aerobics to yoga and everything in between! For the outdoor enthusiast, Sun City Texas is a breath of fresh air. Enjoy jogging paths, plus tennis and bocce courts, all surrounded by the tranquil beauty on the Texas Hill Country. Or take a swing at either 18-hole championship golf course. It has been said, that Legacy Hills and White Wing are two of the best golf courses in Texas. Both provide enjoyment and challenge for beginners and experts alike, as well as offering a multi-tiered practice facility, realistic target greens, and a complete short game practice area. Our golf staff specializes in corporate and group tournaments and outings. Full-service dining and banquet facilities are available for additional enjoyment.

FOR INFORMATION VISIT: *www.delwebb.com* and take a virtual tour of the many Del Webb communities.

INTRODUCTION

Kickin Back in the Kitchen showcases the best cooks in Sun City Texas. Who are these folks and where did they come from? How did they get to Texas and what did they bring along with them?

Kickin back is a Texas term — it means taking it easy, sharing a meal or a drink, having fun in what ever way suits you. One of the best ways to Kick Back is to share food — and for folks lucky enough to live in this diverse community, that food is rich in heritage, and long on taste and comfort.

Blessed with nearly year round great weather, Central Texans can "Kick It Back" just about anywhere — from their own patios to the golf course, the tennis courts, the swimming pool, the lake, and of course their friends living rooms. A Sun City resident who is invited to stop by for a drink might be treated to cocktails from another country — or an invitation to "stay for supper" might mean tasting a 100-year old recipe for a special family treat. Sun City residents have come to Texas from nearly every state and represent diverse professional and personal backgrounds, yet they reflect the heart of Texas — hospitality. Their willingness to include new folks in their lives and to share old traditions, has created new extended families and an ever growing circle of friends. This cookbook is a result of their willingness to share all of that with you.

Enjoy!

ICE

APPETIZERS

&

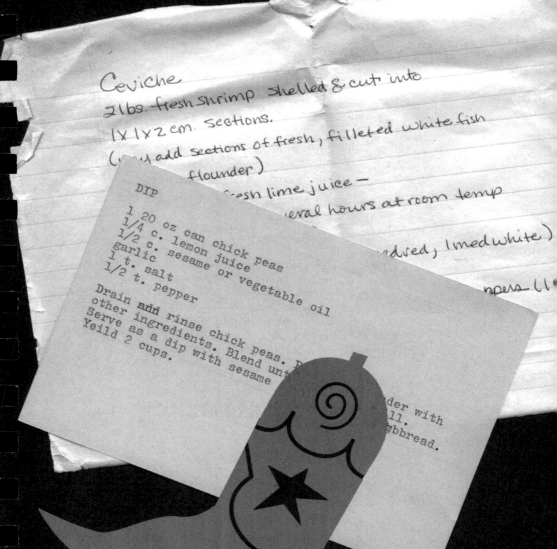

Ceviche

2 lbs. fresh Shrimp shelled & cut into
1 x 1 x 2 cm. sections.
(may add sections of fresh, filleted white fish
        flounder)
        fresh lime juice —
        several hours at room temp
                        (dried, 1 med white)
                        ppers (1

DIP

1 20 oz can chick peas
1/4 c. lemon juice
1/2 c. sesame or vegetable oil
garlic
1 t. salt
1/2 t. pepper

Drain add rinse chick peas. B
other ingredients. Blend unt
Serve as a dip with sesame
Yeild 2 cups.

                        der with
                        ll.
                        bbread.

BEVERAGES

Appetizers

BRAUNSCHWEIGER BALL I

- 1 (16-ounce) can pink braunschweiger (liver sausage)
- 2 tablespoons sour cream or 1 (3-ounce) package cream cheese, softened
- 2–3 teaspoons prepared mustard (wet)
- 1–2 teaspoons horseradish (in jar, pure, not sauce)
- Minced parsley flakes
- Wheat Thin™ crackers

Have sausage and cream cheese at room temperature. Combine sausage, cream cheese (or sour cream), mustard and horseradish. Taste and add more seasonings as desired. Shape into a ball, wrap in waxed paper and chill. Before serving, remove waxed paper and roll ball in parsley flakes. Place on plate. Use a canapé knife to serve with Wheat Thins™. Serves 10-12.

Mary Lee Whipple, Texas

Great spread on crackers for the holidays or for any occasion.

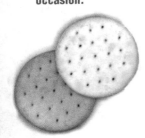

BRAUNSCHWEIGER BALL II

- 1 pound braunschweiger
- 2 (8-ounce) packages cream cheese
- ¼ cup mayonnaise
- 2 teaspoons Worcestershire sauce
- 2–4 drops Tabasco® sauce
- ⅓ cup chopped dill pickle
- ¼ cup chopped onion

Cream braunschweiger and cream cheese until smooth. Add remaining ingredients and mix well. Form into balls and roll in chopped nuts or parsley flakes. Chill. Will keep 4 to 5 days in the refrigerator. Can also be frozen. Makes 3 medium balls.

Michael and Armeda Pauken, Ohio

JUNE'S CHEESE BALL

1 (8-ounce) package cream cheese, softened
2 cups grated sharp Cheddar cheese
1 teaspoon Worcestershire sauce
¾ teaspoon dry mustard
⅛–¼ teaspoon cayenne pepper
⅛ teaspoon garlic powder
Chopped pecans and parsley

Mix cheeses together by hand or with food processor. Add remaining ingredients (except chopped pecans and parsley). Mix well. Form into a ball. Refrigerate 2 hours or more. Before serving, roll ball in chopped nuts and parsley. Serve with multi-grain crackers.

June Isgitt, Texas

CHEESE BALL

2 (10-ounce) packages sharp cracker barrel cheese,
    shredded
¼ teaspoon cayenne pepper
¾ cup beer
1 (3-ounce) package cream cheese, softened
2 tablespoons soft margarine

Combine all ingredients and form into a ball. Allow to set ½ hour or more. Coat with 1 cup chopped walnuts or pecans.

Jan Whittaker, California

PLAINS CHEESE RING

1 pound grated Cheddar cheese
1 cup Hellmann's mayonnaise
½ cup finely chopped onion
1 cup finely chopped pecans
Cayenne pepper

Combine all ingredients. Shape into a ring. Fill center of ring with strawberry preserves. Serve with crackers.

Karen Pevoto, Texas

This recipe can be prepared without freezing. Large spinach balls can also be served as a vegetable side dish.

SPINACH BALLS

2 (10-ounce) packages chopped spinach

2 cups Pepperidge Farm stuffing mix

1 cup minced onion flakes

6 eggs (or 1½ cups Egg Beaters)

¾ cup butter, melted

½ cup Parmesan cheese, grated

1 tablespoon garlic salt

1 teaspoon pepper

½ teaspoon thyme

Cook spinach and drain well. In a large bowl, combine all ingredients, mixing well. Chill until workable. Form balls about 1-inch in diameter. Freeze. Thaw for 15 minutes. Bake in a 350 degree oven for 20-25 minutes.

Mary Lee Whipple, Texas

ALMOND DELIGHT

1 (12-ounce) package cream cheese, room temperature

4 ounces butter, softened

½ cup sour cream

½ cup sugar

1 envelope plain gelatin

¼ cup cold water

Grated rind of 2 lemons

½ cup white raisins

1 cup slivered almonds, toasted, divided

Saltine crackers

Cream softened cream cheese, butter and sour cream. Add sugar. Soften the gelatin in cold water, melt over hot water. Add to cheese mixture. Add remaining ingredients (reserving ¼ cup almonds for garnish), mixing well. Press mixture into a bowl or a mold lined with waxed paper. Refrigerate until ready to serve. To serve, remove from mold and garnish with almonds. Serve with saltine crackers. This is a sweet appetizer and buttery crackers just won't suit.

Cordelia L. Razek, Louisiana

SWEET AND SPICY NUTS

Nonstick vegetable oil spray
3/4 stick unsalted butter
1/2 cup packed brown sugar
1/4 cup water
1 tablespoon chili powder
1 1/2 teaspoons salt
1 teaspoon ground cumin

1 teaspoon dried oregano
1/2 teaspoon ground black pepper
1/4 teaspoon cayenne pepper
2 cups walnut halves
2 cups pecan halves
2 cups whole almonds

Preheat oven to 300 degrees. Spray large baking sheet with nonstick vegetable spray. Melt butter in large nonstick skillet over medium heat. Add next 8 ingredients, stir until sugar dissolves, about 1 minute. Add all nuts, stir until butter mixture coats nuts thickly, about 2 minutes. Spread nut mixture in single layer on prepared sheet. Bake until nuts are glazed and deep brown, stirring often, about 25 minutes. Cool nuts completely on sheet, stirring occasionally. Can be made 1 week ahead. Store airtight at room temperature.

Liz Offord, Texas

SEAFOOD APPETIZER MOLD

2 envelopes unflavored gelatin
1/2 cup cold water
1 (3-ounce) package cream cheese
1 1/4 cups mayonnaise
1 tablespoon fresh lemon juice
2 teaspoons minced parsley
1 cup finely chopped celery
1 teaspoon minced onion
Garlic salt to taste
2 cups cooked tiny shrimp
1 cup flaked crabmeat

Soften gelatin in cold water in double boiler. Heat over hot water until gelatin dissolves, stirring constantly. Beat cream cheese in mixer bowl until light. Add gelatin gradually; mix well. Add mayonnaise and lemon juice. Mix well. Fold in parsley, celery, onion, garlic salt, shrimp and crabmeat. Pour into oiled* 1-quart mold. Chill until set. Unmold onto serving plate; serve with bagel chips or Melba toast rounds.

*It is not necessary to oil a plastic mold.

Ralph and Jeanine Bowles, Washington

INDONESIAN GADO GADO

Assorted raw vegetables and fruits

½ teaspoon grated fresh lime rind

1½ cups unsalted roasted peanuts

4 green onions

4 large cloves garlic

⅓ cup pure smooth peanut butter

2 tablespoons fresh lime juice

2 tablespoons salad oil

2 tablespoons light brown sugar

1¼ cups canned coconut milk

½ of a 2-ounce tin of anchovy fillets

1 small red hot chile

Wash and peel, as needed, vegetables and fruit. Blanch vegetables like string beans or asparagus and then carve, slice, cut into sticks or wedges. Arrange on a platter or divided dishes or bowls and refrigerate while preparing sauce.

Grate lime rind, then cut and squeeze juice and set both aside. Finely chop the peanuts and green onion. Mince or crush peeled garlic and set aside. In a good sized serving bowl, place peanut butter, lime juice, salad oil, brown sugar and coconut milk and mix well. Mash anchovies. Seed and mince the red chile. To peanut butter mixture, add peanuts, onion, garlic, grated lime, anchovies and red chile pepper. Mix thoroughly. To serve, provide oriental sauce dishes or small salad plates.

Elizabeth Miller, Louisiana

ARTICHOKE DIP

1 (16-ounce) can artichokes, drained or dried
  on a paper towel

1 cup Parmesan cheese

1 cup Hellmann's mayonnaise

¼ teaspoon garlic salt

Lemon juice

Blend all together. Heat in a 350 degree oven for 20 minutes. Serve warm with crackers.

Zina Versaggi Graalfs, Florida

ANN'S ARTICHOKE DIP

    1 can Roland artichoke hearts, drained (8 hearts)
    1 can sliced green chiles
    1 small jar pimentos
    1 cup light mayonnaise
    1 egg
    5 to 6-ounces Parmesan cheese
    Garlic salt and pepper to taste

Pulse in food processor until smooth. Place in baking dish and top with bread crumbs. Bake 30 minutes at 350 degrees.

Bernadine Levy, Colorado

DRIED BEEF DIP

    1 cup chopped pecans
    2 teaspoons butter or margarine
    2 (8-ounce) packages cream cheese, softened
    ¼ cup milk
    1 (2½-ounce) jar dried beef, chopped
    ½ teaspoon garlic salt
    1 (8-ounce) carton sour cream
    4 teaspoons minced onion
    Chopped pecans

Saute pecans in butter and reserve. Blend other ingredients (except pecans) and spoon into baking dish. Top with pecans. Bake at 350 degrees for 20 minutes. Serve warm with crackers.

Zina Versaggi Graalfs, Florida

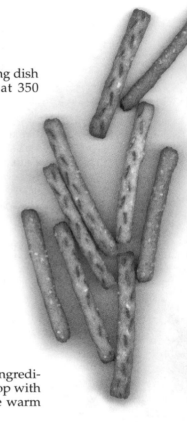

HOT CRAB AND CHEESE DIP

1 (8-ounce) package cream cheese

2 tablespoons milk

1 (6-ounce) can crabmeat

Pinch of salt

1 teaspoon grated onion

1 tablespoon horseradish

1 tablespoon Worcestershire sauce

Tabasco® sauce, to taste

1 teaspoon lemon juice

Slivered almonds

Cream cheese with milk. Add crabmeat, salt, onion, horseradish, Worcestershire sauce, Tabasco® and lemon juice. Pour into buttered casserole and sprinkle with almonds. Bake 30 minutes at 375 degrees. Serve hot with favorite crackers.

Dean Ingram

SHRIMP DIP

1 onion

⅔ cup American or Swiss cheese

1 pound cooked shrimp

1 cup mayonnaise

6 tablespoons milk

2 teaspoons Worcestershire sauce

Dash hot pepper sauce

Use the steel blade of your food processor to mince the onion. Then add cheese and shrimp. Continue to process until smooth. Add remaining ingredients and process until smooth. Remove and chill. Serve with crackers.

Zina Versaggi Graalfs, Florida

JEANETTE'S HOT SHRIMP DIP

1 (8-ounce) package cream cheese

1 can cream of potato soup

1 can small shrimp

2 tablespoons finely minced onion

½ teaspoon horseradish (or more if you like)

½ teaspoon salt and pepper

⅓ cup slivered almonds

8-ounces grated Cheddar cheese, divided

Combine cream cheese and potato soup. Add shrimp, onion, horseradish, salt and pepper. Blend until smooth. Spread half of the shrimp mixture into the bottom of a buttered deep dish pie pan. Sprinkle with almonds and half of the Cheddar cheese. Add remaining shrimp mixture. Sprinkle remaining Cheddar cheese on top. Bake at 350 degrees for 25-30 minutes. Serve warm with crackers.

Zina Versaggi Graalfs, Florida

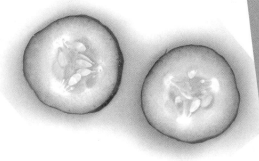

CUCUMBER DIP

1 large cucumber, unpeeled

¼ cup vinegar

½ teaspoon salt

¼ teaspoon garlic powder

1 (8-ounce) carton sour cream

Wash cucumber and remove seeds. Grate using a grater with ¼-inch holes. Add vinegar and salt. Stir, cover and refrigerate overnight. Drain, then add garlic powder and stir in sour cream.

Brenda Martinez, Alabama

BLT DIP

1 cup sour cream

1 cup mayonnaise

1 pound bacon, cooked, and crumbled

1 teaspoon sugar

1 tomato, chopped

Mix all ingredients except tomato. Refrigerate to blend flavors, then stir in tomatoes just before serving. Delicious with Frito Scoops.

Jeri-Lynn Sandusky, Utah

CURRY DIP

1 cup Hellmann's mayonnaise

1 teaspoon garlic salt

1 teaspoon grated onion

1 teaspoon curry powder

1 teaspoon vinegar

½ teaspoon horseradish

Mix together. Serve with raw vegetables. (We like carrots, cauliflower, broccoli and mushrooms).

Carol Ryan, Kansas

HOT TACO BEAN DIP

1 cup sour cream

1 can refried beans or 1 can Campbell's Bean and Bacon Soup

1 cup grated Cheddar cheese

1–3 tablespoons dry taco seasoning

1 (4-ounce) can chopped green chiles

1 teaspoon minced garlic or ¼ teaspoon garlic powder

Mix all ingredients and pour into a baking dish. Microwave until hot and bubbly. Serve with Frito Scoops or tortilla chips.

Jeri-Lynn Sandusky, Utah

MEXICAN DIP

1 (12-ounce) can Mexican corn, drained

8-ounces Cheddar cheese, shredded

4 green onions, chopped or green chiles, chopped

½ cup mayonnaise

½ cup sour cream

½ teaspoon salt

Mix and serve with Fritos.

Mary Q. Smith, Texas

TACO DIP

This recipe was given to me many years ago in Wisconsin. It is a colorful and hearty dip, enough for ten people. Prepare 1 to 2 hours before serving.

Place in a mixing bowl and mix together with seasonings to your taste. Spread mixture on a medium sized plate.

- 1 (8-ounce) package cream cheese, softened
- ⅓ cup sour cream
- Garlic powder
- Onion powder
- Garlic pepper
- Season-all

Top with the following, in the order listed:

- 2 tablespoons finely chopped onion
- 1 cup finely chopped iceberg lettuce
- ½ green pepper, finely chopped
- 3 Roma tomatoes, seeded and finely chopped
- 1 (2.5-ounce) can sliced black olives, drained
- 1 cup shredded Cheddar cheese

Cover and chill. Serve with white corn tortilla chips.

NOTE: Low fat sour cream and cream cheese work well.

Diane Watkins, Wisconsin

FRESH SALSA

3 (16-ounce) cans diced tomatoes

Juice of 1 lime

1 small onion, finely chopped

4-6 garlic cloves, crushed

½ teaspoon salt

½ teaspoon sugar

2 jalapeno peppers, seeded and chopped

4-5 tablespoons pickled jalapeno pepper juice

¼ cup chopped cilantro

Place all ingredients in a blender and pulse to desired consistency. If a chunky salsa is preferred, just combine ingredients and stir.

Pam Redus, Texas

CHRISTMAS KETCHUP

1 (16-ounce) can jellied or whole cranberry sauce

¾ cup sugar

¼ cup vinegar

1 tablespoon fresh, minced garlic

¼ teaspoon ground cinnamon

⅛ teaspoon ground allspice

⅛ teaspoon pepper

1 tablespoon all-purpose flour

2 tablespoons water

1 (8-ounce) package cream cheese

Crackers

Combine cranberry sauce, sugar, vinegar, garlic, cinnamon, allspice and pepper in a medium saucepan. In a small bowl, combine flour, and water until smooth. Add to cranberry mixture. Bring mixture to a boil, stirring constantly. Reduce heat and simmer 5 minutes or until thick and bubbly. Remove from heat. Cool. Store in airtight container in refrigerator. Serve over cream cheese along with crackers. Makes 2¼ cups.

Jeri-Lynn Sandusky, Utah

TROPICAL SALSA

One mango, diced small

2 Roma tomatoes, diced small

1 bunch green onions, sliced small

1 or 2 jalapeno peppers, finely chopped

1 clove garlic, minced

1 small can crushed pineapple or ½ cup fresh pineapple, chopped

5-10 clinatro leaves, minced

½ teaspoon salt (optional)

Mix all ingredients together in a bowl. Let stand in refrigerator for 1 hour before serving. Serve with tortilla chips.

Leny Young, Ohio

JUDY'S APPLE DIP

1 (8-ounce) package cream cheese, softened

¾ cup packed brown sugar

¼ cup granulated sugar

1 teaspoon vanilla extract

Cream all ingredients with a mixer. Serve with apple slices.
Judy Dashiell, Minnesota

CRANBERRY CHUTNEY

Bon appetit and enjoy!

1 (12-ounce) package fresh strawberries

2 cups sugar

1 cup water

1 cup orange juice

1 cup golden raisins

1 cup walnuts or pecans, chopped

1 cup celery, chopped

1 medium apple, chopped

3 tablespoons orange peel

2 teaspoons ginger

Heat cranberries, sugar, water, and orange juice in a 3-quart saucepan until boiling. Reduce heat and simmer for 15 minutes. Remove from heat. Add remaining ingredients. Cool and refrigerate for at least 6 hours.
Leny Young, Ohio

CHRISTMAS CRANBERRY CHUTNEY (Delicious spooned over cream cheese!)

1 (20-ounce) can pineapple chunks, plus water

2 cups sugar

1 pound cranberries

1 cup golden raisins

¼ teaspoon almond extract

¼ teaspoon ground ginger

¼ – ½ teaspoon allspice

½ teaspoon salt

¼ teaspoon nutmeg

¼ teaspoon cayenne pepper

1 cup chopped pecans

Into a large saucepan, drain juice from pineapple and add enough water to make 1 cup liquid. To this liquid, add sugar, cranberries, raisins and spices. Bring to a boil and simmer 25 to 30 minutes. The last 5 minutes, add pineapple and nuts. Chill until firm. Makes 3 pints.

Becky Van Vranken, Washington, DC

This recipe was given to me by Mrs. Henni Vendersleen, a native of Holland whom I met in Houston in the 1980's. Her husband, Nick, was a Royal Dutch Shell Oil employee in Indonesia when World War II began. He was imprisoned for several years by the Japanese and she and her children lived as well as they could until he was released. When he finally reached home, his small daughter ran and hid; Henni had often warned her never to let a strange man tell her he was her father.

GREEN PEAR CHUTNEY

2 cups cut up (unripe) pears, the firmer texture the better

1 cup sugar

½ cup seedless raisins. Cut them up if you want to.

Grated rind of 1 fairly large orange

2 tablespoons apple cider vinegar

1/8 teaspoon (or more) ground cloves

¼ cup pecan pieces (optional)

About 1½ teaspoons minced peeled fresh ginger root. Don't ever use dried. You can add more if you want it more spicy, but note that the flavor develops as it cools.

Boil all ingredients together for an hour over medium heat. Stir at first, then occasionally.

It looks impossibly dry at first, but quickly becomes nicely moist. If you want, you can add a little water, and if you get it too wet, you can thicken it after cooking. (To thicken, dissolve about a tablespoon of cornstarch in twice as much juice, stir it in, then bring it back to a low boil.)

This makes about a pint. In the refrigerator, it keeps virtually forever.

Nancy Nichols Bryan, Arizona

HAPPY HOUR SPECIAL

1 pound ground beef

1 medium onion, chopped

1 cup water

1 package taco seasoning

1 large can tomato sauce

1 package flour tortillas

1 can refried beans

1 (8-ounce) package shredded Cheddar cheese, divided

1 cup sour cream

¼ head lettuce, shredded

1 tomato, diced

Brown meat and onion. Drain off excess grease. Combine water, taco seasoning and tomato sauce. Add to meat mixture. Simmer for about 10 minutes. In a casserole dish, layer meat mixture, flour tortillas, refried beans, and half of the cheese. Bake covered in a 375 degree oven for 45 minutes. Remove from oven and spread sour cream over top. Sprinkle with lettuce, tomatoes and remaining cheese.

Jeri-Lynn Sandusky, Utah

CHILE CHEESECAKE

1 cup crushed tortilla chips

3 tablespoons butter, melted

2 (8-ounce) packages cream cheese, softened

2 eggs

1 (4-ounce) can diced green chiles

1 fresh jalapeno pepper, cored, seeded and diced

4 ounces shredded Colby cheese

4 ounces shredded Monterey Jack cheese

¼ cup sour cream

Chopped tomatoes

Chopped green onions

Diced black olives

Preheat oven to 325 degrees. In a medium bowl, combine tortilla chips and butter. Press into 9-inch spring form pan. Bake 15 minutes; remove from oven, leaving oven on.

In a large bowl, blend cream cheese and eggs. Add green chiles, jalapeno and cheeses. Pour over crust and bake 30 minutes. Do not overcook.

Remove from oven and cool in pan 5 minutes. Run knife around inside edge and remove sides from pan. Spread sour cream over top and decorate with tomatoes, green onions and olives. Serve with tortilla chips. Serves 10-12.

Ralph and Jeanine Bowles, Washington

Can be served as an appetizer or a main dish

COWBOY CAVIAR

2 tablespoons red wine vinegar

1½ – 2 tablespoons Tabasco ®

1½ teaspoons salad oil

1 clove garlic, minced

1 chopped avocado

⅔ cup fresh cilantro, chopped

½ pound Roma tomatoes, chopped

1 (11-ounce) can corn

⅔ cup sliced green onion

Salt and pepper to taste

Mix all ingredients together. Refrigerate until flavors blend. Serve with tortilla chips.

Jeri-Lynn Sandusky, Utah

Will keep up to 2 weeks – if folks will let it last that long!

TEXAS CAVIAR I

New Year's Day Special Dip from the Gold Diggers Investment Club

1 quart black eyed peas

1 small onion, minced

1 tablespoon minced fresh green chile pepper

1 large clove garlic, crushed

½ cup red wine vinegar

⅓ cup vegetable oil

½ teaspoon salt

½ teaspoon sugar

¼ teaspoon freshly ground black pepper

Cook black eyed peas according to package directions. Rinse and drain. Add onion and chile pepper. Mix well. Add garlic, vinegar, oil, salt, sugar and pepper. Mix well. Cover and refrigerate for 2 days. Before serving, garnish with pimentos.

Shirley Thomas, Texas

TEXAS CAVIAR II

- 1 can black eyed peas, drained and rinsed
- 1 can peas, drained
- 1 can whole kernel corn, drained
- 2 cans diced tomatoes, drained
- 2 avocados, peeled, pitted, and chopped
- 1 medium onion, chopped*
- 1 medium green bell pepper, chopped*
- 1 (8-ounce) bottle Italian salad dressing (fat free is just as tasty)
- ¼ teaspoon garlic powder

In a large bowl, mix all ingredients. Refrigerate and serve cold with tortilla chips.

*For convenience, I use frozen seasoning package of onion, red bell pepper, and green bell pepper.

Doris Emmert, Nevada

EGGPLANT CAVIAR

- 1 eggplant
- 1 onion, diced and sautéed in olive oil
- 1 green pepper (if you want a hot dish, use half a can of mild Ortega chiles)
- 1 clove garlic
- 2 tomatoes, peeled and chopped
- 2 tablespoons white wine
- Salt and pepper to taste

Boil whole eggplant for about 45 minutes, or until tender. Cool. Peel and chop eggplant. Saute onion, garlic, and pepper and then add to eggplant. Add tomatoes, wine and seasonings. Cook over low heat until thick. Serve hot or cold on your favorite cracker or bread.

Judy Ingram

BROILER

BR
Clean and halve very young, with salt and pepper. Preheat to the full flame. Put in chick chicken is about 1½ inches fro but finish farther from flame, until tender requires 20 to 30 m

BROILED
Clean large frying chicken and well with 1 cup water and salt a gas and 30 minutes or longer of broil according to above instructic

BRO
Thick chops are preferable for bro preheat the Broiler for 8 to 12 mir as close as possible to flame. Ther meat or not as you desire. Season moved down from flame dependir done meat is desired. Pork and ve Ordinary chops usually require 5 minutes.

GLORIFIED BRO
1½ lbs. good grade hamburg
1 egg
1 medium-sized onion, minced

Mix ingredients, and form into 6 patt with gas on full and Sizzling Platter i Put in patties, and move Platter down from flame. Broil 6 to 12 minutes, dep can be turned down slightly, and Plat broiler flame for very well done patties it is not necessary to turn meat. Serve w hamburgers as individual Salisbury stea Thermowell vegetables around.

To toast buns, split them, butter insides, down. Or toast buns in Broiler.

STUFFED ARTICHOKE HEARTS

Butter, melted

Canned artichoke hearts, drained well

Cream cheese with chives

Parmesan cheese, grated

Melt butter. Drain artichoke hearts and slice in half from bottom to top. Make an indentation in each half with thumb. Fill indentation with cream cheese. Dip each stuffed half in melted butter, then roll in Parmesan cheese. Bake in shallow, glass pan, uncovered, at 350 degrees for 45 minutes. Serve with toothpicks.

Mary Lee Whipple, Texas

HOT CRAB COCKTAIL SPREAD

1 (8-ounce) package of cream cheese

1 tablespoon milk

2 tablespoons Worcestershire sauce

1 (7.5 ounce) can of crab meat, drained and flaked

2 tablespoons chopped green onions

2 tablespoons slivered almonds

Combine cream cheese with milk and Worcestershire sauce. Add crab and onions to cream cheese mix. Turn onto greased 8-inch pie plate or small shallow baking dish. Top with almonds. Bake at 350 degrees for 15 minutes or until heated through. Keep spread warm over candle warmer or chafing dish. Serve with assorted crackers.

Terri Anderson, California

EASY CREAMY CRAB SPREAD

1 (8-ounce) package cream cheese, softened

2 tablespoons finely chopped onion

1 (8-ounce) package frozen crab meat, thawed and well drained (or can used canned)

¾ cup cocktail sauce

Parsley flakes

Mix cream cheese and onion thoroughly. Spread on small platter. Sprinkle well drained crab meat over cream cheese and spread evenly. Spread cocktail sauce over crab-cheese mixture. Sprinkle with parsley flakes. Serve with Ritz crackers or your favorite crackers.

Jan Watson, Illinois

MUSHROOM ALMOND PATE

1 cup slivered almonds

4 tablespoons butter

¾ pound mushrooms, sliced

1 small onion. sliced

1 clove garlic, minced

¾ teaspoon salt

¼ teaspoon ground thyme

⅛ teaspoon white pepper

2 tablespoons salad oil or olive oil

Toast almonds over low heat in a wide frying pan. Stir frequently until lightly browned, about 5 to 7 minutes. Turn out of pan and cool.

Melt butter over medium-high heat. Add mushrooms, onion, garlic, salt, thyme, and pepper. Cook, stirring occasionally, until most of liquid evaporates.

Chop 2 tablespoons of the toasted almonds and reserve. Whirl remaining toasted nuts in a blender or food processor until finely ground. Continue blending, gradually adding oil until creamy and smooth. Add mushroom mixture and whirl until smooth. Stir in remaining nuts. Serve at room temperature with crackers or raw vegetables. If made ahead, cool, cover and chill. Makes about 1½ cups.

Liz Offord, Texas

HUMMUS

1 (17-ounce) can garbanzo beans, drain and save
　　juice to use to thin to right consistency

3 tablespoons olive oil

4 tablespoons tahini

4 tablespoons lemon juice

1 clove garlic

¼ teaspoon paprika, or to taste

Salt and pepper to taste

Combine all ingredients in a food processor and blend until smooth. When smooth, chill in an airtight container. Serve cold with pita. Garnish with olive oil and paprika.

Cordelia L. Razek, Louisiana

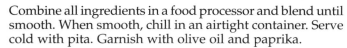

The cheese will
keep safely for up
to three days in
the jar. Keep
refrigerated.

MARINATED MOZZARELLA

2–3 thyme sprigs

2 garlic cloves, sliced thin

1 pound Mozzarella cheese, cut in 1-inch cubes

1 (7-ounce) jar roasted red peppers

1¼ cups olive oil

2 teaspoons Italian seasonings

4 teaspoons rosemary, crushed

½ teaspoon crushed red pepper

Submerge fresh herbs and garlic in boiling water for one minute. Remove from water and dry. In a quart jar, arrange in layers: cheese, roasted peppers, thyme and garlic. In a small bowl, combine olive oil, Italian seasonings, rosemary and crushed red pepper. Stir together. Pour over cheese. Seal jar. Turn upside down to let seasoned oil coat cheese/peppers. Refrigerate overnight before serving. Turn jar occasionally to allow cheese to marinate.

Becky Van Vranken, Washington, DC

CEVICHE

1 pound haddock, cod, or other firm fleshed fish, cut into ⅓-inch squares

5 limes, juiced

⅓ cup olive oil

1 large tomato, diced

1 teaspoon capers, chopped

2 tablespoons pimento stuffed olives, thinly sliced

⅓ cup chopped cilantro

1 jalapeno pepper, finely chopped

Put fish and lime juice in a non-metal container, cover and refrigerate overnight. Fish will "cook". Pour off lime juice and add remaining ingredients to fish. Age in refrigerator 4–6 hours. Place in small bowls, salt and pepper to taste and garnish with thinly sliced onion rings or avocado slices. Try shrimp or scallops in place of fish.

Joe Miller

CRAB MEAT SQUARES

1 (4.25 ounce) can crab meat

½ stick butter

2 tablespoons mayonnaise

½ teaspoon salt

½ teaspoon garlic powder

1 (5-ounce) jar Kraft Olde English cheese spread

Mix all ingredients together. Spread on English muffin halves. Cut each muffin half into quarters and freeze on a cookie sheet for 2 hours or more. Preheat oven to 400 degrees and bake for 8 minutes.

Zina Versaggi Graalfs, Florida

ARTICHOKE SQUARES

2 (6-ounce) jars marinated artichoke hearts

1 small onion, finely chopped

1 clove garlic

4 eggs, beaten

¼ cup bread crumbs

Salt and pepper

⅛ teaspoon dried oregano

1 cup shredded Cheddar cheese

1 cup grated Gruyere or Parmesan cheese

2 tablespoons fresh parsley, minced

Preheat oven to 325 degrees. Drain marinade from 1 jar of artichoke hearts into a medium skillet. Discard marinade from second jar. Chop artichokes. Heat marinade and add onion and garlic. Saute about 5 minutes. In a bowl, combine eggs, bread crumbs, salt, pepper and oregano. Fold in cheeses and parsley. Add artichoke mixture. Pour into an oiled 9-inch square baking dish. Bake for 30 minutes. Cool slightly before cutting into 1½-inch squares. Also good served cold.

Myrna Du Ford, Texas

Can be served as
an appetizer or a
light lunch. Our
daughter Dawn
came up with this
recipe one
Christmas.

DAWN'S BROCCOLI CHEESE SQUARES

3 tablespoons butter

2 (10-ounce) packages frozen broccoli

3 eggs

1 cup all-purpose flour

1 cup milk

1 teaspoon salt

1 teaspoon baking powder

1 pound Cheddar cheese, grated

2 tablespoons chopped onion

Seasoning salt to taste

Preheat oven to 350 degrees. Melt butter in a 13 x 9-inch baking dish. Steam broccoli for about 5 minutes. Transfer to blender or food processor and chop until fine. In a mixing bowl, beat egg. Add flour, milk, salt and baking powder. Mix thoroughly. Stir in broccoli, cheese and onion. Spoon into baking dish and spread evenly. Sprinkle with seasoned salt. Bake until firm, about 30 to 35 minutes. Let set about 10 to 15 minutes before cutting into squares.

Bernadine Levy, Colorado

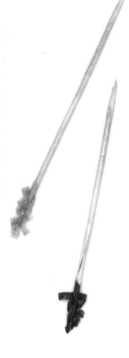

JALAPENO CHEESE SQUARES

4 cups (16-ounces) grated Cheddar cheese

4 eggs, beaten

1 teaspoon minced onion

4 canned jalapeno peppers, seeded and chopped*

Combine all ingredients, stirring well. Spread cheese mixture into an ungreased 8-inch square pan. Bake at 350 degrees for 30 minutes, cut into 1-inch squares.

* Adjust the number of jalapenos to your taste.

Wanda Miller, Texas
Bernadine Levy, Colorado

ZUCCHINI APPETIZERS

3 cups thinly sliced zucchini (3 small)

1 cup biscuit mix

½ cup finely chopped onion

½ cup grated Parmesan cheese

2 tablespoons snipped parsley

½ teaspoon salt

½ teaspoon seasoned salt

1 clove garlic, finely chopped

½ cup oil

4 eggs

½ teaspoon marjoram or oregano

Preheat oven to 350 degrees. Mix all ingredients, spread in greased pan. Sprinkle with Cheddar cheese. Bake in preheated oven about 25 minutes, until golden brown. Use a 13 x 9-inch baking pan. Cut into 2-inch squares.

Betty Sellers, Texas

VEGETABLE BARS

Combine 3/4 cup each of the following and set aside:

Diced tomatoes, chopped green bell pepper, chopped green onion, chopped cauliflower, chopped broccoli, grated carrot, and grated Cheddar cheese

2 (8-ounce) tubes Pillsbury Crescent Roll dough

3/4 cup mayonnaise

1/2 cup sour cream (fat free works well)

1 package Ranch Dressing mix (Uncle Dan's if you can find it)

2 (8-ounce) packages cream cheese, softened.

Preheat oven to 350 degrees. Cover an 11 x 17-inch jelly roll pan with roll dough. Bake in preheated oven for 8 to 10 minutes or until golden brown. Let cool. Combine mayonnaise, sour cream and salad dressing. Add cream cheese and mix until smooth. Spread mixture over cooled crust and top with veggie mixture. Use a sandwich bag to press down veggies. Chill for a few hours and cut into squares for serving.

Ralph and Jeanine Bowles, Washington

Variation from Liz Offord: Add ¼ teaspoon cayenne pepper for a little zing!

OLIVE CHEESE PUFFS

½ pound Cheddar cheese, grated

1¼ cups all-purpose flour

½ cup melted butter

1 (13-ounce) jar stuffed green olives

Preheat oven to 400 degrees. Mix cheese and flour until crumbly. Add melted butter. Take one teaspoon of dough, flatten and put olive inside. Roll into ball. Place on a cookie sheet and bake at 400 degrees for 15 to 20 minutes. Makes 48 appetizers.

Jo Ann Christal, Texas

CHILE CHEESE PUFFS

2 tablespoons margarine

½ cup light or reduced fat cream cheese

2 cups grated sharp Cheddar cheese

Garlic powder to taste

1 cup all-purpose flour

½ teaspoon salt

½ cup chopped green chiles

Preheat oven to 375 degrees. Cream margarine and cream cheese. Stir in Cheddar cheese, garlic powder, flour, and salt. Add green chiles and mix well. Form dough into ¾-inch balls and place on greased cookie sheet. Bake 12 to 15 minutes at 375 degrees.

Judy Krohn, Texas

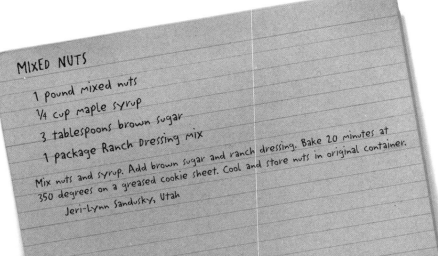

MIXED NUTS

1 pound mixed nuts

¼ cup maple syrup

3 tablespoons brown sugar

1 package Ranch Dressing mix

Mix nuts and syrup. Add brown sugar and ranch dressing. Bake 20 minutes at 350 degrees on a greased cookie sheet. Cool and store nuts in original container.

Jeri-Lynn Sandusky, Utah

CHEESE DELIGHTS

½ cup margarine, softened

2 cups shredded sharp Cheddar cheese

½ teaspoon Worcestershire sauce

Dash of Tabasco® or other hot sauce

1 cup sifted flour

Preheat oven to 350 degrees. Put margarine, cheese, Worcestershire and hot sauce into a bowl. Stir it all up. Now blend in flour and squish around with hands. Form into long, smooth roll (about the size of paper towel tubes). Slice about ¼-inch thick and bake 12 to 15 minutes in preheated oven. Can also be frozen and baked as needed.

Maureen Vogl, Kansas

IDIOT'S CHEESE DELIGHTS

4 ounces butter, softened

2 cups shredded sharp Cheddar cheese

½ teaspoon Worcestershire sauce

Dash Tabasco® sauce

Pinch salt

¼ teaspoon dry mustard

1 teaspoon celery seed

⅛ teaspoon cayenne pepper

1 cup all-purpose flour

Kosher salt

Place all ingredients except flour and Kosher salt into a bowl and stir together. If using a standard mixer, use the flat beater on low speed. Add flour and mix thoroughly. If not using a mixer, it's easiest to use your hands. Form dough into a long smooth roll (about 12 inches) and wrap in waxed paper or plastic wrap. Place in fridge. When ready to bake, remove paper and slice the dough into ¼-inch thick rounds. Place on cookie sheet that has been sprinkled with Kosher salt. Bake at 350 degrees for 12-15 minutes, until lightly browned around the edges. Dough can be frozen before slicing. Makes about 42–1½-inch wafers.

Joyce Crane, Texas

CHRISTMAS PARTY PINWHEELS

3 (8-ounce) packages cream cheese, softened

1 (.4-ounce) package ranch dressing salad dressing mix

½ cup minced sweet red pepper

½ cup minced celery

¼ cup sliced green onions

¼ cup sliced stuffed olives

3 to 4 flour tortillas (10-inch)

Shrimp (optional)

In a mixing bowl, beat cream cheese and dressing mix until smooth. Add red pepper, celery, onions and olives. Mix well. Spread about ¾ cup on each tortilla. Roll up tightly, wrap in plastic wrap. Refrigerate for at least 2 hours. Slice into ½-inch pieces. Serves 15-20.

Can also add shrimp, if desired.

Ralph and Jeanine Bowles, Washington

I often use hot sausage and Italian breadcrumbs and skip the process of rolling them in the beaten egg.

SCOTCH EGGS

1½ pounds bulk sausage

12 eggs, hard boiled and peeled

1 egg, beaten

½ cup dry breadcrumbs

Heat oven to 450 degrees. Divide sausage into 12 equal portions and shape into patties. Wrap each sausage patty completely around 1 hard boiled egg, pressing edges together to seal. Dip sausage into beaten egg and roll in breadcrumbs until completely coated. Place in 15 x 10-inch jelly roll pan. Bake for 30 minutes in preheated oven.

Pat Sampson, Iowa

SAUSAGE CRESCENT ROLL UPS

2 pounds breakfast sausage (either Owen's or
    Jimmy Dean)

1½ (8-ounce) packages cream cheese

A handful of mozzarella cheese

Garlic salt

Salt

3 cans of Pillsbury Crescent rolls

Preheat oven to 375 degrees as noted on the crescent roll
package. Cook up your sausage and crumble it up as it
cooks. Drain the grease. Add all your cream cheese to the
sausage (as the cream cheese melts, stir it into the sausage).
Once the cream cheese is melted into your sausage, sprinkle
a handful of mozzarella cheese over the top of the mixture. (My sister uses Parmesan cheese instead of mozzarella cheese and it's good also). Sprinkle garlic salt and
regular salt to your taste.

Roll out your crescent rolls: each can rolls out 8 perfo-
rated pieces of dough, but you will need to cut each perfo-
rated section with an additional diagonal cut which will
actually give you 16 servings per can of crescent rolls.
Spoon sausage mixture into each section and fold ends over
each other to trap the mixture into the center of the dough.
Place on ungreased baking sheet and bake in preheated
oven until golden brown. Repeat until you have used up
all of your mixture. Makes 48 sausage/cream cheese
thingy's.

Loraine Franklin, Texas

SMOKY BACON WRAPS

1 pound sliced bacon

1 (16-ounce) package miniature smoked sausage links

1 cup packed brown sugar

Cut each bacon strip in half lengthwise. Wrap one piece of
bacon around each sausage. Place in a foil-lined 15 x 10-
inch jelly roll pan. Sprinkle with brown sugar. Bake at 400
degrees for 30-40 minutes. Makes 3½ dozen.

Jeri-Lynn Sandusky, Utah

SHRIMP WRAPPED IN BACON

1 to 1½ pounds large shrimp (21-25 size)

1 small bottle Wishbone Italian dressing

5-6 slices bacon

Shell and devein the shrimp. In a shallow bowl, pour Italian dressing over the shrimp. Marinate ½ to 1 hour. Remove and wrap with bacon slices. Secure with toothpicks. Broil or grill until bacon is cooked.

OPTIONAL DIPPING SAUCE (also great with crab claws)

1 tablespoon plus ½ teaspoon Coleman's dry mustard

1 cup mayonnaise

2 teaspoons Worcestershire sauce

1 teaspoon A-1 sauce

2 tablespoons half and half

⅛ teaspoon salt

Cayenne pepper to taste

Combine all ingredients in a bowl and whisk until smooth. Cover and refrigerate until serving time. Sauce will keep for 1 week.

Zina Versaggi Graalfs, Florida

CHINESE SPARERIBS

½ cup lemon juice

¼ cup cornstarch

1 cup chili sauce

¾ cup pineapple juice

¼ cup soy sauce

½ cup packed brown sugar

6 pounds baby back ribs, cut into pieces and parboiled or pre-baked

Mix lemon juice and cornstarch. Combine with chili sauce, pineapple juice, soy sauce, and brown sugar. Place ribs in shallow baking pan. Season ribs with salt, pepper, and garlic powder. Cover with sauce and bake in covered pan in a 350 degree oven for 1½ hours or until tender. These ribs can be served as an appetizer or a main entrée.

Jeri-Lynn Sandusky, Utah

COCKTAIL MEATBALLS

SAUCE – make first
1 medium onion, chopped

1/4 cup vegetable oil

1-1/2 cups water

1 tablespoon Worcestershire sauce

2 whole cloves

1/4 cup sherry

1 can beef consomme

1 cup stewed tomatoes

2 cloves garlic, pressed (or ¼ teaspoon garlic powder)

1 teaspoon chili powder

1 teaspoon Kitchen Bouquet

Pinch of each: basil, thyme, oregano, celery salt,
 parsley flakes

Saute onion in oil, add remaining ingredients. Cover
and simmer approximately 1 hour. Discard cloves.
Thicken with 1/4 cup cornstarch mixed with 1/2 cup
water. Salt and pepper to taste.

MEATBALLS
2-1/2 pounds lean ground beef

2 eggs

2 teaspoons salt

2 tablespoons grated Parmesan cheese

1 teaspoon marjoram

1/2 teaspoon pepper (scant)

2 cloves garlic, pressed (or ¼ teaspoon garlic powder)

1-1/4 cups fine bread crumbs

2 tablespoons dried minced onion

1 teaspoon chili powder

2 teaspoons Worcestershire Sauce

1/3 cup milk

3 tablespoons parsley flakes

Combine ingredients and mix well. Shape into small
balls. Fry in oil (1/8-inch deep), turning until brown
on all sides and cooked within.
   Combine sauce with meatballs. Serve as cocktail
meatballs or can be served over rice or noodles as a
main dish. Freezes well. Makes ample amount to be
divided in half and frozen for future use.

   Cindy Kelly, Texas

OLIVE NUT SANDWICHES

8-ounces cream cheese, room temperature

½ cup mayonnaise

½ cup chopped green olives

½ cup chopped pecans

½ teaspoon onion powder

White pepper to taste

24 bread slices, buttered lightly

Blend cream cheese and mayonnaise. Add olives, pecans, onion powder and pepper. Mix well. Trim crusts off bread. Spread one slice with sandwich mixture and top with another slice of bread. Cut into halves or thirds. Cover tightly and refrigerate until ready to serve. Serves 12.

Jo Ann Christal, Texas

CHEESE PETIT FOURS

Delicious!

1 loaf Pepperidge Farm thinly sliced white bread (not extra thin)

½ pound butter, softened

2 jars Kraft Olde English Cheese spread

¾ teaspoon Worcestershire sauce

½ teaspoon Tabasco®

1 teaspoon onion powder

Dash cayenne pepper

Dill for garnish

Crust loaf. Beat butter, cheese spread, Worcestershire, Tabasco® and onion powder in mixer until consistency of icing. Spread between each layer of bread and spread on top as well. (Each petit four is 3 slices thick.) Sprinkle each with cayenne and dill. Cut into quarters. Place on cookie sheets and freeze until firm and frozen. Place into plastic freezer bags and keep frozen until ready to bake. DO NOT DEFROST. Bake on greased cookie sheets in a 350 degree oven for 15–20 minutes. Can also line cookie sheet with foil for easy clean up.

Liz Offord, Texas

PORTABELLO QUESADILLAS

4 portabello mushrooms, stems trimmed and discarded

Garlic oil

Salt

Fresh ground pepper

6 (8-inch) flour or whole wheat tortillas

1 cup shredded light Mexican Cheddar cheese

2 teaspoons combination rosemary, thyme and sage

Lightly oil the cooking rack on the BBQ. Brush the mushroom caps liberally with garlic oil and lightly season with salt and pepper. Place mushrooms on the grill and cover. Grill, turning once, until mushrooms are tender, about 6 minutes. Transfer to cutting board and slice into ½-inch strips.

Place 4 tortillas on a work surface and sprinkle each with ¼ cup of the cheese. Top with equal amounts of mushroom strips, sprinkle with herbs, then carefully place each on the grill. Top with remaining tortillas.

Grill the quesadillas until the underside is lightly browned, about 45 seconds. Then, carefully turn and grill the other side. Cut each quesadilla into 6 wedges and serve immediately.

Zina Versaggi Graalfs, Florida

OVEN BAKED QUESADILLAS

6 (6-inch) flour tortillas

6-ounces Monterrey jack cheese, grated

1 yellow or red pepper, diced (or combination)

1 jalapeno, diced, with seeds and stem removed

4 ounces Feta cheese, crumbled (or use soft goat cheese)

Freshly ground black pepper, optional

Preheat oven to 350 degrees. Spray a baking sheet with non-stick vegetable spray. Cover baking sheet with tortillas in a single layer. Sprinkle Monterrey Jack cheese on tortillas, then top with peppers. Sprinkle feta or goat cheese on top of peppers. Sprinkle with a little freshly ground pepper, optional. Bake 5 minutes or until the cheeses are melted. Remove from oven and immediately fold in half. Cut each folded tortilla into 3 triangles.

Winola Van Artsdalen, Kansas

I brought this recipe with me from California when we moved here less than a year ago. I made a promise to myself that I would never share it, as I wanted it to be mine exclusively as it is so unusual and outstanding. But alas; I have given it to numerous new friends, so here it is for everyone. Believe me, you will knock the socks off everyone when you take it as an appetizer.

CALIFORNIA APPETIZER PIZZA

1 Boboli pizza crust (thin, if you can find it)

Top with:
Mixture of Cheddar and Monterey Jack cheeses
Sliced green onions (some of the tops, too)
Dried cranberries
Candied pecans, chopped
Gorgonzola cheese on top

I use no specific amounts of each. Just pile on a lot, particularly cheeses. Bake in a 400 degree oven until slightly browned and bubbly.

Joann Schoen, California

BETTY'S LOW CARB CANAPE – STUFFED MUSHROOMS

40 mushrooms, stems removed
⅓ cup butter, melted
10-ounces bulk sage sausage
1 tablespoon chopped green onion
¼ teaspoon pepper
1 clove garlic, minced
1 tablespoons fresh parsley
8-ounces cream cheese

Place mushrooms in shallow baking dish. Brush with melted butter. Set aside. Brown sausage, onions and garlic in skillet. Drain. Mix in pepper, parsley and cream cheese. Heat to blend all ingredients.

Stuff mushrooms with filling. Bake about 25 minutes at 325 degrees. These can be prepared a day ahead and baked just before the dinner party. Makes 40 pieces.

(68 calories, 6 grams fat, 1 gram carbohydrate per mushroom.)

Betty Sellers, Texas

PICKLED MUSHROOMS

⅔ cup tarragon vinegar

½ cup salad oil

1 medium clove garlic, crushed

1 tablespoon sugar

2 tablespoons water

1½ teaspoons salt

Dash freshly ground pepper

Dash Tabasco® sauce

1 medium onion

2 cans button mushrooms (or 2 pints fresh mushrooms, washed and trimmed)

Combine first 8 ingredients. Slice onion into rings. Add to marinade along with mushrooms. Cover and refrigerate 8 hours or overnight. Stir several times. Drain and serve as appetizer.

Carol Ryan, Kansas

Beverages

SLUSHY BANANA PUNCH

5 medium bananas

½ cup lemon juice

1 large can orange juice

1 large can pineapple juice (not frozen)

4 cups sugar

6 cups water

1 (32-ounce) bottle 7-Up™

Combine bananas with a little water in a blender and blend until smooth. Set aside. Boil sugar and water for 15 minutes until syrup forms. Combine bananas, syrup and juices and freeze. Remove from freezer 2 hours before serving. When ready to serve, mash the frozen mixture with a fork. Put half the frozen mixture and half of the 7-Up™ into a punch bowl. Remaining mixture can be frozen and used for individual servings. Keeps in the freezer for 2-3 months.

Kathy Bratton, Texas

BETSY ROSS PUNCH

1 (6-ounce) can frozen lemonade concentrate

1 (8-ounce) can crushed pineapple

1 (10-ounce) package frozen strawberries

1 tablespoon pomegranate grenadine syrup

3 quarts ginger ale, chilled

Crushed ice

Put lemonade, pineapple, strawberries and grenadine syrup into blender. Blend until completely smooth. Add ginger ale and pour over crushed ice in punch bowl.

Ralph and Jeanine Bowles, Washington

COFFEE PUNCH

1 cup water

3 cups sugar

2 ounces instant coffee

1 gallon low fat milk

½ gallon vanilla ice cream

½ gallon chocolate ice cream

Bring water to a boil. Add sugar and instant coffee, cook until syrupy; allow to cool. Just before serving, add milk and ice cream. Coffee syrup can be made ahead of time and store in refrigerator.

Doris Feldman, Arizona

JUDY'S ORANGE PUNCH

1 (12-ounce) can frozen orange juice

1 (12-ounce) can frozen lemonade

1 large can Hawaiian Punch, orange flavor

1 (32-ounce) bottle 7-Up™ or Sprite™

1 quart orange sherbet

If you use a tray of ice cubes, only add 1 can of water to the frozen juice, otherwise, use 2 cans of water. Combine all ingredients and serve immediately.

NOTE: If you want it a little more tart, add 2 tablespoons Real Lemon.

Judy Dashiell, Minnesota

FRUIT PUNCH

2 small cans frozen orange pineapple juice

16 ounces cranberry juice

Juice from 2 grapefruits

2 cans 7-Up™

Make orange-pineapple juice according to package directions. Combine with cranberry and grapefruit juices. Chill. Add 7-Up™ just before serving. Serves 12.

Sandy Lester, Ohio

PARTY PUNCH

3 cups boiling water
2 cups white sugar
½ cup lemon juice
1 large can pineapple juice
6 cups club soda
1 quart orange sherbet

Mix boiling water and sugar. Cool. Add lemon juice and pineapple juice. Chill for several hours or overnight. Before serving, add club soda and chunks of sherbet.

Sandy Lester, Ohio

We used this punch recipe at our wedding 46 years ago and also when our children got married. It's survived the test of time.

CHAMPAGNE PUNCH

1 gallon Sauterne wine
1 fifth white label rum
2 ounces orange Curacao liquid
10–12 tablespoons sugar
2 fifths sparkling water
1 bottle champagne

Mix wine, rum, curacao, and sugar. Add sparkling water and champagne. Makes approximately 2½ gallons.

Bernadine Levy, Colorado

OPEN HOUSE PUNCH

1 fifth Southern Comfort
1 (6-ounce) bottle lemon juice
1 (6-ounce) can frozen lemonade
1 (6-ounce) can frozen orange juice
3 quarts 7-Up™
Orange and lemon slices

Chill ingredients. Mix in punch bowl, adding 7-Up™ last. Float a block of ice and orange and lemon slices.

Jeri-Lynn Sandusky, Utah

TEQUILA LIME PUNCH

2 cups cold water

1½ cups tequila

1 (6-ounce) can frozen orange-pineapple juice, thawed

½ cup lime juice

2 tablespoons sugar

2 (28-ounce) bottles 7-Up™, chilled

1 lime, sliced

1 orange, sliced

In a large punch bowl, combine water, tequila, orange-pineapple juice concentrate, lime juice and sugar. Slowly pour 7-Up™ down the side of the bowl. Stir punch gently with an up and down motion until mixed. Float the lime and orange slices in the punch. Serve over ice. Makes 24 (½ cup servings)

Jeri-Lynn Sandusky, Utah

FRENCH 75

4 cups fresh, frozen or canned fruit, drained (peaches, strawberries, pineapple, apricots, etc.)

2 tablespoons sugar

1 cup brandy or rum

2 bottles dry white wine, chilled

1 bottle champagne, chilled

Mix fruit and sugar and then pour brandy or rum over fruit. Marinate for 24 hours or more. Place fruit/brandy mixture in a large punch bowl. Add wine and champagne. Remove fruit from punch and serve in a separate dish with toothpicks. Ladle out punch into small wine glasses. Keep chilled.

Jeri-Lynn Sandusky, Utah

MICHILATA

Some people think a Michilata is just a glass with a salted rim and lime juice poured over ice. Here is the real thing.

1 whole lime
½ lemon
4 dashes Tabasco®
1 dash salt
1 dash Lawry's seasoned salt
2 pinches pepper
1 dash Worcestershire
Tomato juice
Tecate (or other Mexican beer)

In a chilled Pilsner glass with a salted rim, squeeze in juice of lime and lemon. Add Tabasco™, salts, pepper and Worcestershire. Fill glass one quarter full with tomato juice. Fill the rest of the glass with beer. Garnish with lime wheel or wedge.

Emily and Bill Lafrance, Louisiana

CRANBERRY MARGARITAS

1¼ cups cranberry juice

½ cup sugar

1½ cups fresh/frozen cranberries

¾ cup lime juice

¾ cup tequila

½ cup orange liqueur (Triple Sec, Cointreau)

3 cups crushed ice (you may also freeze some cranberry juice cocktail and use instead of ice)

Save a few cranberries for garnish. Place all ingredients in a blender and process until smooth. Use a cut cranberry around the rim of the glass and then dip rim in sugar. Pour mix into glasses and garnish with whole berries.

OLD FASHION

½ teaspoon sugar

Dash bitters

1½ ounces Southern Comfort

Dash maraschino cherry juice

½ cinnamon stick

7-Up™

Combine all ingredients, except 7-Up™ in a medium or tall glass. Add ice. Fill with 7-Up™. Garnish with cherry and orange slice.

Jeri-Lynn Sandusky, Utah

COSMOPOLITAN

3 ounces vodka

1 ounce cointreau

Splash lime juice

½ ounce cranberry juice

Shake with crushed ice and serve in a chilled glass.
   Jeri-Lynn Sandusky, Utah

ORANGE COLADAS

1 cup orange juice

⅔ cup light rum

⅓ cup orange flavored liqueur

½ cup cream of coconut, stir before measuring

3 cups ice cubes

Orange slices, halved

Fresh mint sprig, if desired

Pour orange juice, rum, liqueur, and coconut into a blender.
Add ice and whirl on high speed. Pour into cocktail glasses
and garnish with mint and orange slices. Makes 4 cups.
   Jeri-Lynn Sandusky, Utah

MAI TAI

3 ounces Bacardi amber

6 ounces Bacardi light

3 ounces 151 proof rum

6 ounces Meyers dark rum

18 ounces grapefruit juice

18 ounces pineapple juice

4 cap fulls almond extract (small jar)

1½ tablespoons sugar

Mix and serve over ice. Makes 1 pitcher.
   Jeri-Lynn Sandusky, Utah

We used to serve this drink after our tennis matches, when we lived in Okinawa, Japan. Needless to say, after a couple of mai tais, the rest of the day was a waste!

BOB'S (BAILEY'S) IRISH CREAM

    3 eggs, whip into an omelet stage

    1¾ cups brandy

    1 (14-ounce) can Eagle brand condensed milk

    1½ teaspoons vanilla extract

    2 tablespoons Hershey's chocolate syrup

    2 cups whipping cream

Blend all ingredients together using a whisk. Do not over mix, as it will curdle. Keep refrigerated. Serve cold or partially pour over ice cubes. This is awfully close to the real thing.

Bob Heitzman, Iowa

EGG NOG

    2¼ cups egg substitute

    2¼ cups milk (low fat or non fat if you like)

    ½ cup brandy or other spirits

    ⅓ cup confectioners' sugar

    ¼ to ½ teaspoon nutmeg

    3 cups non-dairy whipped topping

Combine and serve! Enjoy!

Peggy Uselton, Colorado

CHRISTMAS BUTTERED RUM

1 cup butter, softened

½ cup packed brown sugar

½ cup sifted confectioners' sugar

1 teaspoon cinnamon

1 teaspoon ground ginger

Dash cloves

1 pint vanilla ice cream, softened

Rum or brandy

Boiling water

Cream butter, sugars, and spices using an electric mixer or food processor. Blend in softened ice cream. Turn into a 4-cup freezer container. Seal and freeze. Mixture will not freeze solid.

To serve: spoon 2 to 4 tablespoons ice cream mixture into each mug. Add 3 tablespoons rum and ½ cup boiling water to each mug. Stir well. Garnish with cinnamon stick, if desired. Makes 12–24 servings.

Jeri-Lynn Sandusky, Utah

FROZEN FRUIT SLUSH

For Christmas, I add maraschino cherries, juice, and maybe some red food coloring.

1 (20-ounce) can crushed pineapple, with juice

1 (30-ounce) can peaches or fruit cocktail (I prefer fruit cocktail)

1 (16-ounce) package frozen strawberries, raspberries or both, with juice

1 (6-ounce) can frozen lemonade concentrate

1 (6-ounce) can frozen orange juice concentrate

1 (12-ounce) can 7-Up ™ or ginger ale

3 mashed bananas

Grapes, optional

Mix all ingredients in a large bowl. I freeze it in smaller portions (such as meal size) as it makes a LOT!

To serve, allow to thaw until it's slushy. Can be used as an appetizer, salad, or dessert.

Leftovers can be re-frozen.

Ruth Fredericksen, Wisconsin

TROPICAL SLUSH

6 cups water, divided

5 medium ripe bananas

2 cups sugar

2 (12-ounce) cans frozen orange juice concentrate, thawed

1 (12-ounce) can frozen lemonade concentrated, thawed

1 (46-ounce) can unsweetened pineapple juice

2 (2 liter) bottles lemon-lime soda

In a blender container, process 1 cup water, bananas and sugar until smooth. Pour into a large container; add the concentrates, pineapple juice, and remaining water. Cover and freeze. Remove from freezer 2 hours before serving. Just before serving, break up and mash mixture with potato masher. Stir in soda. Yield: 40-50 servings (11 quarts)

Ralph and Jeanine Bowles, Washington

...MMM-FETA-FILO

Melt the butter. Mince
...an
...and
...side.
...reserve

MY MOTHER'S APPLE CIDER SLUSH

1½ cups sugar

2 cups water

1 quart apple cider

2 cups orange juice

½ cup lemon juice

...me
...ay
...2 inch
...red)
...ly
...at
...sheets

Boil sugar and water for 5 minutes. Remove from heat and let cool. Add apple cider, orange juice and lemon juice. Freeze to slush consistency. Back in the old days we had to stir this by hand if it got too hard. Now the blender works so well. Serve as a cocktail or as a dessert. Mixes well with vodka. WARNING: Easy to overdo.

Jean Krest, Colorado

ORANGE SMOOTHIES

Half of a 6-ounce can frozen orange juice concentrate
1 cup milk
1 cup water
¼ cup sugar (or sugar substitute)
1 teaspoon vanilla extract
2 cups crushed ice

Place all ingredients in blender, cover and mix until smooth, about 30 seconds. Serve immediately. Serves 2.

Jan Watson, Illinois

CRANBERRY TEA

1 quart water
12 whole cloves
2 (3-inch) cinnamon sticks
4 regular size tea bags
1 (12-ounce) can frozen cranberry juice concentrate, undiluted

Bring first 4 ingredients to a boil in a large saucepan. Pour over tea bags, squeezing gently. Stir in cranberry juice concentrate. Chill. Strain and serve over ice. Yield: 5 cups.

Sue Everett, Texas

ALMOND TEA

Great for hot summer parties.

3 tablespoons unsweetened lemon flavored instant tea
1½ cups sugar
2 cups boiling water
1 (12-ounce) can frozen lemonade
1 tablespoon almond extract
1 tablespoon vanilla extract

Mix all ingredients together. Before serving, add 2½ quarts cold water. Garnish with orange slices. Makes 10-11 cups.

Leny Young, Ohio

SOUPS &

CRANBERRY SALAD

1 lb. cranberries
1 orange
2 red apples
1 1/2 c. sugar
1 package jello

Wash Wash cranberries, put through food chopper.
Wash apples, quarter and core, then put through
chopper. W   orange, remove seeds and grind
it. Use o   . Mix cranberries
apples, o
overnight
and add c
Variation:
Add 1/2

KVĚTÁKOVÁ POLÉVKA (Cauliflower Soup)

3 T. butter
3 T. flour
1/8 t. nutmeg
3 2/3 c. chicken broth
snipped parsley
1 c. water
3 c. small cauliflowerets
1 egg yolk
3 T. heavy cream

About 45 min before serving:
1. In medium saucepan melt butter or margarine;
blend in flour and nutmeg. Slowly stir in chicken
broth and water, them bring to a boil, while
stirring. Now add cauliflowerets; then simmer soup
civered about 25 min or until cauliflower is
tender.
2 In small bowl mix egg yolk with cream, stirring
until blended; add to sop, then bring just to
boiling point; while stirring constantly.
Serve in small bowls, sprinkled with parsley.

B
without st
Salt until
mixture

ZITI SALAD

16 oz. cooked ziti
1/4 c. milk
1/2 c. sour cream
1 1/2 c. mayo
2 packets brown bouillon powder.
1/2 T. salt
1 red onion
2 toma
6 sweet o

2 small gr
large sl
White
fres

th milk whis
bouillon powder. salt
over ziti. Add oth
gar mix well, garnish

SALADS

Soups

SOUP WITH TORTELLINI

1 pound Italian sausage

1 cup onions, coarsely chopped

2 garlic cloves, minced

5 cups beef broth

½ cup water

½ cup red wine or vinegar

1 (16-ounce) can tomatoes, diced

1 cup carrots, thinly sliced

½ teaspoon basil leaves

½ teaspoon oregano leaves

1 (8-ounce) can tomato sauce

1½ cups zucchini, sliced

2 cups frozen meat or cheese filled tortellini or very small ravioli

3 tablespoons fresh parsley, chopped

1 medium green pepper cut into ½ inch pieces

Grated Parmesan cheese

If sausage is in casing, remove casing. In 5 quart Dutch oven, brown sausage. Remove from pan. Saute onions and garlic in reserved drippings until onions are tender. Add broth, water, wine, tomatoes, carrots, basil, oregano, tomato sauce and sausage. Bring to boil. Reduce heat. Simmer uncovered 30 minutes. Skim fat from soup. Stir in zucchini, tortellini, parsley and green pepper. Simmer covered 35 to 40 minutes or until tortellini are tender. Sprinkle Parmesan cheese on top of each serving. Serves 8.

Henry Graalfs, for Jim Dargin, Iowa

TORTELLINI, WHITE BEAN AND SPINACH SOUP

1 can chicken broth with roasted garlic

2 cans chicken broth, without seasoning

1 or 2 cups thinly sliced carrots

1 medium onion, chopped

1 can diced tomatoes with basil, garlic and oregano

1 box frozen, chopped spinach, thawed

1 teaspoon dried Italian seasoning (oregano/basil)

1 (16-ounce) can navy or great Northern beans, undrained

1 (9-ounce) package refrigerated cheese filled tortellini*

Shredded Parmesan cheese

In a 4-5 quart saucepan, combine broth, carrots and onions. Simmer until vegetables are tender. Add tomatoes, spinach and seasonings. Simmer about 10 minutes. Add white beans with liquid, and the tortellini. Boil gently for about 10 more minutes until the tortellini is tender. Stir occasionally. Tortellini will swell as it cooks. Sprinkle with Parmesan cheese before serving.

Juanita Magnuson, Alabama

This is an easy soup to make and it is delicious served with hot cornbread. Leftovers are good the next day.

*Meat filled tortellini may be substituted for cheese-filled tortellini.

CHICKEN TORTELLINI SOUP

1 can Swanson chicken broth

1 can water

1 can cream of chicken soup

1 medium carrot, chopped (about ½ cup)

1 small onion, chopped, (about ⅓ cup)

1 teaspoon dried Italian seasoning, crushed

⅛ teaspoon pepper

1 cup cheese tortellini

1 cup fresh or frozen chopped broccoli

1½ cups chopped, cooked chicken breast

¼ cup finely shredded or grated Parmesan cheese

1 tablespoon snipped parsley

In a large saucepan, combine chicken broth, water, cream of chicken soup, carrots, onion, Italian seasonings and pepper. Heat to boiling. Reduce heat, cover and simmer 20 minutes. Add tortellini and broccoli. Cover and simmer about 15 minutes or until tortellini is tender. Stir in chicken and heat through. Ladle into bowls, sprinkle with Parmesan cheese and parsley. Makes 4 main dish servings.

Betty Stockman, North Dakota

KICKIN' CHICKEN SOUP

2 large boneless chicken breasts or a cooked rotisserie chicken

3 tablespoons Canola oil

1 large onion, chopped

3 cloves garlic, minced

1 jalapeno pepper, minced. Add seeds for more heat

1 (32-ounce) can low sodium chicken broth

3 cups fresh or frozen corn kernels

1 (15.5-ounce) can black beans

Juice of 1 lime

1 teaspoon salt or to taste

½ teaspoon ground red pepper or hot sauce

Freshly ground black pepper

½ cup minced cilantro

Shredded Monterrey Jack cheese

Tortilla chips (optional)

Heat broiler. Cook chicken, turning once, about 10 minutes. Meanwhile, heat oil in stockpot over medium heat. Add onion, garlic and jalapeno. Cook until soft, about three minutes. Add broth, corn, beans, lime juice, salt, red and black pepper. Bring to a boil; reduce heat to simmer.

Slice or shred the cooked chicken. Add to pot. Add cilantro. Heat through, about 1 minute. Ladle into soup bowls. Top each with shredded cheese and crumbled tortilla chips, if desired. Serves 8.

Beck Van Vranken, Washington, DC

BROCCOLI CHEESE SOUP

    1 (2 pound) box Velveeta cheese
    ½ gallon milk
    1½ medium onions, chopped
    1½ cloves garlic, minced
    ¼ cup butter
    1 bunch chopped broccoli, about 4 cups

Melt Velveeta in a double boiler, or non-stick Dutch oven. Add a little milk if cheese starts to stick to pan. In another pan, sauté onions and garlic in butter. When onions are transparent, add broccoli and cook until bright green. Add vegetables and rest of the milk to the melted cheese mixture. Cook over low heat until broccoli is tender, but do not boil. Thin with ¼ cup water, if desired, or add less milk if you want a thicker soup.

Jeri-Lynn Sandusky, Utah

This recipe came from a well-known restaurant and it is one of their most requested recipes. The recipe is so easy to make and it makes enough for a crowd.

CHEESE SOUP

    1 can cream of mushroom soup
    1 can cream of celery soup
    1 can cream of chicken soup
    3 cans evaporated milk
    ½ jar jalapeno Cheese Whiz
    1 (10-ounce) package frozen broccoli (pre-cooked to soften)
    ¼ cup chopped green onions

If you like it very hot, you can add a half of a small can of chopped green chiles

    Combine all ingredients in a soup pot and cook until hot. This makes a large amount of soup. Plenty for 6 to 8 servings.

Mary Baker, Washington

My husband requests this soup often in the fall. Sometimes I add pre-cooked red potato chunks and bacon to it, leaving out the broccoli. Anyway you make it, you'll love the taste.

Denton, Texas was named after my good friend Ernie's great grandfather. This soup is served for the family gathering every Christmas Day.

DENTON'S TORTILLA SOUP

3 tablespoons olive oil

4 large boneless chicken breasts, cubed

4 garlic cloves, minced

2 large onions, chopped

1 (7-ounce) can green chiles, chopped

1¼ teaspoons cumin

¼ teaspoon cayenne pepper

1¼ teaspoons chili powder

Dash black pepper

Dash garlic powder

½ teaspoon dried oregano

¾ teaspoon sweet basil flakes

6–8 cups chicken broth

3 (14.5-ounce) cans Hunt's Choice Cut tomatoes, with juice

1 (6-ounce) can tomato paste

2 (2.25-ounce) cans sliced black olives

⅛ cup or less chopped cilantro

4 green onions, chopped

GARNISH:

Cheddar and Monterrey Jack cheese, grated

Crushed tortilla chips

Avocados

Sour cream

In a large stock pot, heat oil and add chicken and garlic. Cook until chicken is white. Add onions, chiles, cumin, cayenne pepper, chili powder, black pepper, garlic powder, oregano and sweet basil. Simmer for 1 minute. Add chicken broth, chopped tomatoes, tomato paste, black olives, and cilantro. Simmer for 30 minutes. Add green onions and simmer 2 minutes. Garnish as desired. Serves 10. Freezes well.

Nancy DeVries, Illinois

TORTILLA SOUP

2 (10½ -ounce) cans reduced sodium chicken with rice
   soup, undiluted

1 (10-ounce) can Ro-Tel™ tomatoes

Tortilla chips

Cheddar cheese, grated

Combine soup and Ro-Tel™ in a saucepan. Cook over medium heat until thoroughly heated, stirring occasionally. Put chips in bottom of serving bowl, pour soup over chips and sprinkle with cheese.

Kathy Bratton, Texas

TACO SOUP

2 pounds ground beef

1 chopped onion

1 can kidney beans

1 can jalapeno pinto beans

1 can hominy

1 can water or chicken broth, if needed

2 cans stewed tomatoes

1 can Ro-Tel™ tomatoes

1 package taco seasoning

1 package Hidden Valley original ranch dressing

Good over tortilla chips or rice. Also good with Spanish rice or poured over cornbread. Quick, easy and delicious.

You might crush 2-3 cloves of garlic and sauté with onion and beef.

Saute ground beef and chopped onions. Drain fat. Add remaining ingredients. Simmer covered, at least 30 minutes. Better made the day before.

Kathy Bratton, Texas

MEXICAN SOUP

1 can cream of onion soup

1 can cream of potato soup

1 can evaporated milk

1½ cups water

Mix together and simmer.

Add:

1 large can white chicken

1 can chopped green chiles

1 large can diced tomatoes or Ro-Tel™

½ teaspoon black pepper

½ teaspoon garlic salt

Simmer until heated through. Serve in bowls with Monterrey Jack cheese and tortilla chips.

Liz Offord, Texas

SOUTHWEST TACO SOUP

1½ pounds lean ground beef, browned

1 can clear beef broth

2 cans pinto beans

1 can whole kernel corn

1 can stewed tomatoes, cut up

1 can Ro-Tel™ tomatoes

1 package Ranch dressing mix

1 package taco mix

Brown beef. Mix together beef, broth, beans, corn, tomatoes, taco mix and Ranch dressing mix. Open cans and add, juice and all. Simmer 30 minutes.

Liz Offord, Texas

POTATO SOUP

6 raw potatoes, peeled and quartered

1 or 2 diced carrots

1 diced celery stalk

1 heaping teaspoon parsley

2 medium onions, chopped

2 leeks

4 cups water

4 chicken bouillon cubes

2 tablespoons butter

1½ teaspoon salt

Pepper to taste

1 (13-ounce) can skimmed evaporated milk

Place all ingredients except for milk in stew pot and simmer until soft. Add milk and heat to almost boiling. (Do not boil, as it will cause milk to curdle). Top with chopped chives before serving.

Shirley Sterling, Texas

NACHO POTATO SOUP

1 (5-ounce) package au gratin potatoes

1 (11-ounce) can whole kernel corn, drained

1 (10-ounce) can diced tomatoes, drained

1 (4-ounce) can green chiles

2 cups water

2 cups milk

2 cups chopped American cheese

Dash of hot pepper sauce (optional)

Minced fresh parsley (optional)

Combine the potatoes, corn, tomatoes, green chiles and water in a 2-quart saucepan. Mix well. Bring to a boil and reduce heat. Simmer, covered for 15 to 18 minutes or until potatoes are tender. Add milk, cheese, and hot pepper sauce. Cook until cheese is melted, stirring constantly. Garnish with parsley.

Serves 6 to 8.

Liz Offord, Texas

POTATO CHEESE SOUP

This was one of my father's favorite soups.

2 cups diced potatoes

1 cup diced onions

1 cup diced celery

1 cup diced carrots

½ stick butter or margarine

2 cups water

3 chicken bouillon cubes

¼ cup flour

2 cups milk, divided

1 pound Velveeta cheese, cubed

Salt and pepper to taste

Combine potatoes, onions, celery, carrots, margarine, water and bouillon cubes in a large saucepan. Simmer for 1 hour. Make a paste by mixing flour with ¼ cup of the milk. Stir into soup. Add remaining milk. Add cheese and stir. Cook and stir over low heat to prevent cheese from burning. When cheese has melted, add salt and pepper.

This soup does not freeze.

Sue Carmichael, Minnesota

"MUST GO" SOUP OR MAIN DISH

Company coming tomorrow. They want to take you out to lunch but visiting at home is much more satisfactory, so try this MUST GO plan.

Grab all of those neatly bagged leftovers from the freezer — unfortunately not labeled so this could be called MYSTERY SOUP. Partially thaw packages in cold water and toss contents into very large pan. Cover and simmer for two or three hours. Add rice for last half hour or so if using for a main dish. May add frozen brussel sprouts or spinach just before serving. Serve with shredded cheese.

Jean Krest, Colorado

CARROT VICHYSSOISE

1¼ cups peeled and sliced carrots

2 cups peeled and diced potatoes

1 leek, cleaned and sliced, white only

3 cups chicken broth

1 teaspoon salt

⅛ teaspoon white pepper

1 cup cream

Shredded raw carrots, for garnish

Fresh or dried dill, for garnish

In a large saucepan, combine carrots, potatoes, leek, and chicken broth; bring to a boil. Reduce heat and simmer, covered, about 25 minutes or until vegetables are tender. In a blender or food processor, puree the vegetables and their liquid. Place in a bowl, add salt, pepper, and cream; stir to blend. Chill for several hours or overnight. Serve cold with a topping to shredded carrots and dill, if desired. Serves 6.

Liz Hobbs, California

GAZPACHO

1 (16-ounce) can whole peeled tomatoes

2 large garlic cloves

1 teaspoon salt

Dash cayenne pepper

1 teaspoon sugar

1 cucumber, seeds removed

4 cups chicken broth

2 slices pumpernickel bread

2 tablespoons white vinegar

½ green pepper

3 tablespoons olive oil

Blend slowly, a bit at a time, incorporating all of the above ingredients, slowly adding oil. Blend on medium high. Serve with garlic rounds or long crouton sticks to garnish.

Lou Magel, Michigan

KAREN'S WINTER SOUP

1 large onion, chopped
1 ½ pounds chopped sirloin
3 cans Progresso Minestrone soup
3 cans Ranch style beans
3 cans diced tomatoes
1 can Rotel tomatoes

Brown the onion and chopped sirloin. Add the cans of minestrone, beans, and tomatoes. Simmer and enjoy. Eat as is or add Fritos and grated cheese.

Karen Peveto, Texas

HEAT SCALE:
Medium – can be adjusted to mild or hot

For an authentic touch, serve with a plate of fresh dates.

CHICKPEA AND LENTIL SOUP

4 tablespoons olive oil

3 medium onions, chopped

4 medium garlic cloves, finely minced

½ cup finely chopped fresh parsley

2 large jalapeno peppers, finely chopped

2 cups cooked chickpeas (garbanzos)

3 cups canned stewed tomatoes with liquid

½ cup brown or pink lentils, rinsed

9 cups water

1 teaspoon salt

1½ teaspoons ground ginger

1 teaspoon paprika

1 teaspoon ground black pepper

¼ cup brown (or other aromatic) rice

4 tablespoons fresh lemon juice

Heat olive oil in a large Dutch oven and stir-fry onions, garlic, parsley, and jalapeno peppers for 10 minutes. The mixture will release a marvelous fragrance. Stir in remaining ingredients, except rice and lemon juice. Bring to a boil. Stir in rice, cover and cook for 25-30 minutes or until rice is cooked. Stir in fresh lemon juice and serve immediately. Serves 12.

The fresh lemon juice introduces an interesting flavor twist to this recipe.

Judy Krohn, Texas

NORTH WOODS BEAN SOUP

1 cup baby carrots, halved

1 cup chopped onion

2 minced garlic cloves

7 ounces turkey kielbasas, halved lengthwise and cut into
½ inch pieces

4 cups chicken broth

1 teaspoon dried Italian seasoning

½ teaspoon black pepper

2 (15-ounce) cans great Northern (white) beans, drained
and rinsed.

1 (6-ounce) bag fresh baby spinach leaves

Heat a soup pot coated with cooking spray over medium heat. Saute carrots, onion, garlic and kielbasa for 3 minutes, reduce heat to medium and cook for 5 minutes. Add chicken broth, beans and seasonings and boil for 5 minutes.

Place 2 cups of soup in a food processor. Blend until smooth. Return to pot. Simmer 5 minutes. Remove from heat. Add spinach and stir until wilted. Makes 5 hearty, tasty servings.

Connie Timko, Illinois

PEA SOUP

½ pound bacon, diced

½ to 1 cup chopped onion

¼ cup chopped celery

¼ cup shredded or finely chopped carrots

2 crushed garlic cloves

6 cups water

2 cups yellow or green split peas

1 bay leaf

1½ teaspoons salt

¼ teaspoon pepper

1 cup evaporated milk

Saute bacon, onion, celery, carrot, and garlic in a Dutch oven for 3 to 5 minutes or until vegetables are tender. Add water, peas, bay leaf, salt and pepper. Heat to boiling. Reduce heat and cover. Simmer for 2 hours or until peas are soft. Stir occasionally. Remove bay leaf. Stir in evaporated milk. Heat to serving temperature.

Cheryl Wills, South Carolina

LING

ted water
spoon of
prevent
te filling.
d baking
e are re-
25 to 30
d rest of

CHEESE FILLING

½ lb. Mozzarella cheese, diced
2 lbs. Ricotta cheese (or

MEAT FILLING

1½ lbs. chopped meat (beef or

SHRIMP AND CORN SOUP

3 yellow onions, chopped fine

1 medium bell pepper, chopped

3–4 garlic cloves, chopped

2–3 pounds shrimp

1 (14.5-ounce) can Ro-Tel™ tomatoes

1 (8-ounce) can tomato sauce

1 bunch green onions, chopped

3 (14.5-ounce) cans creamed corn

3 (14.5-ounce) cans whole kernel corn, undrained

Saute onions, bell pepper, garlic and shrimp. Put remaining ingredients in a large pot, add sautéed vegetables. Add water to consistency you prefer. Season to taste – bring to a boil and simmer.

Emily LaFrance, Louisiana

ONION SOUP

5 cups thinly sliced onions (do not use red onions)

6 tablespoons butter

2 small garlic cloves, crushed (optional)

½ teaspoon dry mustard

Dash of thyme

1 quart stock or water

1 tablespoon tamari

3 tablespoons dry white wine

Few dashes of white pepper

Salt to taste (1–2 teaspoons)

1 teaspoon honey (optional)

Cook onions and optional garlic in butter. Cook over medium heat until thoroughly heated but not too brown. Add mustard and thyme. Mix well. Add remaining ingredients. Cover and cook slowly for at least 30 minutes. Serve topped with croutons and grated cheese.

Jean Krest, Colorado

MORT'S CLASSIC FRENCH ONION SOUP

4 tablespoons butter

7 cups sliced Bermuda or Spanish onions (3–4 large)

Pinch of sugar

2 cloves garlic, minced

½ cup red wine

6 cups beef broth

1 bay leaf

1 teaspoon thyme

Salt and pepper to taste

1 egg yolk, slightly beaten

1 tablespoon cognac

6 (1-inch thick) slices French bread, toasted

1½ cups shredded Gruyere cheese

½ cup grated Parmesan cheese

Melt butter over low heat; add onions and cook over low heat about 45 minutes or until very tender, but still golden. Turn up heat slightly. Add sugar and cook, stirring until browned.

Add garlic and cook another minute, then pour in wine and cook over high heat 3-4 minutes. Add broth, bay leaf, and thyme. Cook over low heat for 30 minutes. Taste and add salt and pepper as needed.

Stir in a small amount of hot broth into the egg yolk and add to soup, stirring well. Add cognac and divide between four ovenproof soup bowls.

To serve, top with slices of bread and cheese. Run under broiler just until bubbly. Makes 4 servings.

Betty Ann Sheffloe, Nebraska

PUMPKIN VEGETABLE SOUP

1 large onion, chopped

2 tablespoons butter or margarine

4 cups reduced sodium chicken broth

2 medium potatoes, peeled and cubed

2 large carrots, chopped

2 celery ribs, chopped

1 cup cooked fresh or frozen lima beans

1 cup fresh or frozen corn

1 (15-ounce) can solid-pack pumpkin

½ teaspoon salt

¼ teaspoon white pepper

¼ teaspoon ground nutmeg

In a large saucepan, sauté onion in butter until tender. Add broth, potatoes, carrots, celery, lima beans and corn. Bring to a boil. Reduce heat; cover and simmer for 25-30 minutes or until vegetables are tender. Stir in pumpkin, salt, pepper, and nutmeg. Cook 5-10 minutes longer or until heated through. Serves 7.

Jim and Mary Ralston, Illinois

This is fun to serve lunch guests. Serve with a salad.

EASY PUMPKIN SOUP

1 medium sized onion, cut up

Equal amount of celery, cut up

1 (14-ounce) can fat free chicken broth

1 can pumpkin (not pie filling)

Garlic salt, pepper, and any spices you like (I use dill weed and chives, too)

Cook onion and celery in broth until almost tender. Add pumpkin and spices. Cook on low for another few minutes. Then put into blender and blend until smooth. If you prefer, don't use the blender and just have chunky soup. Can be served with low fat sour cream and/or shrimp. Sometimes I add a small potato to the cut up vegetables.

Nancy DeVries, Illinois

SOUTHWESTERN PUMPKIN SOUP

3 cups chicken stock or canned low-salt chicken broth

1 cup whipping cream

1 (15-ounce) can pure pumpkin

3 tablespoons packed dark brown sugar

1 teaspoon ground cumin

½ teaspoon chili powder

½ teaspoon ground coriander

⅛ teaspoon ground nutmeg

¾ cup grated sharp Cheddar cheese

Chopped fresh cilantro

Optional garnishes: Cinnamon, broken tortilla chips, toasted pumpkin seeds, ½ cup honey

This golden-tone soup is wonderfully warming on crisp autumn days. For fun autumn serving flair, use hollowed out pumpkin shells as serving bowls.

In a heavy, medium saucepan, bring chicken stock and whipping cream to a boil. Whisk in canned pumpkin, brown sugar, cumin, chili powder, coriander and nutmeg. Reduce heat to medium and simmer until soup thickens slightly and flavors blend, about 15 minutes. Season to taste with salt and pepper. Ladle soup into bowls. Garnish each serving with Cheddar cheese and cilantro before serving.

Soup can be prepared one day in advance. Cover and refrigerate. Warm over medium-low heat, whisking occasionally.

Robbin Roberts, Texas

TOMATO BASIL SOUP

4 cups tomatoes, peeled or canned

4 cups tomato sauce or V-8 juice or chicken stock

12—14 fresh basil leaves

1 cup heavy whipping cream

¼ pound unsalted butter

Puree tomatoes, sauce, juice, leaves in small batches. Put on stove then add cream and butter. Melt together over low heat. Add cracked pepper to taste. Serves 6.

Carol Ryan, Kansas

Delicious! Enjoy!

This recipe was given to me years ago by a dear friend. We always enjoy it, especially in the winter.

ZESTY VEGETABLE SOUP

1 pound ground meat

1 large onion, chopped

2 cans Italian style stewed tomatoes, chopped, including liquid

2 (13.75-ounce) cans beef broth

1 large can Veg-all, including liquid

1 cup medium egg noodles, uncooked

½ teaspoon oregano

In a large pot, brown meat and onion. Drain off fat. Salt and pepper to taste. Stir in remaining ingredients. Bring to a boil. Reduce heat, cover and simmer 15 minutes.

Instead of Italian tomatoes, use 1 can tomatoes and green chiles. Do not use extra pepper.

Wanda Mueller, Texas

There is an abundance of wild rice in Minnesota where I am from and we use it in many types of recipes.

WILD RICE SOUP

2 tablespoons butter or margarine

⅓ cup chopped onion

⅓ cup flour

2 (14-ounce) cans chicken broth, regular, low sodium or low fat

1 (4-ounce) can mushrooms, do not drain

Salt and pepper to taste

1 (8-ounce) carton whipping cream

¼ cup dry sherry

Parsley to taste

1 tablespoon Worcestershire sauce

1 cup wild rice, cooked and drained

Melt butter, add onion and sauté until transparent. Blend flour into butter/onion mixture. Slowly add chicken broth and mushrooms. Stir until thickened. Add salt, pepper, cream, sherry, parsley, Worcestershire sauce and cooked rice. Cook slowly 5-10 minutes, but do not boil.

Sue Cardinal, Minnesota

RUSSIAN CABBAGE BORSCHT

1½ cups thinly sliced potato

1 cup thinly sliced beets

4 cups stock or water

1½ cups chopped onion

2 tablespoons butter

1 scant teaspoon caraway seeds

2 teaspoons salt

1 stalk celery, chopped

1 large carrot, sliced

3 cups chopped cabbage

Black pepper

¼ teaspoon dill weed

1 tablespoon plus 1 teaspoon cider vinegar

1 tablespoon plus 1 teaspoon honey

1 cup tomato puree

Place potatoes, beets and water in a saucepan and cook until tender. Save the water.

In a large kettle, begin cooking the onions in butter. Add caraway seeds and salt. Cook until onion is translucent. Add celery, carrots and cabbage. Add water from potatoes and beets, cook covered until all vegetables are tender. Add potatoes and beets and all remaining ingredients.

Cover and simmer slowly for at least 30 minutes. Taste to correct seasonings. Serve topped with sour cream.

Jean Krest, Colorado

CORN CHOWDER

4 slices bacon, diced

2 tablespoons butter

3 cups sliced onion

1 bay leaf

¾ cup fresh bread crumbs

4 cups chicken broth

3 to 3 ½ cups diced white rose potatoes

1/8 to ¼ teaspoon red pepper flakes

Salt and freshly ground pepper, to taste

2 cups half and half

1 (10-ounce) package frozen corn

1 (15-ounce) can creamed corn

In a medium sauté pan, sauté bacon and drain; add butter, onion and bay leaf. Cover and simmer for 10 minutes. Stir in bread crumbs. Set aside.

In a large pot, mix broth, potatoes, pepper flakes, and onion mixture. Simmer for 30 minutes. Blend in half and half and corn. Simmer for 3 to 5 minutes. Puree 2 to 3 cups of the soup and stir it back into the pot. Mix well. Serve warm. Serves 8,

Chowder may be refrigerated and reheated at serving time.

Liz Hobbs, California

CRAB AND SHRIMP BISQUE

THE SOUP BASE:

Melt 1/4 cup butter. Blend in 1/4 cup flour, 1/2 teaspoon salt, dash of cayenne, 1/8 teaspoon nutmeg and 1 tablespoon minced parsley. Gradually stir in 1-1/2 cups milk and 2 cups light cream.

THE SEAFOOD:

Cook the soup base over low heat, stirring constantly, until the sauce thickens and is smooth. Flake the contents of 1 pound of crabmeat, discarding the cartilage. Chop and add 1/2 pound of fresh cooked and cleaned shrimp. Small scallops may also be added. Heat through.

Just before serving, add 2 tablespoons sherry. Stir and serve immediately. Garnish with a sprig of parsley.

Zina Versaggi Graalfs, Florida

CREOLE SEAFOOD GUMBO

Optional: Before serving, stir in file.

½ cup flour

½ cup cooking oil

Add flour to oil in a large cooking pot, stir constantly until the roux turns the color of peanut butter; add the following:

1–2 cups chopped onion

3 cloves chopped garlic

1–2 cups chopped celery

1 large can diced tomatoes

1 cup fresh chopped parsley

½ cup chopped bell pepper

6 cups chicken stock

½ teaspoon thyme

½ teaspoon basil

½ teaspoon pepper

1 teaspoon salt

½ teaspoon red pepper or Tabasco® sauce

Simmer for 1 to 2 hours then add:

1 pound cleaned medium shrimp

½ pound cleaned lump crabmeat

Stir to mix, cook until shrimp turns pink. Serve over hot rice.

Millie Royer, Texas

Salads & Dressings

JUDY'S MACARONI AND PUDDING SALAD

2 (16-ounce) cans chunk pineapple

2 eggs, beaten

¾ cup sugar

2 teaspoons all-purpose flour

1 box Pastina (macaroni)

1 large can Mandarin oranges

1 (10-ounce) jar cherries

2 (9-ounce) containers whipped topping

Drain pineapple juice into a pan, add beaten eggs, sugar and flour. Cook and stir over medium heat until thick. Remove from heat. In a separate pan, cook macaroni according to package directions and drain. Pour cooled pineapple mixture over macaroni and mix thoroughly. Cover and store in refrigerator overnight. The next morning, drain juice from oranges and cherries. Reserve orange juice. Add drained fruit and whipped topping to macaroni mixture and cool for several hours before serving. If pudding sauce is too thick, use a little reserved orange juice.

Judy Dashiell, Minnesota

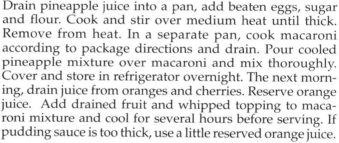

BUTTERMILK SALAD

1 cup buttermilk

1 cup sugar

1 cup chopped nuts

1 large container whipped topping

3 bananas, diced

Combine well and store in freezer. A drop of food coloring makes this a festive salad.

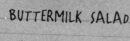

Joyce Latta, Texas

TWENTY FOUR HOUR SALAD

2 cans whole cherries (Queen Anne) halved and pitted

2 cans diced pineapple

2 cans mandarin oranges

2 cups miniature marshmallows

¼ pound almonds, blanched and chopped

2 eggs

2 tablespoons sugar

¼ cup half and half

Juice of one lemon

1 cup heavy cream, whipped

Combine well-drained fruit. Add marshmallows and nuts. Beat eggs until light, gradually adding sugar, light cream and lemon juice. Cook in double boiler until smooth and thick, stirring constantly. Cool. Fold in whipped cream. Pour over fruit mixture. Mix lightly. Chill 24 hours. Do not freeze. Serves 10–12.

Liz Offord, Texas

HEAVENLY HASH

Makes a great salad or a dessert.

1 can sweetened condensed milk

1 (12-ounce) carton whipped topping

1 (21-ounce) can cherry pie filling

1 (11-ounce) can mandarin oranges, drained

1 (20-ounce) can pineapple tidbits, drained

1 cup chopped pecans

1 cup miniature marshmallows

1 cup shredded coconut

Mix condensed milk and whipped topping and refrigerate or freeze overnight. The next day, add remaining ingredients and mix well. Refrigerate until chilled. Serves 12 to 15.

Jo Ann Christal, Texas

FROZEN CRANBERRY SALAD

1 (8-ounce) package cream cheese, softened

2 tablespoons mayonnaise

2 tablespoons sugar

1 can whole cranberry sauce

1 (8-ounce) can crushed pineapple, drained

½ cup chopped nuts

1½ to 2 cups whipped topping

Soften cream cheese; blend in mayonnaise and sugar. Add fruit and nuts. Fold in whipped topping. Pour into a gelatin mold. Freeze at least 6 hours. Serves 10.

Kathy Bratton, Texas

AMBROSIA

I received this recipe from a friend many years ago and have used it ever since. It is wonderful as a side dish for holiday dinners. I don't measure any more – just put it together so it looks right.

Allow 3 days to make

1 can crushed pineapple, (regular size, not small)

1 cup miniature marshmallows

1 can coconut

1 pound red grapes, halved, remove seed if necessary

3–4 oranges, cut up, reserve juice

1 apple, chopped

3 bananas, cut up

First Day: combine pineapple, marshmallows and coconut and let soak overnight in refrigerator.

Second Day: Add grapes and oranges. Return to refrigerator.

Third Day: Add apples and bananas.

Nancy Wright, Arizona

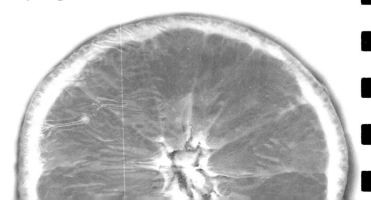

FROZEN SALAD

5 bananas, mashed

1 large can crushed pineapple, drained

1½ cups sugar

¾ cups maraschino cherries, with juice

4 teaspoon lemon juice

1 cup chopped pecans

1 (16-ounce) carton sour cream

1 (9-ounce) carton frozen whipped topping

After you freeze the salads, you can store them in plastic bags and take out what you need. Don't thaw before eating.

Put muffin papers in muffin pans. Combine all ingredients and pour into prepared muffin pans. Freeze. Makes about 40 cupcakes.

JoAnn Christal, Texas

CHERRY COKE™ CONGEALED SALAD

1 (12-ounce) can Cherry Coke™

1 (20-ounce) can crushed pineapple, drain and reserve juice

1 can sweet pitted bing cherries (Oregon), drain and reserve juice

1 (6-ounce) package cherry gelatin

1 cup fresh pitted black bing cherries or frozen (cut in half)

1½ cups chopped pecans

4 tablespoons Cherry Brandy (optional)

1 (8-ounce) package cream cheese, cubed

In a large saucepan, combine Cherry Coke™, reserved pineapple juice, reserved cherry juice and gelatin. Stir well and let simmer for 3 minutes. Pour into a 9-inch decorative bowl. Refrigerate for about 10 minutes to cool. Add cherries, pineapple, and pecans. Refrigerate for 1 hour. Add brandy. Stir slightly. When it's almost congealed, fold in the cream cheese that has been cut into small squares. Do not mash. Refrigerate and wait for those praises. Serves 12.

Can be cut into squares and garnished with whipped cream and a cherry on top for a dessert.

Aline Babb Lewis, Texas

PRETZEL SALAD

2 cups small pretzel pieces

¾ cup melted butter

3 tablespoons sugar

1 (8-ounce) package cream cheese, softened

1 cup sugar

1 small container whipped topping

2 cups water

1 (6-punce) box strawberry gelatin

1 (10-ounce) package chopped frozen strawberries

1 (10-ounce) package whole frozen strawberries

Mix pretzels, butter and 3 tablespoons sugar. Flatten into bottom of a 13 x 9-inch pan. Bake 8 minutes at 400 degrees. Remove and cool. Beat cream cheese, 1 cup sugar and whipped topping. Spread over pretzels and chill. Boil 2 cups water and dissolve gelatin.

Add strawberries and mix until just combined. Let stand until slightly thick. Pour over cream cheese mixture and chill until set.

Betty Sellers, Texas

CRANBERRY GELATIN SALAD

1 (6-ounce) package cherry gelatin

1½ cups boiling water

1 (20-ounce) can crushed pineapple, with juice

1 (16-ounce) can whole-berry cranberry sauce

1½ cups seedless red grapes, halved

¼ cup chopped pecans

In a large bowl, dissolve gelatin in water. Stir in pineapple and cranberry sauce. Refrigerate for 30 minutes. Stir in grapes and pecans. Pour into a 2 quart serving bowl. Refrigerate until firm. Serves 8–10.

Ase Touba, Minnesota

ORANGE CREAM FRUIT SALAD

1 (20-ounce) can pineapple tidbits, drained

1 (16-ounce) can peach slices, drained

1 (11-ounce) can mandarin oranges, sliced

2 medium firm bananas, sliced

1 medium apple, chopped

1 (3.4-ounce) package instant vanilla pudding mix

1½ cups milk

⅓ frozen orange juice concentrate

¾ cup sour cream

In a large salad bowl, combine fruits. Set aside. In a small mixing bowl, beat pudding mix, milk, and orange juice concentrate for 2 minutes. Add sour cream and mix well. Spoon over fruit, tossing to coat. Cover and refrigerate 2 hours. Serves 8-10.

Sharon Odom, Texas

ORANGE ASPIC

2 (11-ounce) cans mandarin orange sections

Orange juice

2 (3-ounce) packages orange gelatin

1 pint orange sherbet or rainbow sherbet

I sometimes add a half package plain gelatin. This sets up quickly. Tasty and refreshing.

Drain oranges over a 2-cup measuring cup, reserving liquid. Add orange juice to measure 2 cups. Bring juice to a boil in a saucepan. Remove from heat. Add gelatin and stir 2 minutes or until gelatin dissolves. Cool. Pour into a large bowl. Add sherbet and mix with an electric mixer until blended. Stir in mandarin oranges. Pour into an 8 x 8-inch pan, chill until firmly set. Serves 8.

Juanita Magnuson, Alabama

HOT FRUIT COMPOTE

1 can pineapple slices, drained

1 can pears, drained

1 can peach halves, drained

1 can apricots, drained

1 jar red spice apple rings, drained but save juice

Drain fruit and let dry on paper towels. Arrange in baking dish.

SAUCE:

1 stick butter

½ cup packed brown sugar

2 tablespoons all-purpose flour

½ cup sherry

2 sticks cinnamon

Dash of curry if you wish

Combine ingredients for sauce and cook until thick. Pour over fruit. Bake in a 350 degree oven for 25 minutes. If it looks dry toward the end of baking, moisten with a bit of spiced apple ring juice. Serves 12.

Can be prepared the day before, cover and refrigerate and then bake.

Liv Volland, Wisconsin

HOT CURRIED FRUIT COMPOTE

1 pound can peach slices

1 pound can pear halves

1 pound can apricot halves

1 pound can pineapple chunks

1 pound can dark sweet cherries

2 teaspoons butter or margarine

⅓ cup packed brown sugar

1½ teaspoons curry powder

Your favorite fruits can be substituted for those listed. Drain fruits and cube. Put all fruits, except cherries, into a 2½-quart casserole. Melt butter and blend in sugar and curry powder. Spoon mixture over fruit. Bake at 325 degrees for 15 minutes. Remove from oven and carefully add cherries. Return to oven for 15 minutes. This is delicious with ham. It makes a wonderful addition to Christmas dinner.

Eleanor Cowan, Texas

Zina Versaggi Graalfs, Florida

CALIFORNIA WALDORF SALAD

Great for a brunch with egg casserole, quiche, roast pork, etc.

2 large firm apples, cut into chunks

Juice from 2 lemons, divided

1 large orange, or 2 tangerines, sectioned

1 stalk celery, chopped

¼ cup raisins or dried currants

⅓ cup toasted cashews

DRESSING:

1 cup yogurt

1 small ripe avocado (1 cup mashed)

⅓ teaspoon grated lemon rind

3–4 tablespoons honey, to taste

Soak apple chunks in half the lemon juice. Combine remaining lemon juice with dressing ingredients in the jar of a blender. Puree until very smooth. Add remaining ingredients to apples and toss with dressing. Taste to adjust lemon-honey balance.

Jean Krest, Colorado

PEAR AND BLEU CHEESE SALAD

1 bunch arugula, torn

1 head Romaine lettuce, torn

3 medium pears, cored and thinly sliced

½ cup buttermilk

½ cup bleu cheese

1 medium garlic clove, minced

¼ teaspoon black pepper, ground

¾ ounce chopped walnuts, about 3 tablespoons, toasted

Combine buttermilk, cheese, garlic, and pepper. Toss greens with dressing. Divide arugula and Romaine among salad plates. Arrange pears on greens. Top with walnuts and serve.

Zina Versaggi Graalfs, Florida

SUMMER SALAD

1 teaspoon grated fresh ginger

1 tablespoon rice wine vinegar

2 teaspoons freshly squeezed lemon juice

¼ teaspoon coarse salt

3 scallions, cut diagonally into ¼ inch pieces

½ small jicama, peeled, cut into ¼ inch matchsticks

½ honey dew melon, peeled, seeded and cut into ½ inch cubes (about 2 cups)

1 orange bell pepper, cut into ¼-inch wide strips

1½ cups fresh blueberries, picked over and rinsed

4 ounces baby arugula

2 teaspoons canola oil

Freshly ground black pepper

Whisk together ginger, vinegar, lemon juice and salt. Set aside. In a serving bowl, combine scallions, jicama, honey dew, bell pepper and blueberries. Pour ginger mixture over salad. Toss to combine. (Salad can be made up to 30 minutes ahead of time, if desired). Just before serving, add arugula and drizzle with oil. Season generously with black pepper. Toss.

Carol Ryan, Kansas

I brought this recipe from Mississippi when I moved to Texas. It is a favorite of family and friends. Make the whole recipe because it will be eaten.

RICE SALAD

2 packages chicken flavored rice (not Uncle Ben's)

¾ cup green pepper, chopped

8 green onions, chopped (use tops if not too strong)

16 pimento stuffed olives

2 (6-ounce) jars marinated artichoke hearts, sliced

⅔ cup mayonnaise

1 teaspoon curry powder

Cook rice, according to package directions, omitting butter. Cool in refrigerator. Add pepper, onions and olives. Drain artichoke hearts and reserve marinade. Add sliced artichokes. Mix artichoke marinade, mayonnaise and curry powder. Add to salad, toss, and chill. Serves 12.

Bunny Petty, Texas

TABOLI

1½ cups soaked, #2 cracked wheat (bulgar)

1 bunch parsley, chopped

1 medium cucumber, sliced and cubed

3–4 medium tomatoes, sliced and cubed

3–4 green onions, thinly sliced

Fresh mint, cut to taste

Olive oil

Freshly squeezed lemon juice

Salt and pepper to taste

In a medium-sized bowl, rinse cracked wheat until water runs off clear. Fill bowl with cold water and let soak for approximately 30–45 minutes. (Soaking time can vary; anything up to 12 hours is fine.) The wheat will plump up. Chop parsley, cucumber, tomatoes and green onions. Place in a large bowl. Cut the leaves off of 16–20 sprigs of fresh mint. Add to vegetables. Use both hands to squeeze water from the wheat and then add it to the salad. Add olive oil, lemon juice, salt and pepper to taste. The cracked wheat will continue to soak up a little more liquid, (olive oil and lemon juice) so be sure to make it juicier than it should be. Store any remaining taboli in a tightly sealed container. It will keep in the refrigerator for up to three days.

This recipe makes a large bowl of taboli. It doubles well for large crowds. After you try it for the first time try adjusting the tomatoes and onions depending upon taste and size. The salad is more visually appealing when everything is cut to about the same size. The packaged cracked wheat can be stored in the freezer for up to a year. Enjoy!

BROCCOLI SALAD

2 to 3 bunches fresh broccoli

1 medium onion, chopped

12 slices bacon, cooked crisp and crumbled

1 cup sunflower seeds

1 cup raisins (soak in hot water, then drain)

1 cup mayonnaise

½ cup sugar

2 tablespoons vinegar

Mix broccoli, onion, bacon, sunflower seeds and raisins in a large bowl. In a separate bowl, blend mayonnaise, sugar and vinegar. Add mayonnaise mixture to salad just before serving.

Judy Krohn, Texas

BROCCOLI-CAULIFLOWER SALAD

1 cup mayonnaise

2 tablespoons white vinegar

1 clove garlic

1 tablespoon sugar

1 teaspoon salt

1 cucumber, peeled

1 pound cauliflower, chopped

1 pound broccoli, chopped

4 green onions or ½ cup chopped red onion

Combine mayonnaise, vinegar, garlic, sugar, and salt. Pour over vegetables. Cover and chill before serving.

Marilyn Erlandson, Pennsylvania

Betty Wolter, New York

CARROT SALAD

3 (No. 2) cans carrots, drained

1 large onion, chopped

1 green pepper, chopped

Mix well and place in a deep bowl, which has a lid.

1 can tomato soup

1/2 cup vegetable oil

1/3 cup vinegar

1 cup sugar

1 teaspoon salt

1 teaspoon pepper

1 teaspoon prepared mustard

1 teaspoon Worcestershire sauce

Bring to a boil. Pour over carrot mixture. Let sit. Will keep for quite a while in the refrigerator.

Ralph and Jeannine Bowles, Washington

just heat so
cken, uncover
utes.

SPINACH SALAD

2 bunches spinach
2 bunches leaf lettuce
½ pound bacon, cooked crisp and crumbled
1½ cups large curd cottage cheese

DRESSING

½ cup sugar
1 teaspoon salt
1 teaspoon dry mustard
1 teaspoon grated onion (can also use dried)
⅓ cup cider vinegar
1 cup vegetable oil, can use less
1 teaspoon poppy seed

Combine all ingredients. Pour over fresh salad greens and serve immediately.

Ralph and Jeaninne Bowles, Washington

SPINACH SALAD

Mix at least 6 hours before using:
1 cup salad oil
5 tablespoons red wine vinegar
½ teaspoon dry mustard
1½ teaspoons salt
1½ tablespoons sugar
2 cloves garlic, crushed
Black pepper

Marinate 1 package sliced mushrooms in dressing for 2–3 hours before serving.

Add two packages spinach, 4 hard boiled eggs, 8 strips bacon (cooked crisp and crumbled). Toss and serve.

Liz Offord, Texas

MAGGIE'S EASY ALL PURPOSE SALAD DRESSING

3 eggs, beaten
½ cup white vinegar

Cook and stir over low flame until thick. Add:

Salt and pepper to taste
1 teaspoon mustard
¼ cup sugar
¼ cup evaporated (not condensed) or regular milk

Stir and strain. The vinegar, sugar and condiments can be adjusted to suit your personal taste. Add mayonnaise if desired.

Can be used on green salads, potato salad and is especially good drizzled over canned salmon.

INDIAN SPINACH SALAD

COUNTRY FRENCH SALAD DRESSING

2/3 cup oil

1/3 cup ketchup

1 tablespoon lemon juice

¾ teaspoon salt

3 tablespoons sugar, or to taste

2 tablespoons cider vinegar

½ teaspoon onion powder

Place the ingredients in a covered pint jar, shake well and refrigerate. Dressing will thicken when chilled.

Cordelia L. Razek, Louisiana

Combine in a jar, cover and chill.

¼ cup white wine vinegar

¼ cup salad oil

2 tablespoons chopped chutney

2 teaspoons sugar

½ teaspoon salt

1½ teaspoons curry powder

1 teaspoon dry mustard

Place 3 bunches of torn spinach in a large bowl. Top with 1 chopped, unpared apple, 1 cup raisins, 1 cup peanuts and 2 tablespoons sliced green onion. Shake dressing, pour over salad and toss.

Terri Anderson, California

SPINACH SALAD WITH SWEET-SOUR DRESSING

1 (10-ounce) bag raw spinach, rinsed and chilled until crisp

1 (8-ounce) can water chestnuts, drained and sliced

1 (16-ounce) cans bean sprouts, drained

8 strips bacon, fried crisp and crumbled

4 hard-boiled eggs, sliced

Tear spinach into piece and combine with the rest of the ingredients, tossing lightly. Add enough sweet-sour dressing to moisten to your taste. Toss again. Serves 6.

SWEET-SOUR DRESSING

1 cup oil

¾ cup sugar

¼ cup vinegar

⅓ cup ketchup

2 tablespoons Worcestershire sauce

1 medium onion, chopped

Blend together and store in refrigerator.

Ralph and Jeannine Bowles, Washington

FRESH SPINACH SALAD

⅓ pound fresh spinach

¼ cup toasted almonds, walnuts or pecans

3 slices bacon, cooked and crumbled

Chopped hard cooked egg, if desired, for garnish

Remove stems from spinach leaves. Wash leaves thoroughly. Pat dry. Tear into bite sized pieces. Combine spinach, nuts and bacon in a large bowl. Set aside.

DRESSING

⅓ cup applesauce

¼ cup sugar

⅛ teaspoon dry mustard

⅛ teaspoon onion juice

¼ teaspoon salt

3 tablespoons cider vinegar

Combine applesauce, sugar, mustard, onion juice and salt in the container of an electric blender. Pulse until well blended. Remove lid and slowly add vinegar while blender is running.

Toss spinach mixture with dressing until well coated. Season to taste with salt and pepper. Garnish with egg.

NOTE: I chunk a piece of onion and add it instead of onion juice. Just put it into the blender and it will turn to juice. Don't use more than one chunk, though. This dressing has no fat and is excellent on all salads.

Marian Butcher, Pennsylvania

If you prefer to sugar coat the walnuts or pecans, just put ¼ cup sugar in a heavy skillet and slowly melt, add nuts and stir. Dry on waxed paper.

MARINATED VEGETABLE SALAD

¾ cup vinegar

½ cup sugar

⅓ to ½ cup corn oil

1 teaspoon salt

1 (16-ounce) can petite green peas

1 (16-ounce) French style green beans

1 (16-ounce) can Shoe Peg corn

1 large green bell pepper, chopped

1 cup chopped celery

1 bunch green onions, chopped

Heat vinegar, sugar, oil and salt in a saucepan until sugar dissolves. Cool. Drain canned vegetables. Combine all vegetables in a bowl. Pour vinegar mixture over vegetables. Chill overnight. Serves 12.

Liz Offord, Texas

MEDITERRANEAN SALAD

3 large oranges, peeled and sliced into cartwheels

½ cup pitted ripe olives

1 medium onion, peeled, thinly sliced and separated into rings

¾ cup pitted dates, cut in half lengthwise

¼ cup lemon juice

¼ cup olive oil

1 teaspoon salt

¼ teaspoon freshly ground pepper

¼ teaspoon coriander

Salad greens

Combine oranges, olives, onion rings and dates in a shallow dish. Combine lemon juice, olive oil, salt, pepper and coriander. Pour lemon juice mixture over orange mixture. Marinate, covered in the refrigerator about two hours or until thoroughly chilled. Serve on salad greens.

Jean Krest, Colorado

TOSSED MANDARIN ORANGE SALAD

½ cup sliced almonds

3 tablespoons sugar

½ head iceberg lettuce

½ head romaine lettuce

1 cup chopped celery

1 (11-ounce) can mandarin oranges, drained

DRESSING:

½ teaspoon salt

¼ cup vegetable oil

Dash pepper

2 tablespoons sugar

1 tablespoon chopped parsley

In a small saucepan, over medium heat, cook almonds and sugar, stirring constantly until almonds are coated and sugar dissolves. Watch carefully, as they bury easily. Cool and store in airtight container. When ready to serve combine almond, lettuce, celery and oranges. In a small bowl, combine dressing ingredients and toss with salad. Serves 8–10.

Carol Ryan, Kansas

PEA SALAD

1 cup mayonnaise

3 tablespoons Parmesan cheese

2 tablespoons sugar

3 cans of peas, drained

Celery, chopped

Onion, chopped

4–5 hard boiled eggs, coarsely chopped

Reserve 1 egg to be sliced and placed on top of salad. Combine mayonnaise, cheese and sugar. Set aside. Combine peas, celery, and onion in a bowl. Pour dressing over peas and mix. Top with egg slices. Refrigerate for 4–6 hours.

Cook Voltz, Ohio

HONEY BACON MUSTARD DRESSING

1/3 hot water

2 tablespoons sugar

1 tablespoon cornstarch

7 pieces thin sliced bacon, diced and cooked crispy

½ cup vinegar

Combine water, sugar and cornstarch and mix until sugar is dissolved. Cook bacon. Add vinegar and bring to a boil. Reduce heat to medium-low and add sugar water. Simmer until sauce thickens.

Then mix together:

1 cup mayonnaise

¼ cup spicy brown mustard

¼ cup honey

When blended, add to the hot bacon dressing and stir to incorporate. Use immediately or cover and refrigerate. Makes 2 ½ cups.

Zina Versaggi Graalfs, Florida

Serves several and is great when you need to "bring a salad"

BRING A SALAD

Layer in a 13 x 9-inch dish:

Light layer of lettuce

Chopped celery

Green onion, finely chopped

1 zucchini, finely grated

½ package frozen peas, cooked with ½ teaspoon salt and drained

Combine:

1 package Hidden Valley Buttermilk Dressing mix

1 (8-ounce) carton sour cream

2 tablespoons mayonnaise

Spread this mixture on top of salad. Top with shredded Mozzarella cheese and sprinkle with Parmesan cheese.

Beth Burt, Texas

RIO GRANDE DANDY GREEN SALAD

1 cup finely chopped celery

1 finely chopped green pepper

½ cup finely chopped onion

1 (2-ounce) jar pimiento, finely minced

1 (1 pound) can French Style green beans, drained

1 (1 pound) can small green peas, drained

1 teaspoon salt

DRESSING:

1 cup granulated sugar

½ cup salad oil

¾ cup cider vinegar

2 tablespoons water

Combine dressing ingredients and set aside. Mix salad ingredients and gently toss with dressing. Cover and refrigerate overnight. Drain well before serving. Makes 6 cups.

Roberta Spurlock, Oklahoma

CORN, TOMATO AND AVOCADO SALAD

½ cup extra-virgin olive oil

2 tablespoons sherry-wine vinegar

1 teaspoon sugar

Coarse salt and pepper to taste

2 (11-ounce) cans whole kernel corn, drained

2 large tomatoes, sliced in ¼ inch slices (red and yellow can be used)

¼ cup fresh basil leaves, coarsely chopped

1 avocado, diced in ¼-inch pieces

8 cups arugula, stems removed (3 bunches)

2 ounces ricotta salata cheese (if not available, use feta)

In a small bowl, whisk together olive oil, vinegar, sugar, salt and pepper. Set aside. In a large bowl, combine drained corn, tomatoes and basil. Drizzle with half of the dressing mix. Add diced avocado and mix gently.

Arrange arugula on salad plates and drizzle with remaining dressing. Add vegetable mixture. Shave ricotta or feta over salad. Serve immediately.

Kay Atkins, Texas

GREEN BEAN AND MOZZARELLA SALAD

2 cups fresh green beans

1 (8-ounce) package Mozzarella cheese

1/2 cup prepared Good Seasons® Zesty Italian salad dressing

6 fresh plum tomatoes, sliced

1/3 cup chopped fresh basil

1/8 teaspoon pepper

Combine all ingredients in a large bowl. Cover. Refrigerate for 1 hour before serving. Serves 4.

Phyllis Rademacher, Iowa

TUSCANY TOMATO SALAD

A good accompaniment to fish or fowl.

Tomatoes

Mozzarella cheese

Sliced black olives

Fresh sweet basil

Cracked peppercorns

Olive oil

Slice ripe tomatoes and layer with cheese in a spiral pinwheel design. Sprinkle with olives, narrowly sliced fresh basil and peppercorns. Drizzle olive oil over entire salad. Serve at room temperature. Serves as many as you intend…depending upon how many tomatoes you use.

Lyn Gogis, California

HONEY CARAWAY DRESSING

¾ cup mayonnaise

2 tablespoons honey

1 ½ tablespoons lemon juice

½ tablespoon caraway seeds

Combine ingredients and chill for 1-2 hours before tossing with salad.

Jeri-Lynn Sandusky, Utah

CREAMY AND SWEET SLAW

1 cup mayonnaise

4 tablespoons confectioners' sugar

½ teaspoon salt

½ teaspoon celery salt

1 teaspoon lemon juice

3 tablespoons white wine

Pepper to taste, if desired

4 tablespoons milk

Mix mayonnaise and sugar until smooth. Add seasoning, stir and add milk, a little at a time until smooth, thick liquid is achieved. You may not need all of the milk.

Pour dressing over 6 cups shredded cabbage. Mix to coat. Chill at least 1 hour before serving.

Cordelia L. Razek, Louisiana

ZIPPY COLE SLAW

**A great alternative
to sweet slaw.**

1 small head green cabbage

½ small onion, chopped

Salt and pepper to taste

2 tablespoons red wine vinegar

3 tablespoons olive oil

Tabasco® sauce to taste (5-6 drops or more, depending
  upon your taste)

2 tablespoons capers, drained

1½ cups mayonnaise, about

Shred cabbage with a knife, not a food processor, it should
be slightly coarse, approximately 4 cups. Toss all ingredients and chill well before serving. Serves 4-6.

Nancy Tarvin, Texas

TANGY COLE SLAW

½ cup mayonnaise

½ cup plain yogurt

3 tablespoons sugar

4 teaspoons prepared horseradish

2 teaspoons dried mustard

½ teaspoon salt

4 scallions, with greens, chopped

2 tablespoons chopped onions

½ teaspoon dill

½ teaspoon caraway seed

1 (16-ounce) package cabbage and carrot slaw mix

Combine dressing ingredients and toss with cabbage. Chill
and serve.

Mary Ralston, Illinois

CABBAGE SLAW

1 large head cabbage, shredded
1 large onion, sliced into rings
1 medium green pepper, diced
1 cup sugar
¾ cup vegetable oil
¾ cup vinegar
1 teaspoon dry mustard
1 teaspoon salt
1 teaspoon celery seed

In a large bowl, combine cabbage, onions, green pepper and sugar. Set aside. In a saucepan, combine oil, vinegar, mustard, salt and celery seed. Bring to a boil. Pour hot dressing over vegetables. Let cool. Refrigerate. Slaw will keep for several days in the refrigerator.

Carol Ryan, Kansas

Celebrate your summer holidays with this refreshing switch from the same old lettuce and tomato salad. Enjoy!

RED, WHITE AND BLEU SLAW

Just combine:

6 cups coarsely shredded green cabbage
½ cup bacon bits
½ cup crumbled bleu cheese

Add:

1 cup Marzetti Slaw Dressing (Original or Light)

Toss to combine and coat everything. Chill to let flavors blend.

Garnish with cherry tomatoes and another ¼ cup of bleu cheese

Sally Loder, OhioLiz Offord, Texas

SWEET POTATO SLAW

½ cup mayonnaise

½ cup sour cream

2 tablespoons honey

2 tablespoons lemon juice

1 teaspoon grated lemon peel

½ teaspoon salt

¼ teaspoon pepper

3 cups shredded, peeled, raw sweet potatoes

1 medium apple, peeled and chopped (I use Granny Smith)

1 (8-ounce) can pineapple tidbits, drained

½ cup chopped pecans or walnuts

In a bowl, combine first seven ingredients; blend until smooth. In a large bowl, combine potatoes, apple, pineapple and nuts. Add dressing and toss to coat. Refrigerate for at least 1 hour. Serves 6–8.

CAESAR SALAD

2 peeled tomatoes

2 heads Romaine, sliced 1 inch wide

4-5 slices cooked bacon

½ cup Romano cheese

1 bunch green onions, chopped

Capers, if desired

Artichoke hearts, if desired

½ teaspoon chopped fresh mint

Pinch oregano

5 tablespoons olive oil

Juice of 1 fresh lemon

Garlic to taste

1 teaspoon fresh ground pepper

½ teaspoon salt

1 soft cooked egg

1 cup croutons

When making any good salad, always put your heavy vegetables in the bowl first. So, first place tomatoes, then Romaine, then bacon, cheese and onions. If desired, add capers or artichoke hearts. Sprinkle mint and oregano over salad. In a separate bowl, combine olive oil, lemon juice, garlic, pepper, salt and egg. Whip vigorously and pour over salad. Add croutons and toss. Never add croutons until after salad has been tossed. Serves 4.

Phyllis Rademacher, Iowa

SEVEN VEGETABLE SLAW

Prepare slaw dressing by whisking the following ingredients together:

- 1 cup salad vinegar
- ½ cup extra virgin olive oil
- 1 tablespoon salt
- 2 tablespoons sugar
- 1 teaspoon black pepper

SALAD INGREDIENTS:

- 1 large head cabbage, shredded
- 1 head cauliflower, broken into floret pieces
- 2–3 cups chopped celery
- 1 large onion, either white of 1015
- 3–4 cloves chopped garlic (can be pressed)
- 1 cup thinly sliced petit carrots
- ½ cup fresh chopped parsley

Place vegetables in a large bowl. Mix well. Pour dressing over vegetables and toss well to mix. Cover and refrigerate overnight. Toss again before serving. Will keep for a week or longer in the refrigerator.

Millie Royer, Texas

SPAGHETTI VEGETABLE TOSS

- 12 ounces spaghetti, cooked and drained
- 2 tomatoes
- 2 zucchini
- 2 tablespoons chopped green onion
- 1 chopped green pepper
- ½ cup salad oil
- 4 tablespoons white wine vinegar
- 4 tablespoons lemon juice
- 4 tablespoons sugar
- 2 teaspoons salt
- 2 teaspoons dried basil, crushed

Combine cooled, cooked pasta and vegetables. In a small bowl, combine oil, vinegar, lemon juice, sugar, salt and basil. Mix well and pour over pasta mixture.

Garnish with cherry tomatoes, cooked shrimp, or cucumbers, if desired.

Ralph and Jeannine Bowles, Washington

TUNA SALAD

1 (9-ounce) can tuna, drained and flaked

1 cup finely chopped celery

1 cup grated cheese, Colby or Cheddar

⅔ cup chopped nuts (walnuts or pecans)

1 cup crushed pineapple, well drained

2 tablespoons Miracle Whip®

¾ cup frozen whipped topping

Combine all ingredients, mixing thoroughly. Chill. Serve on leaf lettuce, with crackers.

Cordelia L. Razek, Louisiana

SEASHELL PASTA TUNA SALAD

1 cup Hellmann's mayonnaise

3 tablespoons lemon juice

½ teaspoon salt

⅛ teaspoon hot red pepper sauce, optional

1 (8-ounce) package seashell macaroni, cooked and drained

2 (6-ounce) cans tuna, drained and flaked

1 cup chopped celery

½ cup minced onion

¼ cup chopped green pepper

In a large bowl, combine mayonnaise, lemon juice, salt and pepper sauce. Stir in macaroni, tuna, celery, onion and green pepper. Cover; refrigerate at least 2 hours before serving. Toss before serving. Makes 6 cups. May add cooked peas.

Anna Laura Doane, Indiana

GREEN POPPY SEED DRESSING

9 green onion tops

½ cup sugar

Pinch salt

1 cup apple cider vinegar

1 teaspoon Dijon mustard

2 cups olive oil

2 tablespoons poppy seeds

Combine onion, sugar, salt, vinegar and mustard in a food processor. Pulse until onion tops are pureed. Slowly add olive oil. Put in a jar and add poppy seeds.

For the salad; combine greens to your taste preference and add the dressing. Enjoy!

Baby spinach leaves

Chopped green onions

Sliced waterchestnuts

Sliced fresh mushrooms

Shredded Parmesan cheese

Bacon bits

Almonds

Zina Versaggi Graalfs, Florida

APPLE AND PRAWN SALAD

Lettuce leaves

1 red apple

1 hard boiled egg

6 stuffed olives

2 radishes

125 gram school prawns

½ cup bottled coleslaw dressing or mayonnaise

Salt and pepper

Line a medium sized bowl with lettuce leaves. Core, but do not peel apple; cut into wedges. Cut egg into thin slices. Halve the stuffed olives. Thinly slice radishes, reserving a few slices for garnish. Add prawns and mix well. Season with salt and pepper. Add dressing and mix well. Place in lettuce lined bowl and garnish with reserved radish slices.

Marian Butcher, Pennsylvania

COLD SMOKEY SALMON SALAD

I make this with left over baked salmon and serve with garlic bread or sticks and sliced tomatoes for a colorful, delicious luncheon.

1 small salmon filet

Salt and lemon pepper to taste

½ to ½ cup white wine

Liquid Smoke seasoning

2 cups macaroni or similar pasta

½ cup finely chopped sweet onions

½ cup diced celery

½ to ¾ cup mayonnaise or plain yogurt

Other herbs and seasonings as desired

Preheat oven to 400 degrees. Rinse salmon and pat dry. Sprinkle with salt and lemon pepper. Place in a 9-inch square baking dish. Add white wine and bake in preheated oven for 20 minutes, until cooked through and flesh is firm. When cool, sprinkle liberally with liquid smoke to taste.

Cook pasta according to package directions. Chill. Break up salmon and combine with cold pasta. Add onions, celery, mayonnaise or yogurt and herbs of choice. Mix carefully. Chill well and serve cold. Keeps well in the refrigerator.

Pat Steige, Alaska

LAYERED SOUTHWESTERN SALAD

½ head lettuce, torn into bite sized pieces

3 cups chopped, cooked chicken breast

1 (15-ounce) can black beans, drained

1 (15-ounce) can whole kernel corn, drained

1 small red or green bell pepper, chopped (or half and half)

½ cup chopped onion

Using a large glass bowl (like a trifle bowl), layer ingredients in order, starting and ending with lettuce.

DRESSING:

1 cup thick salsa (your choice of heat)

1 cup low-fat mayonnaise

⅓ cup low-fat sour cream

3 hard cooked eggs, chopped

1 cup shredded Cheddar cheese (or more to taste)

Combine salsa, mayonnaise and sour cream and spread over salad. Cover completely. Top with eggs and cheese. Store covered in refrigerator if preparing the day ahead. Serve with cornbread or tortilla chips

Darlene Davasligil, Wisconsin

FOUR BEAN SALAD

1 onion, sliced	1 cup sugar
1 can kidney beans, drained	¾ cup salad oil
1 can lima beans, drained	1 cup vinegar
1 can French style green beans, drained	1 teaspoon celery seed
1 can wax beans, drained	1 teaspoon mustard seed
	1 teaspoon salt

In a large bowl, combine onion and beans. In a separate bowl, combine sugar, oil, vinegar, celery seed, mustard seed and salt. Mix and pour over beans. Refrigerate for 24 hours before serving. Keeps for a week or more when refrigerated. Use a slotted spoon to serve so marinade will drain.

Eleanor Cowan, Texas
Anna Laura Doane, Indiana

FIESTA SALAD

1 onion, chopped

2 tomatoes, chopped, reserve a few for garnish

1 head lettuce, shredded

1 cup Cheddar cheese

1 cup Catalina salad dressing

Hot sauce (Tabasco® to taste)

1 (6-ounce) bag toasted corn Doritos™ tortilla chips

1 pound ground beef

1 (15-ounce) can kidney beans

¼ teaspoon salt

1 large avocado, optional

Combine onion, tomatoes, and lettuce. Toss with cheese, dressing, and hot sauce. Crumble tortilla chips and add to salad. Brown ground beef. Drain. Return to skillet. Add beans and salt. Heat and then mix into cold salad. Garnish with extra chips, avocado and extra tomatoes. Serves 6.

Anna Laura Doane, Indiana

TACO SALAD

1½ pounds ground beef

2 packages taco seasoning

2 (8-ounce) packages cream cheese, softened

1 large carton sour cream

1 head iceberg lettuce, finely diced

2 packages shredded taco cheese

3 large tomatoes, diced

Jar of salsa

Brown ground beef and drain. Combine with taco seasoning. Cool. Combine cream cheese and sour cream. Spread on the bottom of a pizza pan. Place meat mixture over cream cheese. Sprinkle shredded lettuce over meat mixture. Sprinkle cheese over lettuce. Top with tomatoes. Serve with salsa on the side.

Marilyn Erlandson, Pennsylvania

TOWER SALAD

Corn chips
Rice, cooked
Chili
Cheddar cheese, grated
Lettuce, shredded
Tomato, chopped
Avocado, chopped
Pecan pieces
Coconut
Raisins
Salsa
Sour cream
Jalapenos

Build salad in order listed. Serve with cornbread. This is a fun salad to serve when you have the neighbors over. Have each person bring one ingredient.

Jan Watson, Illinois

CHICKEN SALAD I

Best if made the
day before, but
still excellent if
you can't.

4 cups diced, cooked chicken

1 cup diced celery

1 small green pepper, diced

½ small onion, diced

½ cup sliced green olives

1 (9-ounce) can pineapple tidbits

1½ cups fresh green grapes, halved

2 tablespoons prepared mustard

1 cup light Miracle Whip® salad dressing

½ cup chopped pecans or walnuts (optional)

½ to ¾ can Chinese noodles

Combine chicken, celery, green pepper, onion, olives, pineapple and grapes. Set aside. In a small bowl, combine mustard and Miracle Whip®. Add nuts, if desired. Combine with chicken mixture. Just before serving, add Chinese noodles. Serve in lettuce cups or lettuce lined bowl. Serves 8–10.

Pat Fenno, Iowa

CHICKEN SALAD II

1 (8-ounce) can pineapple tidbits

6 cups diced, cooked chicken

1 cup sliced grapes

¼ cup dried minced onions or 1 bunch green onions

1 cup diced celery

½ cup sliced almonds, optional

1 tablespoon lemon dill

½ teaspoon salt

¼ teaspoon pepper

1 cup mayonnaise or Miracle Whip® thinned with pineapple juice

Drain pineapple, reserving juice. In a large bowl, combine pineapple and remaining ingredients. Add enough reserved pineapple juice to moisten well. Serves 6–8.

Liz Offord, Texas
Ase Toube, Minnesota

Flavor is best if made a day ahead. Great for brunch, luncheon or showers.

CHICKEN WILD RICE SALAD

1 (6-ounce) package Uncle Ben's Wild Long Grain and Wild Rice

2 cups diced cooked chicken breasts

¼ cup chopped green pepper

½ cup chopped water chestnuts

½ cup mayonnaise

2 tablespoons Russian salad dressing

1 tablespoon lemon juice

¼ teaspoon salt

Cook rice according to package directions. Cool. Add chicken, green pepper and water chestnuts. Set aside. In a small bowl, combine mayonnaise, salad dressing, lemon juice and salt. Pour over chicken mixture and toss. Serve chilled on lettuce leaf with a bowl of sliced almonds and a bowl of raisins to use as toppings. Serves 6–8.

Cindy Kelly, Texas

CHICKEN PECAN SALAD WITH CRANBERRIES

DRESSING

> 2 large egg yolks
>
> 2 tablespoons apple cider vinegar
>
> 2 tablespoons sugar
>
> 1 tablespoon Dijon mustard
>
> ¼ teaspoon salt
>
> ¾ cup Canola oil

Combine all ingredients well and set aside.

SALAD

> 2 whole boneless skinless chicken breasts, poached and diced
>
> ¾ cup dried cranberries
>
> 3 cups chopped celery
>
> 1 cup coarsely chopped pecans or walnuts,
>
> 1 head red leaf lettuce
>
> Salt and pepper to taste

In a large bowl, combine chicken, cranberries and celery. Toss with prepared dressing. Refrigerate 8–10 hours or overnight. Garnish with nuts. Place lettuce leaves on serving plates, top with salad and serve. Salt and pepper to taste.

Mary Q. Smith, Texas

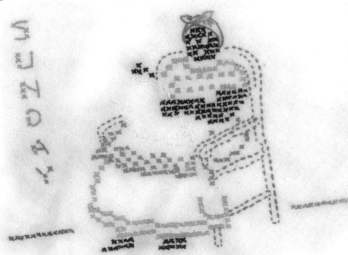

ORIENTAL CHICKEN SALAD

½ cup rice vinegar

¼ cup sugar (or use Splenda®)

2½ tablespoons vegetable oil

2 tablespoons honey

2 tablespoons soy sauce

⅓ cup slivered almonds, toasted

2 tablespoons sesame seeds, toasted

2 packages Top Ramen Oriental Flavored Noodles

8 cups shredded Napa Chinese cabbage

2 carrots, shredded

1 cup thinly sliced green onions

1 can water chestnuts, chopped

2–3 chicken breasts, broiled and chopped into chunks

Combine vinegar, sugar, oil, honey and soy sauce in a small bowl. Set aside and chill. Place remaining ingredients in a giant salad bowl. Crunch noodles into the mixture. Pour chilled dressing over entire bowl and mix. Serves 4–12, depending upon whether it's served as a salad or a side dish.

Lyn Gogis, California

HOT CHICKEN SALAD

2 cups cooked chicken or turkey, cut up

1½ cups chopped celery

3 hard boiled eggs, chopped

½ cup mayonnaise

1 can cream of mushroom soup

½ cup chopped onion

Combine all ingredients. Sprinkle with crushed Ritz® crackers. Dot with butter. Bake at 350 degrees for 30 minutes or until golden and bubbly. This is also good served lukewarm.

Shirley Thomas, Texas

PASTA–TURKEY SALAD

1 (3 to 4 pound) turkey breast, roasted
1 large package tortellini pasta, cooked
1 bunch parsley, chopped fine
Fresh ground pepper
Fresh grated Parmesan cheese

DRESSING:

1 package Italian dressing
Replace vinegar in your Italian dressing with lemon juice
¼ cup olive oil
¾ cup canola oil

Roast turkey according to package directions. Cool and cut into small cubes. Combine turkey, pasta, parsley, pepper and cheese. In a small bowl, combine dressing ingredients and pour over salad.

Kathy Bratton, Texas

ANGEL HAIR PASTA SALAD

1 package angel hair pasta
2 red tomatoes, chopped
1 red onion, chopped
1 zucchini, chopped
6 ounces grated sharp Cheddar cheese
2 teaspoons McCormick Salad Supreme seasoning
⅓ bottle Italian dressing

Cook pasta according to package directions. Chop into small pieces when cooled. Mix with tomatoes, onion, zucchini, cheese and seasoning. Pour dressing over salad and mix well. Chill before serving. Can add shrimp, chicken or ham

Kathy Bratton, Texas

Bob Lilly

NO.
NAME
DESC.
DATE

PICA

Pain Ordinaire

Soften 1 en... of yeast in 1/4 cup lukewarm water. ~~S...~~

1/3 c. water... let the mixture cool.

When it is... the softe...

Mix in g... and stir ; i

make a...

just a...

6ard...

and b...

Place...

and...

dou...

im...

down an...

double in bulk.

Divide th...

rical loa...

let them rise...

in bulk., (...

loaves when...

Brush the so...

for 50 min. o...

6// For a ce...

water on the...

or a faintly swe...

and...

be...

the...

with boiling

...iod.

mixture.

Basic recipe uses 1/2 c. milk ;

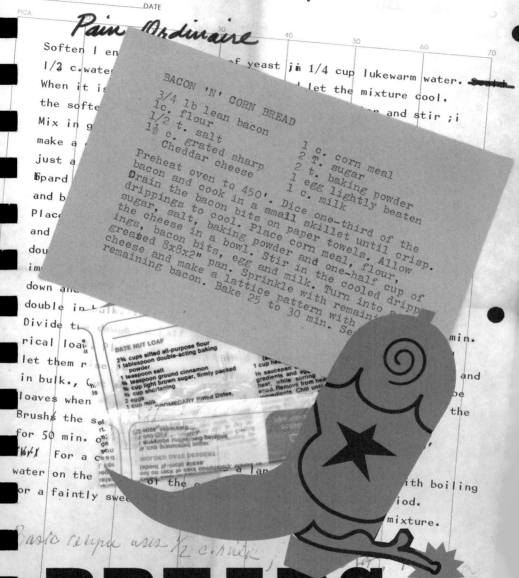

BACON 'N' CORN BREAD
3/4 lb lean bacon
1 c. flour
1/2 t. salt
1½ c. grated sharp
     Cheddar cheese
                              1 c. corn meal
                              2 T. sugar
                              2 t. baking powder
                              1 egg lightly beaten
                              1 c. milk

Preheat oven to 450'. Dice one-third of the
bacon and cook in a small skillet until crisp.
Drain the bacon bits on paper towels. Allow
drippings to cool. Place corn meal and one-half cup of
sugar, salt, baking powder, flour,
the cheese in a bowl. Stir in the cooled drippings, bacon bits, egg and milk. Turn into a
greased 8x8x2" pan. Sprinkle with remaini...
cheese and make a lattice pattern with
remaining bacon. Bake 25 to 30 min. Se...

DATE NUT LOAF
2¾ cups sifted all-purpose flour
1 tablespoon double-acting baking
     powder
1 teaspoon salt
¾ teaspoon ground cinnamon
½ cup light brown sugar, firmly packed
½ cup shortening
2 eggs
1 cup milk
1 8-oz. pkg. DROMEDARY Pitted Dates,

BREADS

YEAST PULL BREAD

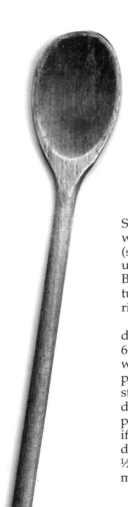

1 cup milk

¾ cup butter

1½ teaspoons salt

½ cup sugar

1 package dry yeast

¼ cup warm water

1 teaspoon sugar

3 eggs, lightly beaten

4 cups sifted flour

2 cubes butter

Sesame seeds

Scald milk. Add butter, salt and sugar; stir. Cool to barely warm. Dissolve yeast in warm water and 1 teaspoon sugar (sugar activates the yeast). Let yeast sit about 10 minutes until it has become bubbly. Add yeast to butter mixture. Beat eggs with a fork until lightly beaten and add to mixture. Add 4 cups sifted flour; the dough will be sticky. Let rise to double in bulk. Punch down. Refrigerate overnight.

Next morning: Melt 2 cubes of the butter in a baking dish. Divide dough into 3 equal parts. Roll each into a piece 6-inches square and ½-inch thick. Cut strips 6 x ⅓-inches wide. Dip each strip in melted butter. Starting in center of pan, roll around. Continue with strips to form a snail. Place strips loosely, then sprinkle sesame seeds on top and press down. Let rise until high but not quite to the top of the pan. Bake at 350 degrees for 15 minutes. Cool and freeze, if for later. When needed, remove and thaw. Bake at 350 degrees for 15 minutes or more, until golden brown. Drizzle ½ cube melted butter over the top and serve. Pull off as much as you like, but don't eat the whole thing!

Bonnie Battles

WHEAT BREAD

1 cup milk

3 tablespoons shortening or butter

½ cup honey

1 cup water (or milk)

4–4½ cups white bread flour

2 cups whole wheat flour

2 tablespoons gluten

1 teaspoon salt

2 tablespoons active dry yeast

Heat milk with butter and honey until butter is melted. Remove from heat, add water (or milk) cool it to the touch. Mix dry ingredients together in mixer bowl.

Add liquids and mix on No. 2 speed of electric mixer until dough comes away from the bowl, mix for 3 or 4 minutes more. Remove dough from bowl and spray the inside of the bowl with cooking spray. Return dough to bowl and coat it with spray, cover and let rise in a warm and draft free location for 50–60 minutes. When dough has risen to double, punch down and remove it from bowl. Let stand for 10 minutes. Make up into 2 equal loaves. Place into 9⅓ x 5½ x 2¾-inch bread pans which have been coated with cooking spray — cover and let rise in a warm, draft free location for about an hour. Bake at 350 degrees for 45–50 minutes. Remove bread from pans and cool on wire racks.

Janice Konetchy, Massachusetts

MIXED HERB BUTTER

½ cup each of 4 fresh herbs: basil, parsley, chervil, fennel, chives, tarragon or rosemary

2 cups butter, softened

½ clove garlic, crushed

1 teaspoon lemon juice

1 teaspoon salt

fresh ground pepper to taste

Finely chop the herbs, but leave some texture. With a mixer, blend the herbs with the butter. Mix in the crushed garlic, lemon juice, salt and pepper. Continue to blend until smooth. Pack the herb butter in a stone crock and store in the refrigerator. Serve at room temperature. Makes 4 cups.

Bernadine R. Levy, Colorado

WHITE BREAD

1 cup milk

2 tablespoons shortening or butter

1½ cups water, cold

6¾ cups flour

2 tablespoons sugar

2 tablespoons gluten

2 teaspoons salt

2½ teaspoons Active dry yeast

Heat milk and butter until melted. Add water to mixture and cool to the touch. Mix all dry ingredients in mixer bowl then add liquids.

Mix on No. 2 speed in an electric mixer. After the dough comes away from the bowl, mix 3 or 4 more minutes. Remove the dough from the bowl and spray the inside with cooking spray. Return the dough to the bowl and coat it with cooking spray, cover and let rise (in a warm, draft free location) for about 50 to 60 minutes. When dough has risen to double, punch down and remove from bowl. Make up into 2 equal loaves. Place into 9⅝ x 5½ x 2¾-inch bread pans which have been coated with cooking spray. Cover and let rise in a warm and draft free location for about an hour. Bake at 375 degrees for 45–50 minutes. Remove bread from pans and cool on wire racks.

Janice Konetchy, Massachusetts

BUTTERHORNS

Mix 1 package dry yeast, ¼ cup warm water, and pinch of sugar. Let rise until foamy. Combine yeast mixture with 1½ cups warm water and ½ cup sugar.

Melt ½ cup margarine and add 2 eggs. Add to yeast mixture. Add approximately 5-6 cups flour, 6 tablespoons powdered butter milk, 1 ½ teaspoons salt and ½ teaspoon baking soda. Knead a little and let rise in a warm place about 1 ½ hours, until double in size.

Cut dough in half and roll in pie form. Cut 16 wedges, spread with soft margarine, roll up and let rise again. Bake at 375 degrees for 10-15 minutes. Serve with butter icing.

BUTTER ICING

Combine 1/3 cup softened margarine with 4 cups confectioners' sugar, about 1 teaspoon almond flavoring and about 2 tablespoons milk to make spreading consistency.

Betty Kuckes, Wisconsin

WHOLE GRAIN RAISIN BREAD

  1 cup milk

  4 tablespoons shortening or butter

  3 cups white bread flour

  3 cups whole wheat flour

  2 cups uncooked quick cooking Quaker Oats

  4 tablespoons brown sugar

  4 tablespoons wheat germ

  2 tablespoons gluten

  3 teaspoons salt

  6 tablespoons active dry yeast

  1 cup raisins

Heat butter with milk until melted. Blend dry ingredients in mixer bowl. Part way through mixing, add raisins.

Add 2 cups cool water or milk to milk/shortening mixture to cool it to the touch, then add to dry ingredients.

Mix on No. 2 speed of electric mixer, and after the dough comes away from the bowl, mix for 3–4 minutes more, adding the raisins. Remove the dough from the bowl. Spray the bowl with cooking spray. Place the dough back into the bowl and coat with cooking spray. Cover and let rise in a warm and draft free location for about 50 to 60 minutes. When the dough has risen to double, punch down and remove it from the bowl and make up into two equal loaves. Place loaves into 9⅝ x 5 ½ x 2 ¾-inch bread pans which have been coated with cooking spray. Cover and let rise in a warm, draft free location for about an hour. Bake at 375 degrees for about 45 to 50 minutes. Remove from bread pans and cool on wire racks.

Janice Konetchy, Massachusetts

DILLY CASSEROLE BREAD

2 package active dry yeast

½ cup warm water

2 cups creamed cottage cheese

4 tablespoons sugar

2 tablespoons instant minced onion

2 tablespoon butter, softened

2 teaspoons salt

½ teaspoon baking soda

2 eggs, beaten

4 teaspoons dill seed

4½ to 5 cups flour

Sprinkle yeast over warm water. Heat cottage cheese to lukewarm combine in mixing bowl with sugar, onion, butter, salt, baking soda, eggs, dill seed and yeast mixture. Add flour to form a stiff dough, beating well after each addition. Cover. Let rise in warm place until double, about 50 to 60 minutes. Stir dough down. Turn into well-greased, round casserole. Let rise in warm place until light, about 30 to 40 minutes. Bake in preheated 350 degree oven until golden brown, about 40–50 minutes. Brush with butter and sprinkle with salt.

Liz Offord, Texas

POPOVERS

2 eggs

1 cup milk

1 cup flour

¼ teaspoon salt

Beat eggs and add milk. Sift flour and salt together and add to egg mixture. Beat constantly to prevent lumps. Add melted butter. Pour into hot greased muffin pans. Bake at 450 degrees for 25 minutes, then reduce heat to 350 degrees and bake 15 minutes. Makes 8.

Jeanne A. Schroeder, Michigan

SAVOY RAISIN SCONES

The Savoy is one of the most famous hotels in London.

2 cups all-purpose flour

⅛ teaspoon salt

4 teaspoons baking powder

5 tablespoons sugar

5 tablespoon unsalted butter

⅔ cups milk

½ cup golden raisins

1 egg, lightly beaten

Sift flour, salt, and baking powder together into the container of a food processor with the metal blade in place. Add sugar and butter. Pulse until the mixture resembles fine crumbs (about 30 pulses). This process can be done by hand, rubbing the mixture together as one would do for making a pastry. Place flour mixture in a medium bowl. Make a well in the center and add milk and raisins. Gently stir, being careful not to over mix. Roll dough to a ⅜-inch thickness. Cut out scones with a 2½-inch cookie cutter. Leftover scraps can be rerolled for cutting. Place rounds on a greased baking sheet. Brush egg on top with a pastry brush. Let stand for 5 minutes. Heat oven to 400 degrees. Bake scones until lightly browned, about 15 minutes. Serve warm with butter and strawberry or raspberry jam. Makes 12.

Susan Barry, Texas

GARLIC CHEESE BISCUITS

2½ cups biscuit mix

⅔ cup milk

1 egg, beaten

½ cup shredded Cheddar cheese

¼ cup margarine, melted

¼ teaspoon garlic powder

Mix baking mix, milk, egg, and cheese into soft dough. Beat vigorously for 30 seconds. Drop dough by spoonfuls onto an ungreased cookie sheet. Bake 8 to 10 minutes at 450 degrees or until golden brown. Mix margarine and garlic powder. Brush over biscuits before removing from pan. Makes 10–12 biscuits.

Lydia Alexander, Texas

CHEESY ONION PAN BISCUITS

2-1/2 cups biscuit mix

1/4 cup grated Parmesan cheese

2/3 cup milk

2 teaspoons instant minced onion

Melted margarine

Mix all ingredients, except margarine until dough forms. Stir 30 seconds. Press in greased or sprayed 8-inch square pan with fingers coated in baking mix. Precut dough into 12 rectangles or 16 squares. Bake at 450 degrees, 10-12 minutes until golden brown. Brush with melted margarine. Cool 10 minutes.

Jan Whittaker, California

BISCUITS

¾ cup any cheese, grated

1 cup heavy cream

1 cup self rising flour

Grease baking sheet and mix the three ingredients together. Drop onto baking sheet and bake at 425 degrees for 15 to 20 minutes.

Mary Q. Smith, Texas

SPECIAL CORNBREAD

2 cups biscuit mix

⅔ cup sugar

6 tablespoons cornmeal

2 eggs

1 cup milk

½ cup melted butter or margarine

Combine dry ingredients. Add eggs and milk. Beat until well combined. Add melted butter. Mix well. Pour into a greased 9-inch pan and bake at 350 degrees for 35 to 40 minutes. Let sit 5 minutes before cutting. Makes 9 servings.

Cheryl Wills, South Carolina

CORNBREAD

¾ cup yellow cornmeal

2¼ cups all-purpose flour

¾ cup sugar

3 teaspoons baking powder

½ teaspoon salt

1 cup milk

¾ cup butter or margarine, melted

3 eggs, beaten

In a large bowl, blend cornmeal, flour, sugar, baking powder and salt. Add milk and butter slowly. Add eggs. Stir just enough to blend mixture thoroughly. Pour into a greased 13 x 9-inch baking pan. Bake at 400 degrees for 20 minutes. Cut into squares.

Jan Whittaker, California

MENNONITE CORNBREAD

**Low in
saturated fat**

Whisk or stir together the following:

1½ cups yellow corn meal

2 cups white flour

4 tablespoons sugar

1 teaspoon salt (this may be omitted or reduced)

7 teaspoons baking powder

Whisk together:

4 eggs

2 cups milk

4 tablespoons canola oil

Pour liquid mixture into dry mixture all at once and whisk or stir until smooth. Don't over mix.

Pour into a 13 x 9-inch baking pan, rubbed with peanut or olive oil and bake at 375 degrees for 25 minutes. The cornbread should be brown on top and firm to the touch when done.

Marilyn Sietsema, Illinois

BROCCOLI CORNBREAD

        2 boxes Jiffy corn muffin mix
        1 box frozen chopped broccoli
        4 eggs
        2 sticks margarine, melted
        1 onion, chopped
        1 cup cottage cheese

Preheat oven to 350 degrees. Mix all ingredients well and bake in 13 x 9-inch greased baking dish about 45 minutes or until done.

Kathy Bratton, Texas
Mary Baker, Washington
Mary Genenwein, Texas

BANANA PRALINE MUFFINS

For topping, combine and set aside:

        3 tablespoons brown sugar
        1 tablespoons sour cream
        ⅓ cup chopped pecans

For muffins, combine:

        1 egg, slightly beaten
        ½ cup sugar
        ¼ cup oil

Then add:

        3 small bananas, mashed.
        1½ cups pancake mix.

Preheat oven to 400 degrees. Fill muffin cups two-thirds full. Drop a half-teaspoon topping on each muffin. Bake for 12 to 15 minutes in preheated oven.

Betty Ann Sheffloe, Nebraska

BANANA NUT MUFFINS

2 eggs

¼ cup buttermilk

½ cup vegetable oil

¾ cup brown sugar (or ½ cup for less sweet)

1 teaspoon vanilla extract

1 cup mashed bananas

¾ cup unbleached flour

¾ cup whole wheat flour

2 teaspoons baking powder

½ teaspoon baking soda

½ teaspoon salt

½ cup chopped walnuts

Preheat oven to 375 degrees. Combine eggs, buttermilk, oil, brown sugar, and vanilla. Mash bananas and add to egg mixture. Combine dry ingredients and walnuts. Blend into egg mixture only until moistened. Spoon into 12 greased muffin cups. Bake in preheated oven for 20 minutes. Makes 12.

This is one of my favorite banana muffin recipes from among the dozen or so I've collected. I especially like muffins for breakfast.

Ghita Carter, Texas

BRAN MUFFINS

4 shredded wheat biscuits softened in 1-1/2 cups boiling water.

3/4 cup margarine

3 cups sugar

4 eggs

4 cups All-Bran cereal

5 cups flour

1 quart buttermilk

5 teaspoons baking soda

1 teaspoon salt

1 cup chopped dates

1 cup chopped pecans

Soften shredded wheat in boiling water. Add margarine, sugar, eggs, All Bran and flour. In a separate bowl, combine buttermilk and baking soda. Add to cereal mixture. Add salt, dates and pecans. Mix well. Place in a 1 gallon container and refrigerate. Bake only what you need by spooning into greased muffin tins without stirring batter. Fill muffin tins two-thirds full. Bake at 375 degrees for 25 minutes. Makes 5 dozen.

Jan Whittaker, California

BOB LILLY'S BRAN MUFFINS

Dry ingredients:

> 2 cups bran flakes (can use oat bran)
>
> 1 cup whole wheat flour
>
> 1 cup raw sunflower seeds
>
> 1 cup raisins (optional)
>
> ¼ cup sesame seeds
>
> 2 teaspoons baking powder
>
> ½ teaspoon salt

Wet ingredients:

> 1 ripe banana, mashed
>
> 1 egg, slightly beaten
>
> 2 tablespoons vegetable oil
>
> ¼ to ½ cup honey
>
> ½ to 1 cup milk or buttermilk

Preheat oven to 350 degrees. Combine dry ingredients and wet ingredients separately. Then mix everything together. Spoon into greased muffin tins, two-thirds full. Bake in preheated oven for 20 to 25 minutes.

Ann Lilly, Texas

WHOLE WHEAT WALNUT MUFFINS

> ½ cup all-purpose flour
>
> ½ cup whole wheat flour
>
> ½ cup brown sugar
>
> 2 teaspoons baking powder
>
> ¼ cup chopped walnuts
>
> ¼ teaspoon salt
>
> 1 egg
>
> ½ cup milk
>
> 3 tablespoons butter, melted

Stir dry ingredients together. Add egg, milk, and butter. Stir until all ingredients are moistened. Spoon into greased muffin cups. Bake at 425 degrees for 20 minutes. Makes 6 large muffins.

Lydia Alexander, Texas

OAT BRAN MUFFINS

1-1/2 cups oat bran
1/2 cup whole wheat flour
3 tablespoons brown sugar
2 teaspoons baking powder
1 teaspoon cinnamon
2 tablespoons honey
1/4 cup plus 2 tablespoons skim milk
1 egg
2 tablespoons vegetable oil
1/2 cup apple juice
1 cup grated apples
1/2 cup golden raisins

Mix oat bran, flour, sugar, baking powder and cinnamon together. Set aside. In a separate bowl, mix together honey, milk, egg, oil and apple juice. Combine wet and dry ingredients; add apples and raisins. Stir until well mixed. Fill cup cake tins about ¾ full. Bake for 20 minutes at 400 degrees.

Lydia Alexander, Texas

PUMPKIN CHIP MUFFINS

4 eggs
1 cup oil
2 cups sugar
2 cups canned pumpkin
2 teaspoons cinnamon
2 cups flour
2 teaspoons baking soda
½ teaspoon salt
1 cup mini chocolate chips

Mix eggs, oil and sugar. Add pumpkin and cinnamon, then flour, soda and salt, mix well. Add chocolate chips. Scoop batter into muffin tins lined with paper or greased. Bake at 350 degrees for 15 to 20 minutes or until set.

Pat Sampson, Iowa

ORANGE PECAN MUFFINS

⅓ cup shortening

½ cup sugar

1 egg

½ cup bran cereal

1 teaspoon grated orange peel

½ cup orange juice

¼ cup milk

1¾ cups all-purpose flour

2 teaspoon baking powder

¼ teaspoon baking soda

½ teaspoon salt

½ cup chopped pecans

Cream shortening and sugar; add egg and beat until light and creamy. Add cereal, orange peel, orange juice, and milk. Sift flour with baking powder, soda and salt. Add dry ingredients to first mixture, stirring just until ingredients are moist. Fold in pecans. Grease muffin cups and fill about two-thirds full with batter. Bake at 400 degrees for 25 to 30 minutes. Makes 12 small muffins or 8–9 large muffins.

Use fresh or frozen blueberries to make these muffins

BLUEBERRY MUFFINS

2½ cups all-purpose flour

2½ teaspoons baking powder

¼ teaspoon salt

½ cup sugar

1 cup buttermilk

2 eggs, beaten

½ cup melted butter or margarine

1½ cups fresh or frozen blueberries, rinsed

2 tablespoons all-purpose flour

Sugar for topping

Sift flour, baking powder, salt and ½ cup sugar. Add buttermilk, beaten eggs, and melted butter; mix until dry ingredients are just moistened. Mix berries with 2 tablespoon flour; bold berries into batter.

Spoon batter into greased muffin pans, filling each cup about two-thirds full. Sprinkle each with a little sugar. Bake at 400 degrees for 20 to 25 minutes. Makes 18–24.

Zina Versaggi Graalfs, Florida

APPLE NUT MUFFINS

1 egg

⅔ cup apple juice or milk

½ cup vegetable oil

1 teaspoon vanilla extract

2 cups all-purpose flour

¼ cup sugar

¼ cup packed brown sugar

1 tablespoon baking powder

½ teaspoon salt

½ cup chopped nuts

1 chopped apple

Cinnamon sugar

In a bowl, beat egg with juice, oil and vanilla. Stir in flour, sugars, baking powder and salt just until flour is moistened. Batter will be a little lumpy. Stir in nuts and apple. Fill greased muffin tins or paper muffin cups about two-thirds full. Sprinkle with cinnamon sugar. Bake at 400 degrees for 20 minutes or until golden brown.

Zina Versaggi Graalfs, Florida

Salado, TX.

CRANBERRY MUFFINS

1½ cups chopped fresh or frozen cranberries

1¼ cups sugar, divided

3 cups all-purpose flour

1½ tablespoons baking powder

½ teaspoon salt

½ cup butter or margarine

2 eggs, lightly beaten

1 cup milk

1 cup chopped pecans or walnuts

1 tablespoon grated orange peel

Toss cranberries with ¼ cup of the sugar. Set aside. In a large bowl, combine flour, baking powder, salt and remaining 1 cup sugar. Cut in butter until mixture resembles coarse crumbs. Combine egg with milk; stir into flour mixture until just moistened.

Gently fold in nuts, orange peel and cranberries. Fill paper-lined muffin tins about two-thirds full. Bake at 400 degrees for 20 to 25 minutes. Makes 18 muffins.

Zina Versaggi Graalfs, Florida

CORN MUFFINS

1 cup all-purpose flour, sifted

1½ cups cornmeal

1 teaspoon baking soda

1 teaspoon baking powder

2 teaspoons salt

¼ cup shortening

2 eggs, beaten

2 cups thick sour milk

Sift dry ingredients together; cut in shortening until mixture resembles meal. In a separate bowl, combine eggs and milk. Stir into flour mixture. Bake in greased muffin pans in a 425 degree oven for 25-30 minutes. Bakes about 18 muffins.

Zina Versaggi Graalfs, Florida

PECAN PEACH MUFFINS

Topping:

> ½ cup chopped pecans
>
> ⅓ cup packed brown sugar
>
> ¼ cup all-purpose flour
>
> 1 teaspoon ground cinnamon
>
> 2 tablespoons melted butter

Muffins:

> 1½ cups all-purpose flour
>
> ½ cup sugar
>
> 2 teaspoons baking powder
>
> 1 teaspoon ground cinnamon
>
> ¼ teaspoon salt
>
> ½ cup butter, melted
>
> ¼ cup milk
>
> 1 egg
>
> 2 medium peaches, peeled and diced (makes about 1 cup diced. Can use frozen thawed or canned)

Preheat oven to 400 degrees. Grease and flour 12 muffin cups or line with paper liners. Combine topping ingredients until mixture is crumbly. Set aside.

Combine flour, sugar, baking powder, cinnamon and salt in a large bowl.

In a separate bowl, whisk together butter, milk and egg. Stir milk/egg mixture into flour mixture and blend just until moistened. Fold in diced peaches. Spoon into prepared muffin cups; sprinkle evenly with topping mixture.

Bake in preheated oven for 20–25 minutes or until a wooden tooth pick inserted in center comes out clean. Remove from pan. Makes 12 muffins.

Zina Versaggi Graalfs, Florida

LEMON MUFFINS

1 cup shortening

1 cup sugar

4 large eggs, separated

2 cups all-purpose flour

2 teaspoons baking powder

1 teaspoon salt

½ cup fresh lemon juice (3 to 4 lemons)

2 teaspoons grated lemon peel

Cream shortening and sugar until light and fluffy. Add egg yolks, beating well. In a separate bowl, combine flour, baking powder and salt; add to creamed mixture alternately with lemon juice, beating well after each addition. End with dry ingredients. Fold stiffly beaten egg whites into batter; stir in lemon peel. Fill greased muffin cups about three-fourths full. Bake in a preheated 375 degree oven for 20–25 minutes, until done. Makes about 15 muffins.

Zina Versaggi Graalfs, Florida

GRANDMA BARRY'S IRISH SODA BREAD

4 cups all-purpose flour

1½ teaspoons baking soda

1 cup sugar

1 teaspoon salt

1 cup raisins

2 tablespoons caraway seeds

1½ cups buttermilk

2 eggs

2 tablespoons butter, melted

Sift flour. Blend flour, baking soda, sugar, salt, raisins and caraway seeds. Set aside. In a separate bowl, combine buttermilk, eggs and melted butter. Mix. Add to flour mixture, gradually. Beat with a wooden spoon and form into a ball. Flatten to form a round loaf, place on a greased cookie sheet or pizza tray. Make the sign of the cross in the top of the dough with a knife. Bake at 350 degrees for 1¼ hours.

Susan Barry, Texas

GINGERBREAD

¼ cup sugar

1 egg

½ cup solid vegetable shortening

½ cup molasses

1½ cups flour

1 teaspoon baking soda

1 teaspoon ginger

1 teaspoon cinnamon

¼ teaspoon nutmeg

Beat all together. Then gradually add ¾ cup boiling water. Bake in 350 degree oven 1 hour in a 13 x 9-inch pan.

Edith Anne Blood, Tennessee

PUMPKIN SPICE BREAD

Can also add white raisins.

3 cups sugar

1 cup vegetable oil

4 eggs, lightly beaten

1 (16-ounce) can solid pumpkin

3½ cups all-purpose flour

2 teaspoons baking soda

1 teaspoon baking powder

1 teaspoon salt

1 teaspoon ground cinnamon

1 teaspoon ground nutmeg

½ teaspoon ground cloves

½ teaspoon ground allspice

½ cup water

In a large bowl, combine sugar, oil, and eggs. Add pumpkin and mix well. In a separate bowl, combine dry ingredients and add to pumpkin mixture, alternately with water. Pour into 2 greased loaf pans. Bake at 350 degrees for 60 to 70 minutes or until bread tests done. Cool in pans 10 minutes before removing to wire rack to cool completely. Yield: 2 loaves.

Sally Loder, Ohio

PUMPKIN RAISIN NUT BREAD

1 cup cooking oil

4 eggs, beaten

⅔ cup water

2 cups pumpkin (1 can)

3½ cups presifted flour

1½ teaspoons salt

1 teaspoon nutmeg

1 teaspoon cinnamon

2 teaspoons baking soda

3 cups sugar

½ cup raisins

½ cup chopped nuts

Preheat oven to 350 degrees. Grease and flour three 8-inch loaf pans. Combine oil, eggs, water, and pumpkin. In a large bowl, sift together flour, salt, spices, baking soda and sugar. Make a well in the center, add pumpkin mixture. Blend until dry ingredients are well mixed. Bake 1 hour.

Kathy Bratton, Texas

COFFEE CAN PUMPKIN LOAF

1 cup fresh pumpkin

3 cups sugar

3 cups flour

1 teaspoon cinnamon

1 teaspoon nutmeg

½ teaspoon salt

2 teaspoons baking soda

1 cup oil

⅔ cup cold water

4 eggs

Sift dry ingredients, then stir in remaining ingredients. Grease and flour three one-pound coffee cans. Pour batter into cans and bake at 350 degrees for 1 hour. Store in the refrigerator.

Dean Ingram

DATE AND WALNUT LOAF

Stir together and let stand until the mixture is lukewarm, about 20 minutes.

  1½ cups packed pitted dates

  1 teaspoon baking soda

  1 cup boiling water

Whisk together thoroughly:

  1⅔ cups all-purpose flour

  ½ teaspoon salt

  ½ teaspoon baking powder

In a large bowl, whisk together:

  2 large eggs or substitute

  ¼ cup vegetable oil

  1 cup packed brown sugar

  1 teaspoon vanilla extract

Stir in the cooled date mixture and the flour mixture just until blended. Fold in 2 cups coarsely chopped walnuts.

Scrape better into a greased 9 x 5-inch pan. Spread evenly. Bake at 350 degrees, 55 to 60 minutes. Bake until a toothpick inserted comes out clean. Let loaf cool in pan on wire rack 5 to 10 minutes before unfolding. Cool completely on a rack before wrapping. This loaf freezes well. Serve with a butter spread.

Myra Hill, Texas

BANANA BREAD

Cream together:

½ cup margarine and 1 cup sugar

Add: 2 well beaten eggs

Add: 1 cup mashed bananas (2 large or 3 small)

Mix together:

Add 2 cups flour

1¼ teaspoon baking powder

½ teaspoon baking soda

1 teaspoon salt

½ cup chopped nuts (optional)

Blend lightly. Pour into greased loaf pan (1 large or 3 small). Bake at 300 degrees for 70 minutes

Betty Kuckes, Wisconsin

BANANA NUT LOAF

1 cup very ripe, mashed bananas

1½ cups sugar

1 egg yolk

1 teaspoon sour cream

1 teaspoon baking soda

½ cup melted margarine

1 teaspoon vanilla extract

½ cup finely chopped pecans

2 cups flour

Combine all ingredients one at a time. Fold 1 stiffly beaten egg white. Spread batter in greased loaf pan. Bake 1 hour at 350 degrees.

Jan Whittaker, California

ORANGE RAISIN PECAN BREAD

1½ cups flour

1 cup sugar

1 tablespoon baking powder

¼ teaspoon salt

1 beaten egg

¾ cup skim milk

½ cup orange juice

2 tablespoons vegetable oil

2 tablespoons grated orange peel

2 cups bran flakes

¾ cup raisins

½ cup chopped pecans

Mix dry ingredients together in a large bowl. In a small bowl, mix egg, milk, juice, oil and orange peel; add to dry ingredients and stir until just moistened. Batter will be slightly lumpy. Stir in bran flakes, raisins and pecans.

Pour batter into a greased loaf pan and bake in a pre-heated 350 degree oven for 50 minutes or until toothpick comes out clean. Cool completely.

Judy Krohn, Texas

STRAWBERRY WALNUT BREAD

- 2 cups finely chopped walnuts
- 3 cups all-purpose flour
- 1 teaspoon baking soda
- 1½ teaspoons ground cinnamon
- 1 teaspoon ground cardamom
- ½ teaspoon salt
- ¼ teaspoon ground nutmeg
- 4 eggs, beaten
- 2 cups sugar
- 1½ cups mashed strawberries (about 3 cups whole berries)
- 1 cup mashed banana
- 1 cup cooking oil
- 1 tablespoon finely shredded orange peel

These are great to give as gifts. I put them into small pans and that makes 4 to 5 loaves.

Grease and flour two 9 x 5-inch loaf pans; sprinkle ½ cup nuts in the bottom of each pan. In a large bowl, combine flour, baking soda, cinnamon, cardamom, salt, and nutmeg. Combine remaining ingredients, add to dry ingredients. Stir until just moistened. Stir in remaining nuts. Spoon batter into prepared pans. Bake in a preheated 350 degree oven for 1 hour. Cool in pans for 10 minutes. Then remove to wire rack to cool. Makes 2 pans.

Yvonne E. Constantino, Texas

EASY MONKEY BREAD

½ cup nuts
½ cup granulated sugar
1 teaspoon cinnamon
3 cans Hungry Jack biscuits
1 stick margarine
1 cup packed brown sugar

Butter a Bundt pan. Sprinkle nuts on bottom of pan. In a small bowl, combine granulated sugar and cinnamon. Using scissors, quarter biscuits and roll in sugar/cinnamon mixture. Drop biscuits into Bundt pan. In a small saucepan, melt butter and combine with cinnamon until sugar is dissolved. Do not boil. Pour mixture over biscuits. Bake at 350 degrees for 30 minutes. Invert onto large plate.

Kathy Bratton, Texas

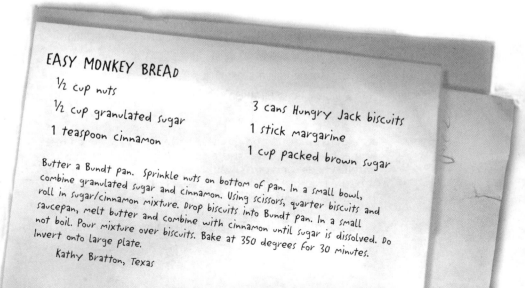

These will keep
successfully if
double wrapped
(tightly with
plastic wrap and
then tightly with
foil) and can be
left in the freezer
for up to nine
months. Enjoy!

ZUCCHINI BREAD

In a large bowl, combine
  4 eggs
  2⅔ cups sugar
  1⅓ cups oil
  2⅔ cups grated zucchini

Sift together and add:
  4 cups flour
  1½ teaspoon baking soda
  ¾ teaspoon salt
  4 teaspoons cinnamon
  ¾ teaspoon baking powder

Add:
  1 cup raisins (dusted with flour)
  1 tablespoon vanilla extract
  1 cup chopped pecans (dusted with flour)

Grease and flour two regular sized loaf pans. Preheat oven
to 325 degrees. Bake one hour or until toothpick comes out
clean.

Judy Krohn, Texas

Do what you can
with what you've
got where you are.

ITALIAN SAUSAGE BREAD

  1 loaf frozen bread dough, thawed
  1 pound ground Italian sausage, removed from casing
  1½ cups grated Mozzarella cheese
  1 teaspoon Italian seasoning
  2 tablespoons Parmesan cheese
  2 eggs

Roll thawed dough on greased surface to 14 x 9-inch rectangle. Brown sausage and drain. Mix sausage with Mozzarella cheese and one slightly beaten egg. Spread sausage
mixture to about 1 inch from edges of dough. Sprinkle with
Italian seasoning. Roll up jelly-roll style and seal edges.
Place in a well-oiled 9-inch spring form pan and let rise
until doubled. Make slits one inch apart in top of dough.

Brush with egg white mixed with water. Sprinkle with Parmesan cheese. Bake at 350 degrees for 30–35 minutes. Cool on rack 10 minutes and then remove from pan. Freezes well for later use.

Myra Hill, Texas

QUICK STICKY PECAN BUNS

- ¼ cup granulated sugar
- 1 teaspoon cinnamon
- ⅛ teaspoon ground cloves
- ½ teaspoon allspice
- ⅓ cup margarine or butter, melted
- ⅓ cup dark corn syrup
- ⅓ cup dark brown sugar
- 16–24 large pecan halves or chopped pecans to cover the bottom of an 8 or 9-inch round or square pan
- 1 package of Rhodes frozen cinnamon rolls

Combine the granulated sugar and spices and set aside. Melt butter in pan and sprinkle the brown sugar over butter. Dribble corn syrup over sugar. Place pecans over mixture. Place 12 to 16 frozen cinnamon rolls in pan, leaving about 1 inch spacing between each roll. Cover with a clean towel and let rise until double. Bake in 350 degree oven for 20–25 minutes. Let cool in pan for a few minutes and then turn out onto a plate. You can make these a day ahead because it takes several hours for the dough to rise.

Jeri-Lynn Sandusky, Utah

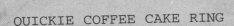

QUICKIE COFFEE CAKE RING

Butter an 8-inch ring mold. Pour 2 to 3 tablespoons honey into pan, coating bottom. Finely chop about 1/2 cup nuts. Open 2 cans refrigerated biscuits. Roll each biscuit in chopped nuts. Place biscuits in mold, slightly overlapping. Pour ¼ cup over biscuits. Bake in a 375 degree oven for about 30 minutes.
Shirley Thomas, Texas

CINNAMON CHEESE ROLL UPS

2 sticks butter

1½ cups sugar

2 teaspoons cinnamon (a little more if you want)

1 (8-ounce) package cream cheese

1 egg

⅓ cup sugar

1½ loaves white thin sandwich bread

Melt butter in a small pie plate. Combine sugar and cinnamon in another small pie plate. Use a mixer to cream cheese, egg and sugar. Remove crust from bread. Spread each slice with cream cheese mixture. Roll jelly roll style. Dip in butter. Then roll in cinnamon/sugar mixture. Bake at 350 degrees for 18–20 minutes. These freeze well before baking.

Bev Tackett, Missouri

BAKED FRENCH TOAST

1 baguette French bread, cut in 1-inch slices

6 large eggs

1½ cups milk

1 cup light cream

1 teaspoon vanilla extract

¼ teaspoon cinnamon

¼ teaspoon nutmeg

½ cup brown sugar, packed

1 tablespoon light corn syrup

¼ cup butter, softened

½ cup walnuts or pecans

Maple syrup

Butter a large baking dish or cookie sheet and arrange bread slices to fill pan. In medium bowl, mix eggs, milk, cream, vanilla cinnamon and nutmeg. Pour over bread, cover and refrigerate overnight. Preheat oven to 350 degrees. Combine brown sugar, butter, nuts, and corn syrup; spread over bread slices. Bake for 40 minutes or until bread is puffed and browned. Serve with maple syrup. Serves 8.

Jeri-Lynn Sandusky, Utah

JUDY'S FRENCH TOAST ROLL UPS

1 (8-ounce) package cream cheese, softened

1 egg yolk

1 cup sugar, divided

24 slices white sandwich bread

1 tablespoon ground cinnamon

3 tablespoons butter, melted

In a medium bowl, beat the cream cheese, egg yolk, and ¼ cup of the sugar until smooth. Set aside. Cut the crust off each slice of bread, then roll out each slice with a rolling pin. Spread the cream cheese mixture over the bread, distributing evenly. Roll each slice jelly-roll style and place seam side down on a baking sheet.

In a shallow dish, mix the remaining ¾ cup sugar and the cinnamon. Brush butter over roll ups, then roll in cinnamon/sugar mixture until coated. Repeat with the remaining roll-ups and place on baking sheet. Cover and freeze for at least 2 hours or up to 2 months.

Just before serving, preheat oven to 400 degrees. Bake for 10 to 12 minutes or until golden brown.

Judy Dashiell, Minnesota

FRENCH/FRENCH TOAST

French bread loaves

French bread egg batter

Chopped nuts

½ cup brown sugar to 1 stick butter ratio

This can be done the night before, if desired, but at 3 hours before cooking.

Slice French bread into 1 to 1 ½-inch slices and place in a baking dish that has been sprayed with non-stick vegetable spray. Fix your favorite French bread egg batter in proportion to the amount of bread. Pour evenly over bread, let set for about 30 minutes. Turn bread slices and pour remaining batter over bread. Cover and store in refrigerator over night or for at least one hour. Bake in a 250 degree oven for 20 minutes. Remove from oven, sprinkle chopped nuts over bread, pour melted butter/brown sugar mixture evenly over bread and place in oven for 5 minutes. Remove from oven and serve. No need for syrup.

Judy Boegler, Texas

PECAN FRENCH TOAST

1 loaf French bread

4 eggs

⅔ cup orange juice

⅓ cup milk

¼ cup sugar

¼ teaspoon nutmeg

½ teaspoon vanilla extract

⅓ cup butter or margarine, melted

½ cup coarsely chopped pecans

Slice bread into 1-inch slices. Lay them in a single layer in a cake pan. Whisk the egg, orange juice, milk, sugar, nutmeg and vanilla together. Pour mixture over bread. Cover with plastic wrap and refrigerate overnight. In the morning, remove casserole and let stand to room temperature. Toss pecans in melted butter and sprinkle over the bread mixture. Bake for 20–25 minutes in a 400 degree oven, or until fluffy. Serve with warmed syrup or cinnamon sugar.

Liv Volland, Wisconsin

APPLE CINNAMON BAKED FRENCH TOAST

1 large loaf French bread

8 extra large eggs

1 cup sugar, divided

3½ cups milk

1 tablespoon vanilla extract

6-8 medium apples

3 teaspoons cinnamon

1 teaspoon nutmeg

⅛ of 1 stick of butter

Slice bread into 1½-inch slices. Spray a 13 x 9-inch glass pan with non-stick vegetable spray. Place bread in glass pan, placing slices tightly together. In a separate bowl, beat eggs with ½ cup of the sugar, milk, and vanilla. By hand, whisk for 30 seconds. Pour one half of the egg/milk mixture over bread. Peel, core and slice apples. Place apple slices over bread. Pour balance of egg/milk mixture over apples. Mix remaining ½ cup of sugar with cinnamon and nutmeg. Sprinkle evenly over apples. Dot with butter. Cover and refrigerate overnight. The next morning, Preheat oven to 350 degrees. Bake for 1 hour.

Mary Ralston, Illinois

OUR FAMILY'S FAVORITE WAFFLES OR PANCAKES

2 cups whole wheat flour

1 tablespoon sugar

1 teaspoon baking powder

½ teaspoon baking soda

⅛ teaspoon ground cinnamon

2½ cups non fat buttermilk

1 teaspoon vanilla extract

3 egg whites, at room temperature

Vegetable cooking spray

¾ cup maple syrup

1 cup blueberries, either frozen or fresh (optional)

Combine first five ingredients in a bow, stir well and set aside. Combine buttermilk and vanilla; Add to dry ingredients, stirring just until moistened. Beat egg whites (at room temperature) at high speed with an electric mixer until soft peaks form; gently fold into flour mixture. Coat a waffle iron or pancake griddle. Spoon half a cup of batter onto pan. When cooked, serve warm with syrup.

NOTE: Aunt Jemima makes a good sugar-free syrup.

Leny Young, Ohio

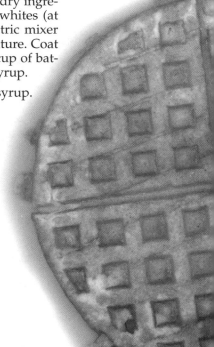

SATURDAY MORNING PANCAKES

1 egg

½ cup buttermilk

½ cup milk

1 tablespoon vegetable oil

⅔ cup all-purpose flour

⅓ cup whole wheat flour

2 tablespoons sugar

¼ teaspoon salt

½ teaspoon baking soda

1 teaspoon baking powder

In a mixing bowl, beat egg, milk, and oil. In a separate bowl, combine dry ingredients and add to egg mixture. Heat a lightly greased griddle over medium high heat. Use a small ladle or large spoon to pour mounds of batter onto griddle. When pancakes puff and bubbles begin to pop, turn over and cook on second side. Makes 12 4-inch pancakes.

Good with apple slices sweetened with cinnamon sugar. We do them in the microwave on high power. Slice apples and cook for 1 minute in microwave. Then, toss with cinnamon/sugar and cook another 2 minutes until tender. No need to peel the apples.

Keith Carter, Texas

APPLE COTTAGE PUDDING

2 teaspoons baking powder

¼ teaspoon baking soda

1 ½ cups whole wheat flour

½ cup sugar

1 large egg

½ cup milk

1 tablespoon butter or margarine, melted

2-4 cups chopped apples — tart apples are best

Good for breakfast

Preheat oven to 400 degrees. Sift baking powder and soda into a large bowl and add to flour. Add sugar and mix well. Add egg, milk and melted butter. Add chopped apples. Mix well. Pour into a 2 quart baking dish. Bake in preheated oven for 35 minutes or until well browned. Serve warm or cool. Serves 8.

Jean Krest, Colorado

JIM'S BUTTERMILK PANCAKES

2 cups buttermilk

2 eggs

1 tablespoon sugar

1 tablespoon baking powder

1 tablespoon canola oil

1 teaspoon baking soda

½ teaspoon salt, optional

Approximately 1 cup flour

For added flavor and nutrition: 3–4 tablespoons soy flour may be used in place of part of the flour

In a large bowl, combine all ingredients well. Use light coating of oil on griddle; cook at low to medium heat. When skillet is hot, spoon enough batter to make pancakes of desired size. Turn when browned. Makes 12–14 medium pancakes.

Jim Van Artsdalen, Missouri

OATMEAL WAFFLES

Another favorite breakfast recipe of ours.

1½ cups all-purpose flour

1 cup oatmeal

1 tablespoon baking powder

½ teaspoon cinnamon

¼ teaspoon salt

2 eggs, slightly beaten

1½ cups milk

6 tablespoons butter or margarine, melted

2 tablespoons brown sugar

In a large bowl, combine flour, oatmeal, baking powder, cinnamon and salt. In a small bowl, combine eggs, milk, butter and brown sugar. Add to flour mixture; stir until blended. Pour batter onto grids of preheated lightly greased waffle iron. Close lid quickly; do not open during baking. Use fork to remove baked waffles.

Keith and Ghita Carter, Texas

CREOLE CREPES

2 large eggs

1 cup milk

1½ tablespoons canola oil

1 teaspoon sugar

Pinch of salt

¼ teaspoon nutmeg

¾ cup plus 1 tablespoon flour

In a bowl, whisk together eggs, milk, oil, sugar, salt and nutmeg; slowly add flour until blended. Do not over beat. Lightly oil crepe pan. Pour 2 tablespoons of batter into pan, tilt to spread, brown on one side about 30 second to 1 minute. Then flip to other side and lightly brown. Can be rolled with cooked vegetables or eaten with butter and syrup. For sweet crepes (dessert) add 3 tablespoons sugar instead of 1 teaspoon , and 1 teaspoon vanilla instead of ¼ teaspoon nutmeg. Sweet crepes can be spread with butter and dusted with confectioners' sugar before rolling in a log. Can also be spread with preserves.

Millie Royer, Texas

BASIC CREPE RECIPE

2/3 cup flour

2 large eggs

1/2 teaspoon sugar

3/4 cup skim milk

1 tablespoon oil

Mix above ingredients together. Preheat a lightly oiled crepe pan or small frying pan. Add a very thin layer of batter, just enough to cover the bottom of the pan. It must be very thin. When underside is slightly brown, turn and brown the other side. Makes 12—16 crepes, depending upon the size of the pan.

Bunny Doucet, New Jersey

TASTY ORANGE SAUCE

⅓ cup sugar

Salt to taste

1 tablespoon cornstarch

1 cup fresh orange juice

1 tablespoon butter

In a top of a double boiler, combine sugar, salt and cornstarch, mixing well. Add orange juice and butter. Turn on heat and cook over rolling boiling water. Cool slightly and serve over crepes or pound cake. Makes 1 cup.

BRANDY NUT SAUCE

1 cup butter, softened

1 cup sugar

1 cup light cream

¼ cup chopped almonds or pistachios

½ cup brandy

In a small bowl, cream butter and sugar. Place in top of double boiler with cream. Heat and stir until light and fluffy. Add nuts. Add brandy a few drops at a time, beating slowly until smooth. Serve warm over crepes or other desserts. Makes about 3 cups.

RASPBERRY AND SHERRY TOPPING

1 (10-ounce) package frozen raspberries, thawed

1 tablespoon cornstarch

2 tablespoons sherry

Place thawed raspberries in a blender and puree. Strain to remove seeds. Combine raspberries and cornstarch in a small saucepan and cook until slightly thick. Cool. Just before serving, stir in sherry. Delicious over crepes, pound cake, cheesecake or ice cream.

Bob Lilly

EGGS &

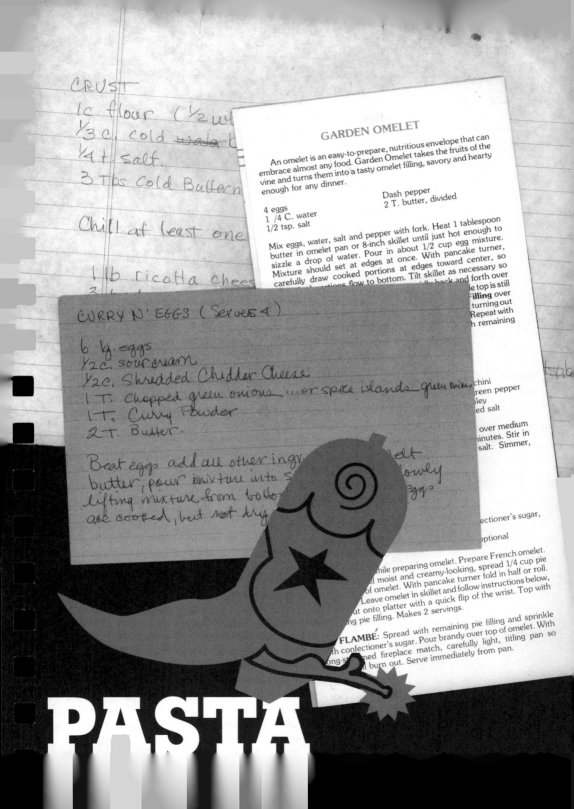

CRUST

1 c flour (1/2 w~~~~
1/3 c. cold ~~water~~ b~~~~
1/4 t. salt
3 Tbs Cold Butter~~~~

Chill at least one ~~~~

1 lb ricotta chees~~~~

GARDEN OMELET

An omelet is an easy-to-prepare, nutritious envelope that can embrace almost any food. Garden Omelet takes the fruits of the vine and turns them into a tasty omelet filling, savory and hearty enough for any dinner.

4 eggs
1 /4 C. water
1/2 tsp. salt

Dash pepper
2 T. butter, divided

Mix eggs, water, salt and pepper with fork. Heat 1 tablespoon butter in omelet pan or 8-inch skillet until just hot enough to sizzle a drop of water. Pour in about 1/2 cup egg mixture. Mixture should set at edges at once. With pancake turner, carefully draw cooked portions at edges toward center, so ~~~~ ~~~~ portions flow to bottom. Tilt skillet as necessary so ~~~~ ~~~~ back and forth over ~~~~ top is still **Filling** over ~~~~ turning out ~~~~ Repeat with ~~~~ remaining

CURRY N' EGGS (Serves 4)

6 lg. eggs
1/2 c. sour cream
1/2 c. Shredded Cheddar Cheese
1 T. Chopped green onions ....or spice islands green onions
1 T. Curry Powder
2 T. Butter.

Beat eggs add all other ingr~~~~ ~~~~elt
butter, pour mixture into s~~~~ ~~~~owly
lifting mixture from bott~~~~ ~~~~ eggs
are cooked, but not dry.~~~~

chini
green pepper
~~~~sley
~~~~d salt

over medium
~~~~inutes. Stir in
~~~~ salt. Simmer,

~~~~ectioner's sugar,

~~~~ optional

~~~~hile preparing omelet. Prepare French omelet.
~~~~l moist and creamy-looking, spread 1/4 cup pie
~~~~ of omelet. With pancake turner fold in half or roll.
~~~~ Leave omelet in skillet and follow instructions below,
~~~~t onto platter with a quick flip of the wrist. Top with
~~~~ng pie filling. Makes 2 servings.

FLAMBÉ: Spread with remaining pie filling and sprinkle
~~~~h confectioner's sugar. Pour brandy over top of omelet. With
~~~~ong-st~~~~ned fireplace match, carefully light, titling pan so
~~~~l burn out. Serve immediately from pan.

PASTA

Eggs

HUEVDES JALAPENOS

1 (10-ounce) jar jalapenos

2 pounds Cheddar cheese, grated

1 dozen eggs, beaten with 1 tablespoon water

Preheat oven to 350 degrees. Butter a 13 x 9-inch pan (glass works best). Place jalapenos in bottom of pan. Sprinkle cheese on top of jalapenos. Evenly pour eggs over jalapenos and cheese mixture. Bake uncovered for 35 to 40 minutes until firm (spongy).

Cook Voltz, Ohio

QUICHE LORRAINE

Serve with broccoli, tomato slices, and French bread. Makes two – freeze one for later or give to a neighbor.

2 deep-dish pie shells, unbaked

1 medium onion, sliced

8 slices bacon, cooked and crumbled

1 cup sliced mushrooms

12 eggs

¾ cup whipping cream

2 tablespoons milk

Garlic powder

¼ teaspoon Tabasco®

Salt and pepper

6 ounces Swiss cheese, shredded

6 ounces Cheddar cheese, shredded

Dill weed or dill seed

Preheat oven to 400 degrees. Line bottom of pie shells with onion, bacon crumbs and mushrooms. Beat eggs, cream milk, garlic powder, Tabasco®, and salt and pepper. Add cheeses. Pour mixture into pie shells. Bake at 400 degrees for 15 minutes, then at 350 degrees for about 30 minutes. Check with toothpick.

Jan Watson, Illinois

QUICHE

1 piecrust

½ pound cooked bacon, crumbled

½ pound Gruyere or Swiss cheese, coarsely grated

4 eggs, slightly beaten

1 teaspoon salt

⅛ teaspoon white pepper

Pinch cayenne pepper

⅛ teaspoon nutmeg

1½ cups light cream

1 tablespoon butter, melted

Preheat oven to 425 degrees. Prepare standard pie crust. Pick sides and bottom with fork. Precook 5–7 minutes. Reduce oven temperature to 350 degrees. Sprinkle bacon and cheese over bottom of cooked pie crust. Combine remaining ingredients. Pour into pie shell and bake at 350 degrees for about 10–15 minutes. Let set for about 10 minutes before serving.

Fay Luker, Texas

QUICHE LORRAINE

1 pie shell, unbaked

½ cup chopped chives or finely chopped onion

8 ounces Swiss cheese, diced (no fat or reduced fat – I use Alpine Lace)

1 can crab meat, drained

½ cup mayonnaise (I use fat-free Miracle Whip™ or Lite)

2 tablespoons flour

½ cup milk (can use skimmed milk)

2 eggs, well beaten

My children used to call this Mother's Crab Pie. Just could not get them to Quiche Lorraine. But, they liked it.

Mix all ingredients and pour into unbaked pie shell. Bake in 350 degree oven for 30 to 35 minutes or until golden brown on top. Let stand for 2 to 3 minutes before serving.

Yvonne E. Constantino, Texas

BRUNCH CASSEROLE

White bread

2 pounds sausage, ham or bacon

1 cup grated Cheddar cheese

½ cup green pepper

⅓ cup chopped onion

12 eggs

1 cup milk

1 teaspoon dry mustard

1 (10½-ounce) can cream of mushroom soup

1 (4-ounce) can mushrooms

⅓ cup milk

The night before, line the bottom of a 13 x 9-inch pan with Texas toast or bread. Brown meat and drain. Crumble with cheese over bread. Saute pepper and onions in drippings. Thoroughly mix eggs, 1 cup milk, and mustard. Stir in veggies and pour over meat and cheese. Refrigerate overnight. Before serving, mix soup, mushrooms and milk. Pour over casserole and bake in a 300 degree oven for 1½ hours or until brown. Cut and serve.

Carol Ryan, Kansas

EGG CASSEROLE I

5 slices buttered bread

¾ cup shredded Old English cheese

4 eggs, slightly beaten

2 cups milk

½ teaspoon dry mustard

Tear bread. Put 2 slices in 13 x 9-inch casserole. Add half the cheese, rest of bread and cheese. Combine eggs, milk and mustard and pour over casserole. Refrigerate overnight. Bake at 350 degrees for 40 minutes. Crumble 5 slices of bacon on top before serving.

Carol Ryan, Kansas

CHEESE FILLING

½ lb. Mozzarella cheese, diced
2 lbs. Ricotta cheese (or
Pot cheese)

MEAT FILLING

1½ lbs. chopped meat (beef or
mixture of beef and pork)
1 egg

...ed water
...spoon of
... prevent
...e filling.
...d baking
...e are re-
... 25 to 30
...d rest of

EGG CASSEROLE II

4-6 slices bacon

½ pound dried beef (or two 2½ ounce packages)

½ cup butter, divided

½ cup flour

1 quart milk

16 eggs

1 cup evaporated milk

Cook bacon in microwave until almost done, then put in skillet with dried beef and ¼ cup butter. Cook a while, then make a white sauce with flour and milk. Cook and stir until sauce is thick. Set aside. Mix eggs and evaporated milk. Scramble in ¼ cup butter. When eggs are done, put in a 13 x 9-inch casserole, alternating eggs and sauce. Bake at 275 degrees for 1 hour.

Carol Ryan, Kansas

BAKED EGGS

4 slices ham

4 eggs

1 teaspoon curry powder or ¼ teaspoon each onion
    powder, thyme and parsley

4 slices Velveeta™ or cheese of your choice

8 ounces shredded Cheddar cheese

1 cup whipping cream

1 tablespoon flour

Butter an 8- or 9-inch baking dish. Cover bottom of dish with four slices of ham, cut to fit as needed. Cover each ham slice with Velveeta™ cheese. Use half of the shredded cheese and make a circle on top of Velveeta™. Add one egg to each circle, being careful not to break yolks. Sprinkle with salt to taste. Mix curry powder or herb blend with cream, and stir in flour. Pour mixture around eggs. Sprinkle remaining Cheddar cheese on top. Bake at 350 degrees for 20-25 minutes depending upon how firm you want your egg yolks. Serve on buttered toast or muffin halves.

Jeri Lynn Sandusky, Utah

Molly is a long time Wisconsin friend.

MOLLY'S EGGS

1 (16-ounce) container sour cream

2 cans mushroom soup

2 dozen eggs

¼ to ½ cup butter

½ cup milk

3 tablespoons sherry

1 pound fresh mushrooms, sliced

Water chestnuts – chopped

1 pound sharp Cheddar cheese

Warm sour cream and soup in microwave, just to spreading consistency. Set aside. Scramble eggs with butter and milk. Add sherry, water chestnuts and mushrooms. Make layers of egg mixture, sour cream and soup.

Refrigerate for 8 hours or overnight. Bake at 300 degrees for 50 minutes. Serves 12

Cooked bacon, sausage, or ham can be used if you wish to add meat to make it heartier.

Liv Volland, Wisconsin

Served at Bay Breeze Bed and Breakfast, Corpus Christi, Texas

ARTICHOKE OVEN OMELET

¾ cup medium or hot picante sauce, or salsa

1 (14-ounce) can artichoke hearts

¼ cup grated parmesan cheese

1 cup grated Monterrey Jack cheese

1 cup sharp Cheddar cheese

6 eggs

1 (8-ounce) carton light sour cream

Grease a 10-inch quiche dish with butter or margarine. Spread picante sauce over bottom. Distribute artichoke hearts over picante sauce. Sprinkle with Parmesan cheese, then add Monterrey Jack and sharp Cheddar cheese. Place eggs in blender and blend until smooth. Add sour cream and blend well. Pour egg mixture over cheese mixture. Bake uncovered at 350 degrees for 30 to 40 minutes or until set. Let sit for 5 minutes before cutting into wedges. Serve with watermelon slices and English muffins.

Perry Tompkins, Texas

PERRY'S SHRIMP OMELET

Served at Bay
Breeze Bed and
Breakfast, Corpus
Christi, Texas

3 tablespoons butter or margarine

½ cup sliced mushrooms

1¾ cups frozen, cooked bay shrimp, thawed

Lemon pepper to taste

4 eggs

½ cup low fat milk

2 tablespoons cream cheese with chives

In a sauté pan, melt 2 tablespoons or butter and sauté the mushrooms. Add shrimp and sprinkle lemon pepper generously over all. Saute for 5 minutes, or until shrimp are warm. Whisk eggs with milk in a medium bowl. Melt 1 tablespoon butter with 2 tablespoons cream cheese in a 10-inch skillet. When the skillet is hot, add eggs and sprinkle with lemon pepper. Let eggs cook until almost set. Use a slotted spoon and add mushroom-shrimp mixture over half the nearly set egg mixture. Fold over the other half of the nearly set eggs and sprinkle with a few shrimp. Cut in half and serve.

Perry Tompkins, Texas

POTATO OMELET FRITTATA

3 tablespoons olive oil

1 onion, finely chopped

½ bell pepper, finely chopped

3 large potatoes, peeled, sliced thin

Salt and pepper to taste

2 tablespoons grated Italian cheese

7 eggs, well beaten or egg beaters

Put olive oil in a large pan and heat. Saute onion and bell pepper, add potatoes and sauté until golden brown. Sprinkle with salt and pepper. Mix cheese with eggs and pour mixture over potatoes, lifting potatoes so eggs can reach bottom of pan. Make sure potatoes are covered with eggs. Cook until top is solid; turn frittata to other side to finish cooking.

Bernadine Levy, Colorado

EGG/SAUSAGE BREAKFAST CASSEROLE

6 eggs, beaten

2 cups half and half cream

2 slices white bread, crusts removed, cubed

1 pound bulk sausage, cooked, drained and crumbled

1 cup grated Cheddar cheese

Salt (scant teaspoon)

Mustard (scant teaspoon)

½ pound sliced mushrooms

Mix beaten eggs and half and half. Set aside. Layer bottom of a greased casserole with bread cubes, cooked sausage, cheese, salt and mustard. Pour egg mixture over all. Refrigerate overnight. Place mushrooms on top of casserole. Bake at 350 degrees, uncovered for 1 hour and 10 minutes. Serves 6.

Zina Versaggi Graalfs, Florida

Served at Bay Breeze Bed and Breakfast, Corpus Christi, Texas

GREAT GARLIC CHEESE GRITS

1 cup uncooked instant grits

4 cups water

½ cup butter or margarine

1 (6-ounce) roll garlic cheese

¼ cup shredded Cheddar cheese

¼ cup Worcestershire sauce

Pepper to taste

2 eggs

Paprika

Cook grits in a saucepan in salted, boiling water until thick, stirring occasionally, for about 7 minutes. Remove from heat. Add butter, cheeses, sauce, and pepper. Stir until butter and cheese melt. Mix eggs and milk in a small bowl, and add the cooked grits. Mix well and pour into a 13 x 9-inch casserole dish. Bake at 350 degrees for 30–40 minutes until bubbly and slightly brown.

Perry Tompkins, Texas

Pasta

PASTA FLORENTINE

1 (10-ounce) package frozen chopped spinach

1 pound lean ground chuck

1 medium onion, chopped

1 clove garlic, minced

1 (16-ounce) jar spaghetti sauce with mushrooms

1 (8-ounce) can tomato sauce

1 (6-ounce) can tomato paste

8 ounces small shell pasta, cooked

2 tablespoons vegetable oil

1 cup shredded sharp cheese

½ cup Italian seasoned breadcrumbs

2 eggs, beaten

Shredded Parmesan cheese

Freezes well. Assemble casserole and place into freezer. Thaw and bake. Enjoy!

Microwave frozen spinach until thawed. Drain over a bowl. Press the back of a spoon into spinach, draining liquid into bowl. Measure juice and add enough water to make 1 cup. Set aside.

Brown beef and drain well. Return to skillet and add onion and garlic, stirring well. Add spinach liquid, spaghetti sauce, tomato sauce and paste. Bring to slow boil, reduce heat and simmer 10–15 minutes. Stir often to prevent burning. Toss cooked, drained pasta with oil. Stir in spinach, cheese, breadcrumbs, and eggs. Spread into a lightly greased 13 x 9-inch dish. Top with beef mixture. Sprinkle Parmesan cheese all over top. Bake, covered, at 350 degrees for 30 minutes or until thoroughly heated. Serves 8–10.

Juanita Magnuson, Alabama

BAKED SPAGHETTI

1 cup chopped onion

1 cup chopped green pepper

1 (28-ounce) can tomatoes with liquid, cut up

1 (4-ounce) can mushroom stems and pieces

1 (2.25 ounce) can sliced rip olives, drained

2 teaspoons dried oregano

1 pound ground beef, browned and drained

1 hot Italian sausage link, cooked and sliced thin (optional)

12 ounces spaghetti, broken, cooked and drained

2 cups shredded Cheddar cheese

1 (10.75-ounce) can cream of mushroom soup, undiluted

¼ cup water

¼ cup Parmesan cheese

In a large skillet, sauté onion and green pepper in butter until tender. Add tomatoes, mushrooms, olives and oregano. Add ground beef and sausage, simmer uncovered for 15 minutes. Place half of the cooked spaghetti in a 13 x 9-inch baking pan. Top with half vegetable/meat mixture. Sprinkle with 1 cup cheese. Repeat layers. Mix soup and water until smooth. Pour over casserole. Sprinkle with Parmesan cheese. Bake uncovered at 350 degrees for 40 minutes.

Suzanne Lukens, Washington
Becky Van Vranken, Washington, D.C.

Hint: may want to drain some of the broth after cooking the spaghetti so it won't be too runny!

TANGY CHICKEN SPAGHETTI

2 fryers (or 1 large hen)

1 (12-ounce) package vermicelli

1 pound Velveeta™ cheese, cubed

1 onion, chopped

1 bell pepper, chopped

1½ sticks margarine

1 can Rotel™ tomatoes (or add according to taste)

1 cup tiny peas, drained (optional)

Salt and pepper to taste

Boil chicken and reserve broth. Bone chicken, cook

spaghetti in reserved broth. Add 3 or 4 chicken bouillon cubes, if not rich enough taste. Add cheese to hot spaghetti. Set aside. Saute onion and bell pepper in butter until tender. Add to spaghetti and cheese. Add tomatoes, peas and chicken. It's ready to eat. No baking!

Sharon Odom, Texas

LASAGNA WITH SAUSAGE AND SPINACH

1 pound Italian sweet sausage, remove from wrapper, chop and fry

1 (15-ounce) container Ricotta cheese, light

2 cups shredded Mozzarella cheese

2 eggs

1-3/4 cups grated Parmesan cheese

2 (16-ounce) jars Classico spaghetti sauce, tomato basil style

12 lasagna noodles, cooked

2 (10-ounce) packages frozen spinach, chopped or leaf, thawed, then pressed between paper towels

1 (14-ounce) jar sun dried tomato Alfredo sauce

Fry sausage, drain and set aside. Combine Ricotta, Mozzarella, eggs, and ¼ cup Parmesan. Set aside. Pour 1½ cups of spagetti sauce into a lasagna pan. Add a layer of lasagna noodles. Add a layer of spinach, then cheese mixture, and top with crumbled sausage and a layer of spagetti sauce. Repeat layers, ending with sauce. Top with remaining 1½ cups Parmesan cheese. Bake covered at 350 degrees for 45 minutes. Uncover and bake for 15 minutes. Let stand for 15 minutes before cutting.

Margaret Purkey, Texas

EASY OVEN LASAGNA

¾ pound ground beef, browned and drained

½ cup water

1 teaspoon salt

2 jars marinara sauce (Prego or Ragu)

½ package (8-ounces) lasagna noodles, uncooked

1 cup ricotta or small curd cottage cheese

12 ounces Mozzarella or Monterey Jack cheese

½ cup grated Parmesan cheese

Bring ground beef, water, salt, and marinara sauce to a boil. In an 11 x 7-inch baking dish, layer sauce, lasagna noodles and cheese. Repeat layers, ending with sauce. Top with Mozzarella and Parmesan cheese. Cover with foil and bake at 375 degrees for 1 hour.

Betty Kuckes, Wisconsin

EGYPTIAN MACARONI OR LASAGNA

1½ pounds ground beef

1 large onion, chopped

1 bay leaf

1 (8-ounce) can tomato sauce

1 pound penne pasta or elbow macaroni

1 tablespoon butter or margarine

2 tablespoons flour, heaping

Salt and pepper to taste

2 cups milk or light cream (half and half)

1 or 2 eggs

Brown ground beef with onion. Drain. Return to skillet and heat with bay leaf and tomato sauce. Cook pasta according to package directions. Drain and set aside. Make white sauce by melting butter in a small saucepan, blend in flour, salt and pepper. Cook and stir over low heat until mixture is smooth and bubbly. Remove from heat. Stir in milk. Add one or two eggs. Cook and stir over low heat until mixture thickens a little. Remove bay leaf.

Cover bottom of large glass or metal baking pan with a little of the white sauce. Layer half the macaroni over white sauce. Add a layer of meat mixture then top with rest of macaroni. Pour remainder of white sauce over the top of the macaroni and spread to cover. Sprinkle with Parmesan cheese. Bake at 400 degrees for at least 1 hour. White sauce will brown. Serve by cutting into squares.

Maureen Vogl, Kansas

TOMATOES, FETA CHEESE AND BASIL WITH FETTUCCINE

6 ripe tomatoes, diced

3 garlic cloves, minced

1 cup fresh basil, chopped

½ teaspoon salt

Black pepper

⅓ cup olive oil

4 ounces mild goat cheese (Feta), crumbled

1 pound fresh fettuccine or ¾ pound dried fettuccine or
    linguini (I use less)

Combine tomatoes, garlic, basil, salt and pepper, olive oil, and cheese in a large bowl and toss gently. Let sit 30–60 minutes. Cook pasta al dente according to package directions. Drain well in a colander. Stir pasta into sauce and toss well. Serve immediately. Serves 4.

Gene and Peggy Uselton, Colorado

SUN DRIED TOMATO PESTO

1/2 cup sun dried tomatoes,
    softened in water and drained

1/2 cup toasted walnuts or pecans

1/2 cup olive oil

3/4 cup grated Parmesan cheese

6 cloves garlic

Salt and pepper to taste

Place all ingredients in a food processor and process until ingredients are thoroughly chopped. Taste for salt and pepper. Refrigerate or freeze. Wonderful with crackers and wine. We serve this pesto with Ritz crackers.

Bernadine Levy, Colorado

This recipe makes enough sauce for 3 or 4 batches of ravioli. I always freeze containers of the sauce left over in separate containers. A quart of sauce for a batch of ravioli (or more if you like it really saucy).

RAVIOLI SAUCE

1 package turkey Italian sausage

1 minced Texas sweet onion

1 heaping tablespoon fresh minced garlic

1 (14-ounce) can diced pasta style tomatoes

1 (14-ounce) can diced tomatoes with basil and garlic

1 teaspoon crushed dried oregano (fresh is good if you have it)

1 teaspoon crushed rosemary (again, fresh is good)

Add fresh basil if you like

2 tablespoons sugar

Salt and pepper to taste

Remove sausage from casing and break off into "teensy weensy" pieces. In a large pot, sauté sausage, onion and garlic. Drain. Return to pot and add remaining ingredients. Simmer for 30–45 minutes.

Lyn Gogis, California

TOMATO GRAVY

1 large white onion, finely chopped

½ cup olive oil

2 (6-ounce) cans Italian tomato paste

2 (8-ounce) cans tomato sauce

12 ounces water

4 cloves garlic, crushed

1 tablespoon sweet basil

¾ cup imported Italian cheese, divided

1 teaspoon sugar

Salt and pepper to taste

Fresh pork hock, optional

Saute onion in olive oil until tender. Add tomato paste, stirring while frying on low heat. (Be careful not to burn.) Stir often until paste begins to change color, approximately 15 to 20 minutes. Add tomato sauce, water, garlic, sweet basil, ½ cup cheese, sugar, salt and pepper. (Do not add too much salt now. After gravy cooks with cheese, you can correct seasonings.) Stir and then place lid on pot, turning heat to low. Cook slowly for at least 2 hours, preferably 3. Stir occasionally. If gravy becomes too thick, add a bit more water. At this point, add meatballs. Add ¼ cup Italian cheese, continue cooking slowly for another hour. Correct seasonings before serving if necessary. Serve with pasta. A fresh pork hock, cooked from the beginning with the gravy, adds a delicious taste. This recipe can be doubled or tripled easily and gravy frozen for later use. Serves 6.

Bernadine Levy, Colorado

BERNIE'S MEATBALLS

2 pounds ground chuck

1 pound pork, freshly ground

1 large white onion, grated

Salt and pepper to taste

3 eggs, well beaten

¼ cup water

½ cup Italian breadcrumbs

1 recipe Tomato Gravy

½ cup Italian cheese

Combine meat, onion, and seasonings. Add eggs with water and mix well, but gently. Add breadcrumbs and cheese. Mix and shape into round balls or little footballs, being careful not to pack meat. Gently shape the meat with the palms of your hands. Fry until lightly brown but not completely done, or bake at 300 degrees on a cookie sheet, until lightly brown. Add to gravy and cook 1 hour. Serve with pasta and sprinkle with Italian cheese.

Bernadine Levy, Colorado

As a child growing up in an Italian family, my grandmother fixed meatballs and spaghetti every Sunday. There were no written recipes. As I got older, I watched carefully to get the amounts to write the recipes to pass on to our family. I prefer to bake the meatballs.

BUL GO KI
(Barbecue Beef)
Cooking Time 30 min.
1 H̶   balaw on flank steak

Coq au Vin

½ lb. lean salt pork
12 T butter approx.
5 t. peanut oil
3 four-pound chickens
· cut into serving pieces
= salt and fresh l
½ c. Cog
1 b 1

add the pork pieces and coe
stirring often, until browned a
crisp. Using slotted spoon, rer
pieces and set aside. Leave
fat in the skillet.
2 A
to the
ned a
to use

bnyt
nd
nem
son l
pr

BAKED HALIBUT WITH HERB BUTTER
2 lbs halibut
1T. chopped green onion
1 clove garlic
1/4 t. sweet basil
1/4 t. pepper
2 T. parsley
1/4 c. butter, melted
2 T. lemon juice
1 t. salt
Place halibut in buttered baking dish.
Sprinkle with parsley and green onion. Combine
melted butter, garlic lemon juice, sweet basil,
salt and pepper. Drizzle over halibut and
bake at 350° 20 minutes or until
flakes whne tested with a fork

3/
1/

Pla
to
drai
cross
2 cups
then c
onion

MEATS

Beef & Pork

PEPPER STEAK

2 pounds round steak cut in ½-inch strips

2 tablespoons olive oil

2 cloves garlic – 1 whole, 1 minced

Large can sliced mushrooms

2 large green peppers cut in strips

2 large onions, chopped

2 teaspoons salt

½ teaspoon pepper

¾ cup red wine

Brown strips of round steak in skillet with olive oil and 1 whole garlic clove. Add mushrooms, green pepper, and onion. Cook until vegetables are tender. Add black pepper, salt and minced garlic. Add wine. Cook slowly for 1½ hours. Serve with noodles.

Bernadine Levy, Colorado

This marinade is also good on skirt steak.

BARBECUED FLANK STEAK

Flank steak, 2–3 pounds or smaller

½ cup soy sauce

6 tablespoons honey

4 tablespoons red wine vinegar

2 teaspoons each of garlic powder, ground ginger, and garlic salt

½ cup salad oil

1 medium onion, chopped

Combine all ingredients and pour over steak that has been slightly scored. Marinate all day or overnight. Barbecue 7 minutes on each side. Cut diagonally into thin slices.

Mary Q. Smith, Texas

BRAISED BEEF TIPS

This is easy and delicious.
From the American Heart Association Cookbook, 1970.

¼ cup corn oil

⅓ cup finely chopped shallots or green onion

½ cup diced green pepper

¼ pound fresh mushrooms, sliced

2 pounds beef tips, cut into small chunks or thin slices

½ cup red wine

1 cup beef broth or bouillon cubes

1 tablespoon Worcestershire sauce

½ cup chili sauce

In a large skillet, heat oil, add shallots or green onions, peppers and mushrooms. Saute until golden. Add beef tips. Braise very slowly until tender. Pour off fat. Add red wine and beef broth, Worcestershire sauce, and chili sauce. Bring to a boil and cook slowly until liquid is reduced to half the original volume. It should thicken slightly.

Marian Butcher, Pennsylvania

SPICY BRISKET OF BEEF

3 pounds fresh beef brisket

1 teaspoon salt

¼ teaspoon pepper

1 sliced onion

1 stalk celery

½ cup chili sauce

¼ cup water

1 can of beer

¼ cup chopped parsley

Place beef in casserole. Season and cover with onion, celery and chili sauce. Add ¼ cup water and roast uncovered in 325 degree oven until brown. Pour beer over meat, cover and bake at same temperature for about 3 hours or until tender. Remove meat; strain off all fat. Add chopped parsley. Cut into thin slices and serve with juices. Serve with hashed brown potatoes and buttered carrots. Serves 4.

Fay Luker, Texas

I have put this in at night and baked all night. You certainly feel hungry when you wake up. You let it cool and slice it, and then cool and reheat when you need it.

BEEF BRISKET BARBEQUE

Boneless brisket, 4–5 pounds

1½ teaspoons salt

½ cup ketchup

¼ cup vinegar

½ cup finely chopped onion

1 tablespoon Worcestershire sauce

1½ teaspoons liquid smoke

1 bay leaf, crumbled

¼ teaspoon pepper

Rub meat with salt. Place in ungreased baking dish or use 1 large oven cooking bag. (With this, you have no mess.) Stir remaining ingredients together and pour over meat. Cover tightly with foil, if using a baking dish. If using an oven baking bag, first put about 2 tablespoons flour into the bag. Add meat, then cover with sauce. Close the bag and put it in a pan with a lip, so if there is a run over, it goes into the pan. (In the twenty years I've been making this dish, this has only happened a couple of times.) Also, remember to put a few slits in the bag. Bake at 325 degrees for about 3 hours or until done.

Yvonne E. Constantino, Texas

SAKE MARINADE

1 cup sake

¼ cup chopped green onion

1 tablespoon soy sauce

1 clove minced garlic

Combine and marinate meat for 2–24 hours. Boil reserve down and brush on meat.

Terri Anderson, California

KOREAN BARBECUE

½ cup soy sauce

¼ cup sugar

1 tablespoon sesame oil

1 large clove garlic, minced

2 stalks green onion, chopped

Dash of black pepper

2 pounds flank steak, thinly sliced. Or, use chicken pieces

Combine marinade ingredients. Pour over meat. Marinate beef for at least a half hour. Chicken should marinate in refrigerator for several hours or overnight. Grill as desired.

Becky Van Vranken, Washington, DC

POT ROAST DINNER

Boneless chuck roast, 2 pounds
4 large potatoes (cut in fourths)
2 large carrots (cut in 4-inch sticks)
1 large onion (cut in 8 pieces)

Spray large casserole dish or roaster with cooking spray.
Arrange vegetables around meat. Cover evenly with 1 can
condensed soup (tomato, cream of chicken, cream of celery or cream of mushroom). Bake covered 5 hours at 250
degrees.

Jan Whittaker, California

EYE OF ROUND

1 eye of round
1 package Lipton Beefy Onion Soup
½ cup red wine

Preheat oven to 350 degrees. Use a glass roaster. Place meat
in roaster. Combine soup and wine and pour over roast.
Bake 2 hours at 350 degrees. Reduce heat to 250 degrees
and cook 1 additional hour. After the first hour of baking,
carrots, mushrooms and potatoes can be added.

Loraine Franklin, Texas

VEAL CUTLET PARMESAN

2 eggs
Salt and pepper to taste
1 cup bread crumbs
3 tablespoons grated Parmesan cheese

1 pound veal cutlets
6 tablespoons olive oil
1 cup Ragu tomato sauce
½ pound Mozzarella cheese slices

Beat eggs thoroughly. Add salt and pepper to taste. Mix bread crumbs with Parmesan
cheese and dip cutlets into egg first, and then into bread crumbs. Fry in hot oil about
4 to 5 minutes on each side until golden brown. Place browned cutlets in baking pan,
pouring layer of sauce over them, then a slice of Mozzarella cheese on top. Bake in
slow oven for 15 minutes or until cheese turns slightly brown. Serves 4.

Bernadine R. Levy, Colorado

ALL AMERICAN MEATLOAF

3 slices white bread

1 large carrot, peeled and cut into ¼-inch pieces

1 rib celery cut into ½-inch pieces

½ medium yellow onion, peeled and roughly chopped

2 cloves garlic, smashed and peeled

½ cup flat leaf parsley leaves loosely packed

½ cup plus 3 tablespoons ketchup, divided

4½ teaspoons dry mustard, divided

8 ounces ground pork

8 ounces ground veal

8 ounces ground round

2 large eggs, beaten

2 teaspoons salt

1 teaspoon ground black pepper

1 teaspoon Tabasco® sauce

½ teaspoon chopped fresh rosemary plus more needles for sprinkling

2 tablespoons dark brown sugar

1 tablespoon olive oil

1 small red onion, cut into ¼-inch thick rings

STEP ONE: Preheat oven to 400 degrees. Remove crusts from bread and place in the bowl of a food processor. Process about 10 seconds till fine crumbs form. Transfer breadcrumbs to a large mixing bowl. Do not substitute dried breadcrumbs in this step as they will make your meatloaf rubbery.

STEP TWO: Place carrot, celery, yellow onion, garlic and parsley in the bowl of the food processor. Process about 30 seconds. Stop and scrape down sides of the bowl once or twice. Chopping vegetables this way saves time and ensures that vegetables will be small enough to cook through and will not be crunchy. Transfer to bowl with breadcrumbs.

STEP THREE: Add ½ cup ketchup, 2 teaspoons dry mustard, pork, veal, beef, eggs, salt, pepper, Tabasco®, and rosemary to breadcrumbs. Using your hands, knead the ingredients till thoroughly combined, about one minute. Be careful not to overknead; doing so will result in a heavy and dense meatloaf. The texture should be wet, but tight enough to hold a free-form shape.

STEP FOUR: Set a wire baking rack into an 11 x 17-inch baking pan. Cut a 5 x 11-inch piece of parchment paper over center of rack to prevent meatloaf from falling through. Using your hands, form an elongated meatloaf covering the parchment.

STEP FIVE: Place the remaining 3 tablespoons ketchup, 2½ teaspoons dry mustard, and brown sugar in a bowl. Mix until smooth. Using a pastry brush, generously spread the glaze over meatloaf. Place oil in a medium saucepan set over high heat. When oil is smoking, add red onion. Cook, stirring occasionally until onion is soft and golden in places. Add 3 tablespoons water. Cook and stir until most of the water is evaporated. Transfer onion to a bowl to cool slightly, then sprinkle onion over meatloaf.

STEP SIX: Bake 30 minutes, then sprinkle rosemary needles on top. Continue baking loaf until an instant read thermometer inserted into center of the meatloaf registers 160 degrees, about 25 minutes more. Let meatloaf cool on rack, 15 minutes.

Henry Graalf's sister, Jan Dargin, California

MICROWAVE MEATLOAF DEVINE

1 (8-ounce) can tomato sauce

¼ cup packed brown sugar

1 teaspoon prepared mustard

1 egg, lightly beaten

1 medium onion, minced

¼ cup cracker crumbs

¼ cup canned mushroom pieces, drained

1½ pounds ground beef

1½ teaspoons salt

¼ teaspoon pepper

Can be made with 1 pound ground beef. Easy meatloaf recipe that's good enough for company.

Combine tomato sauce, brown sugar, and mustard in a small bowl. Set aside.

Combine egg, onion, cracker crumbs, mushrooms, ground beef, salt and pepper in a mixing bowl. Add half of the tomato mixture and blend thoroughly.

Shape into an oval loaf and place in an oblong baking
(continued on page 164)

dish. Make a depression in top of loaf. Pour remaining tomato sauce over top of meat.

Cook uncovered, on high power, 18 to 20 minutes, or until center of loaf is cooked. Cover meat and let stand about 10 minutes before serving.

Kay Alexander

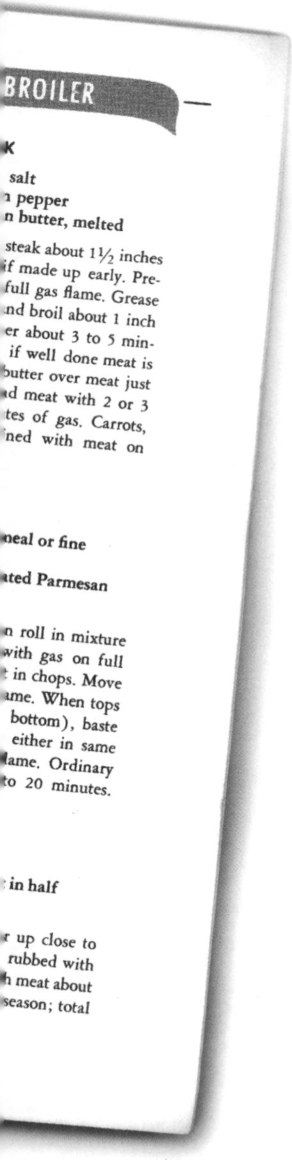
BROILER
salt
pepper
butter, melted
steak about 1½ inches
if made up early. Pre-
full gas flame. Grease
and broil about 1 inch
er about 3 to 5 min-
if well done meat is
butter over meat just
d meat with 2 or 3
tes of gas. Carrots,
ned with meat on
neal or fine
ated Parmesan
n roll in mixture
with gas on full
in chops. Move
ame. When tops
bottom), baste
either in same
lame. Ordinary
to 20 minutes.
in half
up close to
rubbed with
h meat about
season; total

SICILIAN STYLE MEATLOAF

1½ pounds ground chuck

Salt and pepper to taste

1 small can of tomato sauce. Do not use puree.

*Reserve ⅓ of the can of tomato sauce to be used later on the top of the meatloaf.

2 tablespoons fresh Parmesan cheese

2 tablespoons breadcrumbs

1 tablespoon chopped onion

1 teaspoon minced garlic

1 tablespoon chopped Italian parsley

2 eggs

Mix all ingredients together and adjust for consistency. If too dry, add a little water. If too wet, add more breadcrumbs. Press mixture out onto a piece of waxed paper to make one large loaf or two small loaves, keeping in mind the finished produce will be folded into thirds.

FILLING

3–4 slices partially cooked bacon

2 hard boiled eggs, sliced

4 slices Genoa salami, each slice cut in half

3 slices provolone cheese, each slice cut in half

Pine nuts (optional)

Layer the above ingredients, including the pine nuts, on top of the flattened meat mixture. Carefully roll the meat into ⅓ sections by picking up two sides of the waxed paper and dragging each side to the center of the meatloaf. Seal in the ingredients by pressing down on all sides of the meatloaf. Wrap each meatloaf with 2 slices of bacon and place in the refrigerator for about one hour.

Cover the bottom of a baking pan with oil and heat to

400 degrees. Carefully place the meatloaf in the pan and bake for 10 minutes at 400 degrees. Reduce heat to 350 degrees and bake for an additional 30 minutes. During the last 10 minutes of cooking time, pour the remaining tomato sauce over the meatloaf and continue cooking. If you do not have enough sauce to cover the top of the meatloaf, try adding some ketchup. Allow the meatloaf to set for 15 minutes before slicing and serving.

Be very careful when transferring the uncooked meatloaf to the pan with the hot oil.

Zina Versaggi Graalfs, Florida

SICILIAN SUPPER

1 pound ground beef

½ cup grated onion

1 (6-ounce) can tomato paste

¾ cup water

½ teaspoon salt

¼ teaspoon pepper

¾ cup milk

1 (8-ounce) package cream cheese, cubed

½ cup grated Parmesan cheese

½ cup chopped green pepper

½ teaspoon garlic salt

2 cups noodles, cooked and drained

Brown meat and drain grease. Add onion. Cook until tender. Add tomato paste, water and seasonings. Simmer for 5 minutes. Heat milk and cream cheese. Add green pepper, garlic salt and noodles. In a 1½-quart casserole, layer half the noodle mixture, then half the meat mixture. Repeat. Sprinkle with Parmesan cheese. Bake at 350 degrees for 30 minutes.

Marilyn Erhandson, Pennsylvania

TACO CASSEROLE

1 (8-ounce) package Pepperidge Farm cornbread stuffing

1 (14¾-ounce) can cream style corn

1 can water, divided

Vegetable cooking spray

1½ pounds ground sirloin

½ onion, chopped

1 (15-ounce) can black beans

⅔ cup salsa

1 package Taco seasoning

1 (8-ounce) package reduced fat Mexican cheese blend

Preheat oven to 375 degrees. Combine stuffing, corn and half of the water. Mix well. Press mixture into a 13 x 9-inch pan that has been coated with cooking spray. Bake for 10 minutes. Remove from oven and set aside.

Cook meat and onion in skillet until brown and crumbly. Drain well and return to pan. Add remaining half can of water, beans, salsa and taco seasoning. Stir well. Spoon mixture over stuffing mixture and top with cheese. Cover and bake at 375 degrees for 20 minutes or until cheese is crumbly. Cut into squares. Serves 8.

Lyn Gagis, California

STEAK TARTARE

1 pound ground sirloin

1 medium onion, grated

1 clove garlic, minced

1 egg

1 tablespoon olive oil

1 teaspoon vinegar

Mustard powder to taste

Accent to taste

1 tablespoon capers

Salt and pepper to taste

Mix all ingredients and chill. Serve on small rye bread rounds.

Dean Ingram

TAMALE PIE

Serve with guacamole and chips of your choice.

12 tamales

½ pound hamburger meat, browned and drained

1 can corn

1 can chili

4 corn tortillas

1 medium onion, chopped

2 cups Fritos corn chips

2 cups shredded Colby cheese

1 (8-ounce) can tomatoes, chopped

1½ cups sour cream

Celery salt (to taste)

Pepper (to taste)

1 teaspoon chili powder

Arrange a layer of tamales on bottom of casserole dish, then a layer of each of the other ingredients. Layer ingredients until casserole is full. Top with additional shredded cheese. Bake at 375 degrees for 30 to 45 minutes until casserole is hot and cheese has melted on top.

Dean Ingram

MOM'S FIVE LAYER CASSEROLE

2 cups sliced raw potatoes

2 teaspoons salt

1½ pounds ground beef

¼ cup sliced onions

2 cups sliced raw carrots

½ cup uncooked rice

1 (12-ounce) can stewed tomatoes

2 tablespoons butter or margarine

Put potatoes in a casserole. Sprinkle with a little of the salt. Add meat, a bit more salt, onions and carrots. Partially cook the rice with the tomatoes. Top casserole with rice/tomato mixture. Dot with butter. Cover and bake in a 350 degree oven for about 2½ hours or until done.

Henry Graalfs, Iowa

SWEDISH MEATBALLS

1½ cups fresh bread crumbs

1 cup heavy cream

2 tablespoons butter or margarine, divided

1 small onion, chopped

1 pound ground beef

½ pound ground pork

3 tablespoons chopped fresh parsley, divided

1½ teaspoons salt

¼ teaspoon black pepper

¼ teaspoon ground allspice

1 cup beef broth

1 cup sour cream

1 tablespoon all-purpose flour

Combine breadcrumbs and cream in a small bowl; mix well. Let stand 10 minutes. Melt 1 tablespoon butter in a large skillet over medium heat. Add onion. Cook and stir 5 minutes or until onion is tender. Combine beef, pork, breadcrumb mixture, onion, 2 tablespoons parsley, salt, pepper and allspice in large bowl. Mix well. Cover and refrigerate 1 hour.

Pat meat mixture into 1-inch thick square on a cutting board. Cut into 36 squares. Shape each square into a ball. Melt remaining 1 tablespoon butter in same large skillet over medium heat. Add meatballs. Cook 10 minutes or until browned on all sides and no longer pink in center. Remove meatballs from skillet; drain on paper towels.

Drain drippings from skillet and discard. Pour broth into skillet. Heat over medium-high heat, stirring and scraping up any browned bits. Reduce heat to low.

Combine sour cream and flour; mix well. Stir sour cream mixture into skillet. Cook 5 minutes, stirring constantly. Do not boil. Add meatballs. Cook 5 minutes more. Sprinkle with remaining 1 tablespoon parsley. Garnish as desired. Serves 5–6.

Mary Ralston, Illinois

STUFFED CABBAGE

1 pound chopped beef, browned

1 cup cooked rice

1 onion, chopped fine

¼ cup milk

1 teaspoon salt

¼ teaspoon pepper

1 medium head cabbage

TOPPING:

1 cup bouillon

1 cup tomato sauce

NOTE: Mashed potatoes, boiled red potatoes or broad egg noodles are wonderful accompaniments.

Brown chopped beef, remove from heat and drain excess fat. Return to pan and combine with rice, onion, milk, salt and pepper. Turn off heat. Steam cabbage leaves in water until slightly tender. Fill cabbage leaves with chopped beef and rice mixture. Roll up and set in baking dish and add bouillon and tomato sauce. Bake at 350 degrees for 1½ hours.

Jean Krest, Colorado

CROCK POT CORNED BEEF AND CABBAGE

1 medium onion, cut into wedges

4 medium potatoes, peeled and quartered

1 pound baby carrots

3 cups water

3 garlic cloves, minced

1 bay leaf

2 tablespoons sugar

2 tablespoons cider vinegar

½ teaspoon pepper

1 (2½–3 pound) corned beef brisket, with spice packet

1 small head cabbage, cut into wedges

Place onion, potatoes and carrots in a 5 quart slow cooker. Combine water, garlic, bay leaf, sugar, vinegar, pepper and contents of spice packet. Pour over vegetables. Top with brisket and cabbage. Cover and cook on low heat for 8–9 hours or until meat and vegetables are tender. Remove bay leaf before serving.

Becky Van Vranken, Washington, DC

Jan's grandmother and mother made this one-dish meal often and called it "hash". When Jan cooked it for Bob, he renamed it.

OVEN STEW

2 pounds beef, cubed (do not brown)

2 medium onions, quartered

1 cup celery, sliced

2 cups diced carrots

6 medium potatoes, cubed

Layer in large container, with beef on bottom, potatoes on top. Spread 1 can tomato soup over top. Bake covered at 250 degrees for 5 hours. Serves 8.

May substitute different meat, soup, vegetables.

Jan Whittaker, California

BAKED BEEF STEW

1 cup water

3 tablespoon tapioca

¼ cup sugar or 5 packages sugar substitute

1½ teaspoons salt

½ teaspoon pepper

1 tablespoon Kitchen Bouquet browning sauce

2 pounds top sirloin cut into cubes

4 medium carrots cut into cubes

2 celery ribs cut into cubes

1 medium sweet onion cut into cubes

1 can green beans, drained

Mix water, tapioca, sugar, salt, pepper and browning sauce in a small bowl and set aside. Place meat and vegetables in a greased crock pot or a pan suitable for the oven and pour the contents of the small bowl over all, coating the meat and vegetables thoroughly. If choosing to cook in a crock pot, cook on low for 8 to 9 hours. In a 375 degree oven, bake for 2 hours.

Mary Baker, Washington

LOW FAT, LOW SALT BEEF STEW

1 or 2 tablespoons peanut oil or olive oil

2 to 2½ pounds of beef eye of round or choice stew meat

1 level tablespoon Mrs. Dash's Original Seasoning

2 level tablespoons of flour

Golden potatoes, baby carrots, shallots, or small
cooking onions

2 tablespoons low-sodium soy sauce

1 cup beef broth

2 heaping tablespoons of flour

Rub bottom of Dutch oven or deep sauté pan with oil.

Cut off fat from beef leaving only a little interstitial fat. Dice into 1-inch chunks. Place meat in plastic bag and sprinkle with Mrs. Dash's Original Seasoning and flour. Mix meat and spices together by shaking the bag.

Heat oil over medium high heat in Dutch oven. When a drop of liquid sizzles, add meat, tossing occasionally with wooden spoon until meat and flour mixture are lightly browned and produce a tempting aroma. This may take about 15 minutes. At this point, gravy will have started to form. Put lid on Dutch oven and simmer over heat low enough to slightly bubble. Continue to cook until meat is fork tender. Watch closely to make sure sauce does not dry and add a small amount of water or low-sodium beef broth if necessary. Stir from time to time.

Meanwhile, peel potatoes and cut into 1-inch pieces. Cook these until just barely tender. Cook carrots until tender crisp. Cook shallots or other small cooking onions until just tender.

When meat has reached desired tenderness, remove and set aside temporarily. Add soy sauce to meat juice.

Using a 16-ounce sized peanut butter jar, fill with beef broth and 2 tablespoons of flour. Screw the lid on tight and shake until smooth. Add to meat juice while stirring and heating, adding additional beef broth or water from vegetables until sauce is desired thickness. Taste frequently. Add more beef broth if you wish more sauce. Add cooked vegetables and a handful of frozen peas and simmer until heated through. Pepper may be added just before adding vegetables.

Marilyn Sietsema, Illinois

This recipe freezes well in zip-lock bags. When you wish to use it from the frozen state, cut bag open, add to pan with a small amount of water and let warm until heated through. A handful of frozen baby peas may be added when stew is ready to be served and brought back to a simmer. This will give it a freshly made taste.

MINNESOTA "MARY JO" CHILI

2½ pounds ground meat*

3 tablespoons chili powder

1 medium onion, chopped

3 large pieces celery, chopped

2 cans of diced tomatoes

Salt and pepper to taste

1 (15½-ounce) can kidney beans, undrained

Brown ground beef in a large skillet. Drain excess grease. Add chili powder, onion, and celery. Cook on low until onion is transparent. Add tomatoes, salt and pepper. Simmer for 25 minutes over low heat. Add beans and simmer another 15 minutes. *Can also use ground turkey

Barbara Rhoades, Texas

MILLIE'S CHILI

I sometimes add Rotel tomatoes in place of one of the cans of tomatoes. I also add more chili powder upon occasion.

1 pound fresh ground pork

2 pounds fresh ground chuck

½ cup cooking oil

2 medium onions, chopped

¼ cup chopped garlic (4–5 cloves)

6 tablespoons chili powder

1–2 teaspoons salt (optional)

1 tablespoon oregano (optional)

1 tablespoon Worcestershire sauce

2 (8-ounce) cans tomato sauce

1 (15-ounce) can petite diced tomatoes

2 cups beef bouillon (stock)

2–4 cups hot water

Add pork and chuck to cooking oil and sauté until brown. Add onions, garlic, chili powder, salt, oregano and continue to sauté. Add Worcestershire sauce, diced tomatoes, beef bouillon and 2–4 cups water. Slower simmer for 3–4 hours, adding water as needed. Serve with tortilla chips.

OPTION: In the last 30 minutes of cooking, add 1 or 2 cans of red kidney beans.

Millie Royer, Texas

CRUNCHY TOP HAM AND POTATO CASSEROLE

2 pounds Southern style hash brown potatoes, thawed

1 can cream of chicken soup, undiluted

½ cup butter, melted

2 cups sour cream

2 cups cubed cooked ham

½ teaspoon pepper

½ cup chopped green onion

1½ cups shredded Cheddar cheese

Topping (see below)

TOPPING

2 cups crushed potato chips

¼ cup melted butter

Combine all ingredients, except topping and mix well. Place in a 13 x 9-inch baking dish. Combine chips and butter, sprinkle over casserole. Bake at 350 degrees for 1 hour.

Elaine Fawcett, Texas

I never liked stew until I discovered this recipe and now I can't wait for cold weather to make it. I love crock pot recipes.

HAM-RICE CASSEROLE

Our favorite casserole.

2 cups cubed leftover cooked ham

2 cups cooked rice

½ cup (heaping) grated mild Cheddar cheese

½ cup evaporated milk

1 can cream of asparagus soup

2-4 tablespoons chopped onion

Salt and pepper to taste

TOPPING:

1 cup slightly crushed cornflakes

4 tablespoons melted butter

Combine all ingredients and place in baking dish, cover with topping and bake uncovered at 375 degrees for 20-25 minutes until top is golden brown and casserole is bubbly. Serves 4-6.

Nancy Tarvin, Texas

LING

led water
spoon of
prevent
te filling.
d baking
e are re-
25 to 30
ld rest of

CHEESE FILLING   MEAT FILLING

BELGIAN ENDIVE WRAPPED IN HAM

8 Belgian Endive

8 slices cooked ham or turkey, sliced thin

Mustard

3 tablespoons butter

2 tablespoons chicken buillon

Bay leaf and Italian seasonings

Bechamel Sauce

Select firm heads of endive. Cut off a thin slice at the base and make a cross on the bottom about ¾–inch deep. Clean the endive by removing the outer leaves.

Melt the butter and turn the endive around in it. Do not let them take color (about 5 minutes on low heat). Add water to half their height; add seasonings and bouillon. Cover and simmer for at least 15 minutes until the base is soft. Do not allow the water to evaporate. Drain well.

Spread a thin layer of mustard on each slice of ham. Place one endive on the ham and roll up, placing bundles tightly in a buttered dish tightly. Pour Bechamel sauce over the endive and bake at 325 degrees for about 15 minutes.

Make a thick Bechamel sauce as the endive will release some liquid.

BECHAMEL SAUCE

3 cups half and half or milk

⅓ cup butter

2 tablespoons grated onion

⅓ cup all-purpose flour

2 sprigs fresh parsley

6 black peppercorns

Pinch of freshly grated nutmeg

Salt

1 cup grated Gruyere or Emmenthal cheese

Warm half and half in a saucepan over very low heat. Meanwhile, melt butter in another saucepan and saute onion until golden brown; do not allow to burn. Stir in flour and cook over low heat for 3 minutes or until bubbly. Gradually add the half and half, whisking constantly.

Cook until sauce thickens; add parsley, peppercorns,

nutmeg and salt. Keep heat very low and continue cooking 20–25 minutes, uncovered, stirring frequently. Strain through a fine sieve. Add the gruyere to sauce, reserving ¼ cup of the cheese for the top of the casserole. Makes 3 cups.

Zina Versaggi Graalfs, Florida

HAM AND SWEET POTATO CASSEROLE

Par-boil sweet potatoes about 20 minutes ahead of time. Skin and cut in 1-inch pieces and arrange in a 13 x 9-inch baking pan. Top with butter. Pour 1 cup orange juice over potatoes; sprinkle with 1 cup brown sugar and cinnamon. Top with slices of ham. Sprinkle with basil and parsley. Cover with aluminum foil. Bake in a 325 degree oven for 45 minutes.

Betty Ann Sheffloe, Nebraska

SWEET JALAPENO BBQ RIBS

   3 pounds country style pork ribs

   ½ teaspoon garlic powder

   ½ teaspoon salt and pepper

   1 (10½-ounce jar) red jalapeno jelly

   1 medium onion, chopped

   1 (5-ounce) jar A-1 steak sauce

   2 jalapeno peppers, seeded and finely chopped (optional)

Sprinkle ribs with garlic powder, salt and pepper. Place ribs on a rack in a broiler pan. Broil 5½ inches from heat for 18–20 minutes or until well browned, turning once. While ribs are broiling, combine jelly, onion, steak sauce, and if desired, chopped jalapenos in a saucepan. Cook over low heat until jelly melts. Simmer for a few minutes; remove from heat. When ribs are brown, remove them to a baking dish. Pour sauce over ribs, cover, and return to a 350 degree oven for 1 hour.

Jeri-Lynn Sandusky, Utah

PINEAPPLE SAUCE

1 (20-ounce) can pineapple slices

¼ cup sugar

1 tablespoon cornstarch

Dash salt

1 egg yolk, slightly beaten

2 tablespoons butter

Drain pineapple juice into a measuring cup. Add water to juice to equal 1 cup liquid. Combine sugar, cornstarch, salt and reserved liquid. Cook until thickened. Stir small amount of hot mixture into egg yolk. Return to hot mixture. Cook 1 minute. Stir in butter. Cut 2 slices of pineapple into chunks and add to the sauce.

This sauce is excellent served with ham, leg or lamb, or grilled pork chops.

Jeri-Lynn Sandusky, Utah

A favorite recipe from my Belgian friend, Suzanne Janssens

OVEN BARBECUE SPARERIBS

4–5 pounds ribs, cut into serving size pieces

salt and pepper

lemon sices

1 onion, chopped

Spread ribs meaty side up in a shallow baking pan. Sprinkle with salt and pepper. Place 1 lemon slice on each rib. Sprinkle chopped onion over all. The lemon and onion are what give the meat a delicious flavor — so be generous.

Bake in a 400 degree oven, uncovered for 45 minutes (or less) to brown. Remove from oven and reduce oven temperature to 325 degrees. Baste with sauce as directed below.

SAUCE:

1 teaspoon chili powder

1 tablespoon celery seed

¼ cup packed brown sugar

¼ cup vinegar

¼ cup Worcestershire sauce

1 cup tomato paste

2 cups water

Combine all ingredients and bring to a boil. Pour over ribs, roast for 1½ hours, uncovered. Baste, turn ribs. If sauce thickens too much, add a little hot water.

Ruth Rice, Texas

New Year's Eve Special

HOPPING JOHN

1 pound bacon

1 pound hot sausage

1 large onion, chopped

2 small cans chopped green chiles

1 box Uncle Ben's Herb flavored Wild Rice

1 (size) can water

Fry bacon until crumbly. Drain and set aside. Fry sausage, onion and 2 chopped green chiles until sausage is cooked. Drain and set aside.

Prepare rice according to package directions. Add bacon and sausage mixture to rice. Add water and simmer 20 minutes or to desired consistency. Serve as a dip or as a meal with cornbread.

Kathy Bratton, Texas

CURRIED PORK CHOP DINNER

6 pork chops

Seasoned salt

Butter or vegetable oil

1 can cream of mushroom soup

4 medium cooked potatoes, thickly sliced

1 large onion, thinly sliced

1 teaspoon curry powder or to taste

¾ cup water

1 teaspoon beef bouillon or 1 bouillon cube

Season pork chops with seasoned salt and pepper. Brown pork chops in butter or oil for about 6–8 minutes per side. Remove from skillet and brown onions until translucent. Add water and bouillon. Stir until bouillon is dissolved, then stir in mushroom soup and curry powder. Add cooked potatoes to sauce. Place pork chops on top of potatoes and cover. Simmer about 10 minutes.

Jeri-Lynn Sandusky, Utah

STUFFED PORK CHOPS

2 strips bacon

2 tablespoons chopped onion

1 cup soft bread crumbs

1 cup chopped, peeled raw apple

¾ cup chopped cooked prunes

6 pork chops, 1-inch thick

Salt, pepper, flour

½ cup pineapple juice

½ cup Sauterne

Mince bacon and cook until almost crisp. Add onion and cook 3 minutes on medium heat. Add crumbs, apples, and prunes. Cut a slit in each pork chop, fill with the stuffing and fasten with a toothpick. Sprinkle with salt, pepper, and flour. Brown in a heavy skillet; pour off fat and add the pineapple juice and wine. Cover and either bake at 325 degrees or cook on the stove on low heat until tender, about 1 hour. Add more juice or water if necessary.

Fay Luker, Texas

Check your local Chinese market for good curry powder.

HAM GLAZE

1 cup light or dark brown corn syrup

½ cup packed brown sugar

3 tablespoons spicy mustard

½ teaspoon ground ginger

Dash ground cloves

Combine all ingredients and bring to a boil over medium heat. Simmer 5 minutes, stirring constantly. Brush onto baked ham, frequently during the last 30 minutes of baking.

Jeri-Lynn Sandusky, Utah

HONEY BOURBON GRILLED TENDERLOIN

Utterly Delicious! Great for chicken, too!

3 (¾ pound each) lean pork tenderloins

½ cup diced onion

½ cup lemon juice

¼ cup bourbon (optional)

¼ cup honey

¼ cup low sodium soy sauce

1 tablespoon minced peeled ginger root

2 tablespoons olive oil

4 cloves garlic, minced

½ teaspoon salt

¼ teaspoon pepper

Vegetable cooking spray

3 tablespoons all-purpose flour

1¼ cups water

Trim fat from pork. Use a large zip lock bag and combine onion, lemon juice, bourbon, honey, soy sauce, ginger root, olive oil and garlic. Add pork. Seal bag and marinate in refrigerator for 30 minutes.

Remove pork from bag and reserve marinade. Sprinkle salt and pepper over pork.

Prepare grill. Place pork on the grill which has been coated with vegetable cooking spray. Cover and cook for 30 minutes or until meat thermometer registers 160 degrees, turning and basting pork occasionally with a half cup of the marinade. Cut pork into ¼-inch slices.

Place flour in a small saucepan. Gradually add remaining marinade and water, stirring with a wire whisk until blended. Bring to a boil over medium heat, and cook and stir 3 minutes or until thickened. Spoon gravy over pork. Serve with garlic mashed potatoes. Yummy!

Zina Versaggi Graalfs, Florida

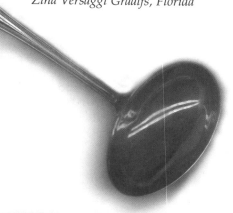

BARBECUED PORK

2 pounds boneless pork

1 teaspoon brown bean sauce

2 cloves garlic, chopped fine

1 tablespoon hoisin sauce

1 tablespoon Chinese bead molasses or Kitchen Bouquet

½ cup chicken stock (or 1 chicken bouillon cube in ½ cup water)

1 tablespoon salt

6 tablespoons soy sauce

½ teaspoon five flavored spice powder

1 tablespoon pale dry sherry

½ teaspoon red food coloring

Pork loin, tenderloin or fresh ham may be used. Cut pork into 1½ to 2-inch x 3 x 3-inch strips (or whole tenderloin). Trim fat.

Place all ingredients, except pork, five spice powder, dry sherry and food coloring in a saucepan. Heat until mixture blends (do not boil). Remove from heat. Add five spice powder, sherry and food coloring. Pour over pork strips and marinate for at least 6 hours (preferably overnight).

Can use a plastic bag placed in a mixing bowl so mixture can be turned while marinating.

Preheat oven to 350 degrees. Place pork strips on a broiler pan with a half inch of water underneath and roast for 45 minutes, basting with marinade every 10 to 15 minutes. Increase heat to 450 degrees and roast 15 minutes longer.

Ralph and Jeanine Bowles, Washington

MUSTARD BARBECUE GLAZE

This recipe was published in the November/December 2003 issue of Taste of Home magazine. I submitted this recipe to the magazine as a barbecue sauce, to be used to glaze oven-baked or grilled spareribs and chicken.

2/3 cup dark brown sugar, firmly packed

½ cup coarse grained, Dijon mustard

5 tablespoons cider vinegar

2 tablespoons molasses

1 tablespoon dry mustard

Combine all ingredients in a small saucepan and simmer on low heat for 2-3 minutes. Double recipes if you like lots of sauce.

Jeri-Lynn Sandusky, Utah

SOUTHWEST PORK STEW

1 pork loin, about 1 pound*

1½ teaspoons ground cumin

¼ teaspoon salt

¼ teaspoon cinnamon

⅛ teaspoon ground red pepper

2 teaspoons vegetable oil

1 cup chopped onion

1 cup chopped green, red or yellow pepper

2 cloves minced garlic

3 cups cubed, peeled potatoes

1 cup no-salt V-8 juice

½ cup water

1 (14-ounce) can undrained Mexican style stewed tomatoes with jalapeno peppers

1 (10-ounce) package frozen corn, thawed and drained

Fresh cilantro

Sour cream

Cut pork into cubes. Set aside. Combine cumin, salt, cinnamon and pepper in a bag. Add pork and shake until pork is coated.

In a large pot, add 2 teaspoons vegetable oil; cook pork for 5 minutes. Add onion, green pepper and garlic and sauté for 3 minutes.

Add potatoes, V-8 juice and water. Simmer for 25 minutes. Add corn and continue to simmer for an additional 35 minutes. Garnish with cilantro and sour cream.

Add other fresh vegetables as desired.

*You can substitute chicken for the pork loin, but pork is better.

Betty Dougherty, Texas

RAISIN SAUCE

1 cup raisins

1¾ cups water

1/3 cup packed brown sugar

1½ tablespoons cornstarch

¼ teaspoon cinnamon

¼ teaspoon cloves

¼ teaspoon dry mustard

¼ teaspoon salt

1 tablespoon vinegar

Bring raisins to a boil in water. Lower heat and simmer 5 minutes. Add sugar which has been mixed with cornstarch and spices. Cook, stirring until thickened. Blend in vinegar. Makes 1½ cups. Serve hot. Wonderful with ham.

Jan Watson, Illinois

ROAST LAMB

OPTIONAL MARINADE:

> 3–4 tablespoons olive oil
>
> 2 tablespoons soy sauce
>
> Juice of ½ lemon, plus grated peel if you wish
>
> About ½ teaspoon rosemary
>
> 1–2 cloves garlic, pureed (optional)

Rub the unboned* side of the lamb with a tablespoon of olive oil and place oiled side down, in a baking pan. Rub the rest of the oil and the soy, lemon juice and optional peel, rosemary, and optional garlic into the top side. Cover with plastic wrap and marinate until you are ready to cook the lamb—an hour or more, if possible. I marinate overnight or through the day prior to dinner.

To roast lamb in oven: I prefer to roast the lamb and then finish it off under the broiler. Place the marinated lamb flat, boned side up, in a roasting pan in the center of a preheated 375 degree oven. Roast for 20 to 25 minutes or until a meat thermometer inserted in center reads 120 degrees. (I do not turn the lamb on its other side.) Baste with oil and broil for 2–3 minutes until lightly brown. Let sit for 8–10 minutes outside the oven before carving.

*May also use a boned roll of lamb.

Barbara Konetchy, Massachusetts

A hearty red, such as Cotes du Rhone, Beaujolais or Zinfandel complements this meal.

SAUSAGE A LA RUSSE

1 pound pork sausage meat
1 onion, minced
1 large green pepper, minced
1 can (14½ or 19 ounce) diced tomatoes

1 cup uncooked broken macaroni
2 tablespoons sugar
1-1/2 cups sour cream
Salt and pepper
Chopped parsley

Cook sausage meat until lightly browned, breaking up with a fork. Pour off most of the fat (if there is any). Add onion and green pepper and cook 2 or 3 minutes longer. Add tomatoes, macaroni and sugar. Bring to a boil; reduce heat, cover and simmer 30 minutes. Add sour cream; heat and add salt and pepper to taste. Put in serving dish and sprinkle with parsley. Serves 4-6.

Barbara Konetchy, Massachusetts

VENISON STEAKS WITH WILD MUSHROOM SAUCE

Demi-Glace can be ordered from gourmet specialty shops or found in fine markets.

4 venison steaks (about 1½ pounds)

1 teaspoon fresh or dried chopped chives

1 sprig fresh thyme or large pinch of dried thyme

1 bay leaf

½ cup dry red wine

½ cup vegetable oil

Place venison steaks in a shallow baking dish. Mix all ingredients in a small bowl and pour over steaks. Marinate for several hours or overnight, turning at least once.

Place the steaks on a grill about six inches above the hot coals. For extra flavor, throw in a few mesquite or hickory chips that have been soaked in water for at least 30 minutes. Turn steaks once, checking for doneness (5 minutes per side for rare; 10 minutes for well done). Place steaks on a warmed platter and serve with Wild Mushroom Sauce.

WILD MUSHROOM SAUCE

2 tablespoons finely chopped shallots

½ stick butter

8–10 ounces sliced fresh wild mushrooms or 1 ounce of reconstituted dried wild mushrooms

1 cup red wine

1.5 ounces Demi-Glace Gold

¼ cup heavy cream

½ cup hot water

Salt and freshly ground pepper

Saute shallots in butter for 1–2 minutes or until translucent. Add mushrooms and cook until mushrooms are tender, about 3 minutes. Remove mushrooms and set aside.

Add red wine and reduce by half. Add Demi-Glace Gold and whisk until dissolved.

Return mushrooms to pan and add heavy cream and reduce briefly; then add enough water to reach desired sauce thickness. Add salt and pepper to taste. Makes 3–4 servings.

Zina Versaggi Graalfs, Florida

HENRY'S MOOSE STEW

A favorite at the Minnesota Vikings tailgate parties!

1 medium onion, chopped

½ teaspoon minced garlic

½ teaspoon baking soda

1 pound moose steak or other wild game (venison, elk, antelope) cut into bite sized pieces

Beef broth or water

1 medium package carrots, sliced

3 ribs celery, diced

3 medium potatoes, diced

3 medium turnips, diced

1 cup flour

Salt and pepper to taste

1 package frozen corn

1 package frozen peas

2 teaspoon lemon juice (optional)

Chop onion and sauté with garlic in vegetable oil until soft. Add baking soda and stir well. Add boiling water, just to cover, stirring occasionally until onions are mashed. Transfer mixture to a roasting pan.

Preheat oven to 350 degrees. Season flour with salt and pepper. Then dredge the meat in the flour and brown in a frying pan in oil. Add to the onions and garlic. Add water or beef broth as necessary to keep a stew consistency (about 3 cups). Cook covered for about one hour. Add carrots, celery, potatoes and turnips and any other vegetables you like. Adjust the seasonings. Add more liquid, if necessary. Stir well and bring to a low boil again in the oven. Cook until meat and vegetables are tender. Add frozen corn, peas and lemon juice and cook for an additional 30 minutes. If there is too much liquid, thicken by adding flour or corn starch.

Henry Graalfs, Iowa

Chicken

HAWAIIAN CHICKEN

1 (3 pound) chicken, cut up

¼ cup butter

¼ cup packed brown sugar

⅓ cup ketchup

¼ cup vinegar blended with 2 teaspoons cornstarch

1 teaspoon salt

1 teaspoon Worcestershire sauce

1 teaspoon soy sauce

1 (9-ounce) can crushed pineapple, undrained

Put chicken in casserole dish. Combine remaining ingredients, except pineapple, for sauce, cook until thickened and pour over chicken. Add pineapple. Bake uncovered at 325 degrees for two hours.

Jan Watson, Illinois

The roasted chicken is a beautiful deep burnished brown when done. Has a mouthwatering aroma!

TERIYAKI ROASTED CHICKEN

One whole roasting chicken

ROASTING SAUCE:

¼ cup soy sauce

¼ cup balsamic vinegar

¼ cup honey

1 teaspoon fresh grated ginger

1 heaping tablespoon fresh grated garlic (or 4 cloves fresh)

Mix sauce together and spoon over chicken and bake in a 350 degree oven for about 1½ hours or until done. Baste chicken 3 or 4 times with juices throughout roasting time. Serve with rice and green beans or asparagus. Serves 4–6.

Lyn Gogis, California

IMPERIAL CHICKEN

2 chickens, halved

1 teaspoon salt

¾ cup butter, melted

2 teaspoons Worcestershire sauce

2 teaspoons curry

2 teaspoons oregano

1 teaspoon dry mustard

1 teaspoon garlic powder

½ teaspoon paprika

2–3 dashes Tabasco® sauce

⅓ cup dry sherry

Developed by Dr. Ruth Rice. Won first prize and placed in International Wild Rice Cookbook.

Season the chicken with salt. Place skin side down in a shallow baking dish. Blend all remaining ingredients and pour over chicken. Bake at 350 degrees for 1½ hours or until tender. Temperature may be increased during the last 15 minutes to crisp chicken. Serve with wild rice, oven roasted vegetables, and a nice red wine.

Winola Van Artsdalen, Kansas

CHERRY SAUCE

1 jar cherry preserves

2 tablespoons red wine vinegar

Cook and stir over medium heat until bubbly. Serve with ham steaks, chicken, lamb or duck.

Jeri-Lynn Sandusky, Utah

CHICKEN ADOBO

Brown 2–3 pounds chicken pieces in vegetable oil.
Stir in:

½ cup soy sauce

½ cup water

¼ cup vinegar

Sprinkle with:

¼ teaspoon pepper

¼ teaspoon ginger

¼ teaspoon allspice

¼ teaspoon garlic powder

1 tablespoon dried onion

1 tablespoon sugar

Cook one hour on low or simmer. Serve with white rice.

Jan Whittaker, California

CHI COLA CHICKEN

    6 to 8 chicken pieces, any kind

    ½ cup sliced onions

    1½ cups ketchup

    1 (12-ounce) can of cola, regular or diet

Six to eight chicken pieces, any kind, halved and browned in flour, salt, and pepper. Place browned chicken in a baking dish. Mix ½ cup sliced onions, 1½ cups ketchup, and one (12-ounce) can of cola (regular or diet) together in a large bowl, as it will "fizz" up. Pour over chicken and bake at 350 degrees for one hour. Serve over rice.

    Jeri-Lynn Sandusky, Utah

RUSSIAN CHICKEN

I have used this with a whole chicken cut up, chicken legs and thighs, or with boneless skinless chicken breasts. I just bake the chicken at 350 degrees for 15–20 minutes, drain the liquids and fats, then put the sauce over the top and finish cooking for another 15 minutes or until done. Serve with rice.

SAUCE

    1 package Lipton's Onion Soup mix, no liquid

    1 bottle Russian Salad dressing

    1 small jar apricot jam (use a large jar if you prefer)

Mix ingredients.

    Lyn Gogis, California
    Ralph and Jeanine Bowles, Washington

SALSA COUSCOUS CHICKEN

This has become our family's favorite chicken dish.

- 3 cups hot cooked couscous or rice (cooked according to package directions)
- 1 tablespoon olive or vegetable oil
- ¼ cup coarsely chopped almonds
- 2 garlic cloves, minced
- 8 chicken thighs, skin removed
- 1 cup Old El Paso Garden Pepper or Thick N Chunky Salsa
- ¼ cup water
- 2 tablespoons dried currants
- 1 tablespoon honey
- ¾ teaspoon cumin
- ½ teaspoon cinnamon

While couscous is cooking, heat oil in a large skillet over medium-high heat until hot. Add almonds; cook 1 to 2 minutes or until golden brown. Remove almonds from skillet with slotted spoon; set aside. Add garlic to skillet; cook and stir for 30 seconds. Add chicken; cook 4 to 5 minutes or until browned, turning once. In medium bowl, combine salsa and remaining ingredients; mix well. Add to chicken; mix well. Reduce heat to medium; cover and cook 20 minutes or until chicken is fork-tender and juices run clear. Stir occasionally. Stir in almonds. Serve chicken mixture with couscous. Serve 4.

Ralph and Jeanine Bowles, Washington

TURKEY IN THE SACK

Oil the inside of a double strength grocery sack. Set oven to 325 degrees. Brush full thawed bird with oil or butter, being careful to brush inside wings. Stuff the body cavity of the bird with a few stalks of celery, some carrots, and a chopped onion. Secure the bag using strong string or staples. Place bird on rack in broiler pan. 12 pounds and under, cook 20 minutes per pound. 12 pounds and up, cook 15 to 18 minutes per pound. After turkey is done, remove from oven. Poke holes in bag so juices run into pan for gravy. Let turkey sit for 20 minutes before carving.

Liz Offord, Texas

CREAMY CHICKEN AND MUSHROOMS

1 pound boneless, skinless chicken breasts

1 teaspoon olive oil

½ cup chopped shallots

1 (8-ounce) package sliced mushrooms

½ cup dry white wine

1 cup fat free milk

2 teaspoons all-purpose flour

3 ounces spreadable cheese (garlic and herb flavor)

2 tablespoons chopped parsley

¼ teaspoon black pepper

Pasta, cooked according to package directions

Parsley for garnish

Spray a large skillet with non-stick spray. Cook chicken over medium heat for 4 minutes. Remove chicken from pan and set aside. Add olive oil and shallots to pan and cook for 1 minute. Add mushrooms and cook for 4 minutes. Add wine. In a small bowl, combine milk and flour with a whisk. Add to skillet and cook for 3 minutes. Add chicken, cheese, parsley and pepper. Reduce heat and simmer for 3 minutes. Serve over cooked pasta. Garnish with parsley. Serves 4.

Connie Timko, Illinois

CHICKEN BREASTS IN WHITE WINE

4 chicken breasts

8 slices Swiss cheese

1 can cream of chicken soup

¼ cup dry white wine

1 cup dressing mix

1 cup melted butter

Preheat oven to 350 degrees. Arrange chicken in greased 13 x 9-inch baking dish. Top with cheese. Combine soup and wine. Pour over chicken. Sprinkle with dressing mix. Pour melted butter over mixture. Bake in preheated oven for 1 hour.

Lorraine Franklin, Texas

CHICKEN CACCIATORE

1 large Vidalia onion, sliced
2 chicken breasts
1 can stewed tomatoes
Italian seasoning or parsley
Parsley

Combine and cook in a large skillet for 20 minutes.

Mushrooms, sliced
1 red bell pepper, sliced
1 cup white or red wine.

Add to onion/chicken mixture. Cover and cook for 25 more minutes. Serve over pasta. Double recipe if using 4 chicken breasts.

Bunny Doucet, New Jersey

JUDY'S CHICKEN REGGIES

2–4 skinless chicken breasts, cut into bite sized pieces
2 small cans mushrooms (or fresh)
1 can hot cherry peppers
1 can black olives
2 (28-ounce) cans crushed tomatoes or tomato puree
½ cup red or white wine
1 cup grated mozzarella cheese
1 pint half and half or heavy cream
1½ pounds rigatoni, cooked according to package
    directions

Sauté chicken breast pieces in oil or margarine. Add mushrooms, hot cherry peppers and black olives and continue to sauté. Add tomatoes and wine, reduce heat and simmer for a half hour. Add cheese, salt and pepper to taste, and half and half. Add cooked rigatoni. Sprinkle cheese on top and brown in oven.

Judy Dashiell, Minnesota

VERY EASY CHICKEN CORDON BLEU

12 boned chicken breasts

12 thin slices ham

12 chunks Swiss Cheese (large enough to be rolled inside each breast)

2 cans cream of celery soup, undiluted

Pound breasts until thin. Place a slice of ham and a piece of cheese on each breast. Roll each piece and secure with a toothpick. Place rolled breasts in a shallow pan which has been lined with foil. Stir the two cans of soup until creamy. Pour over all and bake for 1 to 1½ hours at 325 degrees or until breasts are tender and sauce bubbles. Do not overcook.

Judy Ingram

SESAME CHICKEN

½ cup sesame seeds, toasted

½ cup soy sauce

¼ cup packed brown sugar

1 teaspoon ground ginger

½ teaspoon pepper

4 cloves garlic, minced

4 green onions, thinly sliced, divided

8 skinless, boneless chicken breasts, cut into bite sized pieces

4 to 6 cups cooked rice, with parsley added

Make a marinade mixture by combining the sesame seeds, soy sauce, brown sugar, ginger, pepper, garlic and half of the green onions. Add chicken to marinade mixture; cover and chill 1 to 4 hours.

Arrange the chicken in a single layer in a baking pan. Pour marinade over the chicken. Broil 6 inches from heat until golden, about 10 minutes. Turn chicken and broil 5 minutes longer or until meat is no longer pink. Serve with parsley-rice, garnishing with remaining sliced green onions. Serves 6–8.

Liz Hobbs, California

CHICKEN DELIGHT

4 whole chicken breasts

3 packages frozen broccoli spears

2 cans cream of chicken soup, undiluted

1 cup Hellmann's mayonnaise

1 teaspoon lemon pepper seasoning

1 teaspoon lemon juice

4 ounces grated Cheddar cheese

½ to 1 stick butter

1 cup bread crumbs

Bake or boil chicken breasts. Cool and remove meat. Cook broccoli half the time stated in package directions.

Line a 13 x 9-inch pan with broccoli. Place chicken on broccoli. Combine soup, mayonnaise, lemon seasoning and lemon juice and spread over chicken. Top with grated cheese. Melt butter and combine with bread crumbs and sprinkle over all. Bake in a preheated 325 degree oven for 45 minutes to 1 hour.

NOTE: Can be made 2 days ahead. Remove from the refrigerator 2 hours before serving.

Mary Ralston, Illinois

CHICKEN PARISIENNE

Place 4 chicken breasts in a baking dish and season to taste.

Blend 2 cans cream of mushroom soup, ½ cup cooking sherry and 3 ounces fresh sliced mushrooms and heat.

Spoon some of the mixture over seasoned chicken and bake at 350 degrees for 1 hour and 15 minutes.

During the last 15 minutes, add remaining soup mixture.

Terri Anderson, California

CHICKEN MARSALA

3 tablespoons olive oil

1 tablespoon margarine

2 tablespoons minced garlic

4 chicken breasts, skinless and boneless

¼ cup flour

8 ounces sliced mushrooms

½ cup Marsala wine

½ cup chicken stock (mix 1 teaspoon chicken base with
    ½ cup water)

Heat oil and margarine in a skillet and sauté the garlic until it becomes light brown. Cover chicken cutlets with flour and sauté in oil mixture until golden brown on both sides. Remove from skillet and set aside. Add mushrooms and sauté until wilted. Pour wine into the skillet and mix up the brown bits that are on the bottom. Add the chicken stock and stir well, reducing the liquid in the pan just a little. Return chicken to pan and simmer on low heat for 15 minutes.

Zina Versaggi Graalfs, Florida

VIVA LA CHICKEN

6 chicken breasts, cooked

10–12 corn tortillas, cut into 1-inch strips

1 can cream of chicken soup

1 can cream of mushroom soup

1 cup milk

1 onion, grated

1 (7-ounce) can green chile salsa

1 pound Cheddar cheese, grated

Combine soups, milk, onion and salsa. Set aside. In a greased 13 x 9-inch baking dish, layer ingredients as follows: Half of the tortilla strips, chicken, soup mixture then layer the remaining tortillas, chicken, and soup mixture Top with grated cheese. Refrigerate overnight. Bake in a preheated 300 degree oven for 1¼ hours. Serves 12.

Edith Ann Blood, Tennessee

CHICKEN A LA KING

2 (6-ounce) cans sliced mushrooms, drained reserving
     ½ cup liquid
1 cup diced green pepper
1 cup margarine
1 cup all-purpose flour
2 teaspoons salt
½ teaspoon pepper
2 cups milk
2½ cups chicken broth
4 cups chopped, cooked chicken
2 (4-ounce) jars pimento

Cook mushrooms and green pepper in margarine; stir in flour, salt, pepper and liquids into mushroom mixture. Cook over low heat until thick. Add chopped chicken and pimento. Stir to combine. Serve over broccoli cornbread.

Mary Genenwein, Texas

CHICKEN ROLL UPS

1 can cream of mushroom soup
1 can cream of chicken soup
½ cup milk
½ cup grated Cheddar cheese
½ teaspoon salt
¼ cup margarine, melted
½ cup chicken broth
2 (8-count) packages Pillsbury Crescent Rolls
3 or 4 chicken breasts, cooked and chopped
1 can water chestnuts, chopped

Mix first seven ingredients together and put half of the mixture in a 13 x 9-inch baking dish. Spread crescent rolls flat and place a small amount of chicken and water chestnuts on each. Roll up from the broad side and place in dish. Pour remaining sauce over the top. Bake at 350 degrees for 45 minutes.

Peggy Laverentz,

CHEDDARY CHICKEN POT PIE

1 can cream of chicken soup

½ cup milk

½ cup chopped onion

1 (3-ounce) package cream cheese, softened

¼ cup chopped celery

¼ cup shredded carrots

¼ cup grated Parmesan cheese

½ teaspoon salt

Combine all ingredients and cook until cheese melts.

3 cups cooked chicken

1 (10-ounce) package frozen broccoli, cooked and drained.

Add chicken and broccoli to soup mixture and pour into a 2-quart casserole.

1 egg

1 cup shredded Cheddar cheese

1 tablespoon vegetable oil

1 cup buttermilk pancake mix

½ cup milk

Blend all ingredients and spoon over chicken mixture. Bake in a 375 degree oven for 20–25 minutes. May be frozen, just thaw and reheat.

Liz Offord, Texas

CHICKEN CASSEROLE

2 cups diced chicken

2 cups uncooked macaroni

½ cup grated cheese

2 cans cream of mushroom soup

2 cups milk

½ cup minced onion

Mix together and pour into a 13 x 9-inch casserole. Cover and refrigerate overnight. The next day, bake in a preheated 350 degree oven for 1 hour.

Phyllis Kelso, Minnesota

CHICKEN ROYAL

1 cup sliced mushrooms

2 tablespoons butter

1 large onion, chopped

1 clove garlic, minced

½ green pepper, chopped

2 cups diced cooked chicken

⅓ pound wide noodles, cooked according to package directions

1 cup chopped walnuts

1 can ripe olives, chopped

2 cans mushroom soup

1½ cups water or chicken broth

Salt, pepper, and garlic salt to taste

½ cup grated Parmesan cheese

Preheat oven to 350 degrees. Sauté mushrooms in butter. Add onion, garlic and green pepper. Cook until tender. Combine chicken and noodles with the mushroom mixture. Add walnuts and olives. Place mixture in a greased, 2-quart casserole. Combine soup and water and pour over mixture. Add seasonings. Bake in preheated oven for 45 minutes to 1 hour. Remove from oven and sprinkle with cheese.

JoAnn Christal, Texas

GREEN CHILE CASSEROLE

1 ½ pounds turkey sausage

2 cans cream of chicken soup

1 (16-ounce) container sour cream, fat free

1/8 teaspoon pepper

1/8 teaspoon garlic powder

6-8 large flour tortillas or 10-12 corn tortillas

1 (4-ounce) can chopped green chiles

1 small onion, chopped

1 ½ cups grated Cheddar cheese

1 ½ cups grated Monterey Jack cheese

Preheat oven to 350 degrees. Lightly spray a 13 x 9-inch casserole dish with non-stick spray. Cook and chop meat. Mix soup, sour cream, pepper and garlic. Place a layer of tortillas in prepared pan; spread a layer of soup mixture. Then layer chiles, onion, meat, Cheddar and Jack cheese. Repeat, ending with cheese. Bake for 20-30 minutes. Cool before cutting and serving.

Bernadine Levy, Colorado

This has a great taste!

CHICKEN OR TURKEY CASSEROLE

1 package seasoned bread stuffing*

1 stick margarine, melted

1 cup water

2½ cups diced cooked chicken or turkey

½ cup chopped onion

¼ cup chopped olives or green onion tops

½ cup mayonnaise

¾ teaspoon salt

2 eggs slightly and add

1½ cups milk

1 can mushroom soup

Cheddar cheese, grated

Lightly mix together, stuffing, margarine, and water.* Place half of mixture into a buttered 12 x 8-inch pan.

Mix chicken or turkey, onion, olives or onions, mayonnaise and salt thoroughly. Place on top of stuffing mixture and top with remaining stuffing. Slightly beat eggs and add milk. Pour evenly over entire mixture. Cover with foil and refrigerate overnight. Take out one hour before baking. Spread soup over the top. Bake uncovered in 325 degree oven for 40 minutes. Sprinkle with grated Cheddar cheese. Return to oven for 10 minutes.

*Can use left over stuffing
Betty Wilkins, Colorado

CHICKEN AND RICE CASSEROLE

3 to 5 boneless, skinless, chicken breasts

Salt, pepper, and garlic salt to taste

1 to 3 pats butter or margarine

1 can cream of chicken soup

1 cup uncooked rice

1⅔ cups water

Trim and season chicken breasts with salt, pepper, and garlic salt. Let set for 10–20 minutes.

Heat a corning skillet; lightly spray with non-stick cooking spray. Heat to medium-high heat. Add a couple of pats of butter. Put seasoned chicken breasts in skillet and lightly brown on all sides. Pour cream of chicken soup and 1 can water in skillet. Stir to combine. Add dry rice and half the water for the rice recipe. Mix evenly, cover and bring to a boil. Remove from heat and place in a 300 degree oven for about 30 minutes. Check tenderness of rice, if still hard, put back in oven for 15 minutes. If most of liquid is gone, add about ½ cup water and mix in. Add more if needed. Casserole is done when rice is done.

Judy Boegler, Texas

CHICKEN CASSEROLE SOUFFLE

9 slices white bread

4 cups diced chicken

½ pound fresh mushrooms

¼ cup butter

1 (8-ounce) can water chestnuts, sliced

¼ cup mayonnaise

9 slices sharp cheese

4 eggs, well beaten

2 cups milk

1 teaspoon salt

1 can cream of mushroom soup

1 can cream of celery soup

1 (2-ounce) jar chopped pimento

Bread crumbs

Line a deep 13 x 9-inch pan with bread. Place chicken on top. Sauté mushrooms in butter. Place on top of chicken. Add chestnuts and dap mayonnaise on top. Add cheese. May be frozen at this point.

Combine eggs, milk, and salt and pour over top. Mix soups and pimento. Spoon on top.

Cover with foil and refrigerate overnight. Bake covered at 350 degrees for 1 hour. Uncover and sprinkle with breadcrumbs. Continue baking for 20 minutes. Serves 6.

Arlene Perkins, Illinois

CHICKEN VEGETABLE BAKE

½ cup flour

1½ teaspoons salt

¼ teaspoon pepper

1 teaspoon paprika

2½ to 3 pound chicken, cut up

1 tablespoons brown sugar

¼ teaspoon ginger

Dash of salt

½ onion, sliced

½ cup coarsely chopped carrots

1 (3-ounce) can mushrooms, sliced (or use fresh)

⅓ cup frozen orange juice concentrate, thawed

¾ cup water

Combine flour, salt, pepper, and paprika in a bag. Add chicken 2 or 3 pieces at a time and shake to coat. Reserve 2 tablespoons of flour mixture. Brown chicken in hot oil. Remove chicken to a 2-quart casserole, add onions, carrots and mushrooms. Blend flour mixture and brown; add sugar, ginger and a dash of salt into drippings in the skillet. Stir to make smooth sauce paste. Add orange juice concentrate and water. Cook and stir until bubbly. Pour over chicken. Cover and bake at 350 degrees for 1 to 1¼ hours.

Jean Krest, Colorado

CHICKEN RO-TEL™ CASSEROLE

2 pounds chicken

1 (7-ounce) box Vermicelli (broken up)

1 large onion, chopped

1 green pepper, chopped

3 tablespoons butter or margarine

1 pound Velveeta™ cheese, cut up

1 can Ro-tel™ tomatoes

1 small can green peas, drained

1 small can mushrooms, drained

1 tablespoon Worcestershire sauce

Boil chicken in water seasoned with salt and pepper. Reserve 4 cups of the broth. Remove chicken meat from bones. Boil vermicelli in chicken broth. Sauté onion and green pepper in butter. Combine undrained vermicelli with cheese, tomatoes and juice.

Add remaining ingredients. Pour into a 13 x 9-inch baking dish. Bake in a preheated 350 degree oven for 45 minutes until bubbly. Freezes well.

Phyllis Kelso, Minnesota

COMPANY CASSEROLE

1 cup wild rice

½ cup chopped onion

½ cup butter

¼ cup flour

1 (6-ounce) can mushrooms

1½ cups light cream (may use low fat half and half)

3 cups diced, cooked chicken

¼ cup diced pimento

2 tablespoons snipped parsley

½ cup slivered, blanched almonds

1½ teaspoons salt

¼ teaspoon pepper

Prepare the wild rice according to package directions. Sauté onion in butter until tender. Remove from heat and stir in flour. Drain mushrooms, reserving the liquid. Add enough chicken broth to make 1½ cups. Slowly stir into flour mixture. Add cream. Cook and stir over medium heat until thick. Add wild rice, mushrooms, chicken, pimento, parsley, salt and pepper. Place in a 2-quart casserole. Sprinkle with almonds. Bake in a 350 degree oven for 20–25 minutes. Serves 8.

Betty Wilken, California

Bob Lilly

Mesilla, N. M.

CHICKEN SPECTACULAR

3–4 cups cooked diced chicken

1 box Uncle Ben's Wild and Long Grain Rice, original

1 can cream of celery soup

1 cup mayonnaise

1 (2-ounce) jar pimento

1 small onion, diced

1 (8-ounce) can sliced water chestnuts, drained

1 (16-ounce) can French-style green beans, drained

1½ cups grated sharp Cheddar cheese

1 (2.25-ounce) package slivered almonds

Cook and cut up chicken. Prepare rice according to package directions. Place chicken and rice in a large bowl and combine with all ingredients, except cheese and almonds. Mix well. The mixture will be soupy and stir easily.* Pour mixture into a lightly greased 2½-quart casserole dish. Top with cheese and almonds. Bake covered in a 350 degree oven for 30 to 40 minutes, or until bubbly and hot. Serves 6–8.

*I usually add another can of soup and it can be any other flavor you like. Cream of chicken soup with herbs is very good or cream of mushroom soup with roasted garlic.

NOTE: If you don't have almonds, you can use a can of French Fried Onion Rings. Just add during the last few minutes of cooking — but watch them because they burn easily.

The dish freezes well — don't bake before freezing.

Juanita Magnuson, Alabama

CHICKEN BROCCOLI CASSEROLE

3 whole chicken breasts
salt and pepper
2 boxes frozen broccoli
2 cans cream of chicken soup
¾ cup mayonnaise
¾ teaspoon curry powder
2 teaspoons lemon juice
1 cup American cheese, grated
½ cup Italian bread crumbs

Salt and pepper 3 whole chicken breast, cover with foil and bake in a 350 degree oven for 1 hour. Cool and cut into bite sized pieces.

Partially cook the frozen broccoli with salt and pepper. Drain and place in bottom of an ungreased 13 x 9-inch baking pan. Layer chicken on top. Mix together soup, mayonnaise, curry powder, and lemon juice and pour on chicken. Top with cheese and bread crumbs. Bake covered in a 350 degree oven until bubbly and top is lightly browned. Uncover for last few minutes to brown top. Serves 6–8. Can be frozen and reheated.

Cindy Kelly, Texas

CORNBREAD STUFFING

Crumble cornbread when it is cool. Crumble or cut up an equal amount of left over bread, hamburger buns, or anything you want to get rid of. Add at least 2 tablespoons of poultry seasoning and toss with crumbs. Taste, you may want to add more seasoning.

Finely chop one small onion and four stalks of celery (less or more works fine). Cook these vegetables in a small amount (teaspoon or so) of butter, peanut oil or whatever. Add some chicken broth and simmer until celery is tender.

Add the vegetables to the cornbread mixture. Then, add enough broth to make the mixture fluffy, not soppy. Taste again, as you may want to add more poultry seasons (or sage, thyme, marjoram, rosemary or pepper if you are using these instead of the poultry seasoning). You can add more salt here, too, if you wish.

Optional: Add 1 cup of chopped pecans and/or six slices of chopped Canadian bacon.

Can be used with left over or canned chicken or turkey. Place stuffing in oiled baking dish, top with meats and cover with left over gravy or gravy made from low sodium chicken broth. Cover with aluminum foil and bake at 350 degrees until bubbly, about 45 minutes.

Marilyn Sietsema, Illinois

CHICKEN ENCHILADAS WITH TOMATILLO SAUCE

⅓ cup half and half

1 (6-ounce) package cream cheese, softened

2 cups shredded cooked chicken

¾ cup finely chopped onion

½ teaspoon salt

2 dozen tomatillos, husked

3 cups chicken broth

4–6 Serrano peppers, stemmed, seeded and minced

2 tablespoons cornstarch

About ⅓ cup water

1 teaspoon salt

2 tablespoons chopped fresh cilantro

12 (8-inch) corn tortillas, softened in vegetable oil

¾ cup shredded Cheddar cheese

¾ cup shredded Monterey Jack cheese

Combine half and half and cream cheese, beating until smooth. Add chicken, onion and salt to cheese mixture. Blend well. Set aside. Boil tomatillos and peppers in chicken broth for 7–10 minutes. Dissolve cornstarch in water. Add to broth, along with water, salt and cilantro.

Spoon a thin layer of sauce into a 13 x 9-inch baking dish. Spread each softened tortilla with a thin layer of tomatillo sauce. Place ¼ cup chicken mixture down center. Roll and place seam side down in pan. Spoon tomatillo sauce over all. Cover with foil. Bake in a 350 degree oven for 20 minutes. Remove foil. Sprinkle with Cheddar and Monterey Jack cheese. Bake 5 minutes.

This sauce makes enough for at least 1½ times the chicken recipe.

Liz Offord, Texas

CHICKEN ENCHILADAS I

1 large fryer, cooked, skinned and deboned or
can use 2-3 breasts, cut in chunks

1 large onion, chopped

1 stick margarine

1½ cups chicken broth

1 can cream of mushroom soup

1 can cream of chicken soup

1 (4-ounce) can green chiles

1 jar chopped pimento

Cheddar cheese, grated

1 large package Doritos (large size)

Sauté chicken and onions in margarine. In a
bowl, combine broth, soups, chiles and pimento.
Add 1 cup of the grated Cheddar cheese. Spray
an oblong glass casserole with cooking spray.
Line casserole with Doritos; layer chicken,
cheese and soup mixture alternately. Top with
Doritos. Bake at 350 degrees for 30 minutes.
Top with grated cheese and return to oven until
cheese melts.

Jane Davidson, Texas

CHICKEN ENCHILADAS II

1 (10-ounce) can mild enchilada sauce

1 (8-ounce) can tomato paste

12 corn tortillas

2 cups vegetable oil

1½ cups chopped chicken

¾ cups grated cheese plus ¼ cup for topping

¼ cup minced onion

Heat enchilada sauce and tomato sauce together until sim-
mering. Dip each tortilla in hot oil to a count of 3, turn
with tongs, drain on paper towels. Place tortillas in a shallow baking dish. Fill each tortilla with about 2 tablespoons
chopped chicken, 1 tablespoon grated cheese, and 1 teaspoon minced onion. Roll up and cover with enchilada/
tomato sauce. Top with remaining ¼ cup grated cheese.
Cover baking dish with foil and bake in a preheated 350
degree oven until cheese melts, about 10–15 minutes.

Brenda Martinez, Alabama

MYRNA'S CHICKEN ENCHILADAS

Simmer 1 pound boneless chicken breast with salt, pepper, onion, 1 bay leaf until done. Shred meat with 2 forks. Remove bay leaf.

FILLING:

> Chicken
>
> ½ cup chopped onion
>
> ½ cup shredded Monterey Jack cheese
>
> ½ cup reduced fat extra-sharp cheese

SAUCE:

Combine and set aside:

> 1 can Campbell's Cream of Chile Pablano Soup
>
> ¼ cup milk
>
> ¼ cup chopped cilantro
>
> 1 can Ro-Tel® Diced tomatoes in sauce with chiles (not the tomatoes with chiles)
>
> ¼ cup each Monterey Jack and reduced fat extra sharp cheese for topping
>
> 8 (6-inch) corn tortillas

To assemble:

Place a small amount of sauce in bottom of casserole dish. Place small amount of hot water from cooked chicken in bowl. Quickly dip a tortilla in water or chicken broth. This is to save calories. You can also soften the tortilla in a little hot oil in a small skillet over medium heat. Spoon filling down center of tortilla, roll and place seam side down in baking dish. Cover with sauce. Cover baking dish with foil and bake for 20 minutes in a preheated 375 degree oven. Remove cover and top with ¼ cup of each cheese. Bake 5 minutes or until hot and bubbly. Top with sour cream.

Myrna DuFord, Texas

CHICKEN & BLACK BEAN ENCHILADAS

- 1 boneless skinless chicken breast, cut into strips
- 3 slices bacon
- 2 cloves garlic
- 1½ cups picante sauce, divided
- 1 (16-ounce) can black beans, do not drain
- 1 red bell pepper, chopped
- 1 teaspoon cumin
- ½ cup sliced green onion
- 12 flour tortillas
- Monterey jack cheese

Cut chicken into short, thin strips. Cook bacon in a large skillet until crisp. Remove to paper towel. Crumble. Pour drippings from skillet. Place chicken pieces and garlic in skillet and cook until chicken is not longer pink. Stir in ½ cup picante sauce, beans, red pepper, cumin and salt. Simmer until thick. Add green onions and reserved bacon. Spoon ¼ of the mixture on each tortilla. Roll up. Put in greased oblong casserole. Pour remaining picante sauce over enchiladas. Bake at 350 degrees for 15 minutes. Top with cheese and bake for 5 minutes. Remove and serve. Serves 6.

Anna Laura Doane, Indiana

GREEN SALSA CHICKEN CHILI

- 1 pound chicken, cut into bite sized pieces
- ½ cup chopped red or yellow sweet onion
- 3 cans white Northern beans (white kidney beans)
- 1 jar mild green salsa
- ½ cup fresh cilantro, chopped
- 1 can diced tomatoes with garlic
- 1 cup water

Sauté chicken in oil. Add onion and sauté about 2 minutes. Add beans, salsa, cilantro, tomatoes and water. Simmer until hot. Serve over rice. Garnish with chopped cherry tomatoes. This recipe can be doubled.

Lyn Gogis, California

LEWIS AND CLARK'S WHITE CHILI

2 pounds boneless, skinless chicken breasts

1 tablespoon olive oil

4 garlic cloves, minced

2 (4-ounce) cans chopped mild green chiles (May substitute hot green chiles)

2 medium onions, chopped

1 teaspoon ground cumin

¼ teaspoon cayenne pepper

1 teaspoon ground oregano

¼ teaspoon ground cloves

4 cans Great Northern beans, rinsed and drained

4 cups chicken stock or canned broth

20 ounces Monterey Jack cheese, grated and divided

Sour cream, optional

Chopped jalapeno peppers, canned (optional)

Place chicken in large saucepan. Add cold water to cover and bring to simmer. Cook until tender, about 14 to 20 minutes. Remove from saucepan and dice into ½-inch cubes. Using the same pan, discard water and heat oil over medium heat. Add onions and sauté until translucent. Stir in garlic, chiles, cumin, cayenne pepper, oregano, and cloves. Sauté for 2 to 3 minutes. Add chicken, beans, stock and 12 ounces of the cheese. Let simmer for 15 minutes. Ladle into large bowls and top each with 1 ounce of the cheese. Serve with a side of sour cream and chopped jalapeno peppers, if desired. Serves 6–8.

Barbara Langford, Texas and Washington

BOWL OF THE WIFE OF KIT CARSON

¾ cup dry garbanzos (chick peas)

2 pound fresh turkey legs — or thighs, skin removed

3 bay leaves

1 teaspoon oregano

¼ teaspoon each salt, pepper, onion powder

¾ cup rice

1½ cups chopped onion, ½-inch dice

1 (4-ounce) can chopped mild green chiles

2 tablespoons chopped fresh parsley

Additional salt, pepper, and oregano

3 large avocados

12 ounces Monterrey Jack cheese

Water

This was an original dish at The Fort Restaurant near Morrison, Colorado. The Fort is a replica of the old adobe Bent's Fort on the Santa Fe Trail in the plains east of Pueblo, Colorado.

In a large pot, put 4 cups cold water and the dry garbanzos. Soak overnight. Drain in the morning. Put 5 cups cold water in the same pot, add drained garbanzos. Make a hollow in the center and put turkey pieces inside. Add bay leaves, oregano, salt, pepper and onion powder. Cook 30 minutes and check the turkey and garbanzos for doneness. Cook longer, if necessary, checking that the water level stays above food surface. When done, remove from heat.

In another pot, put 3 cups water, rice, and onion and cook until done, 15–18 minutes. Remove turkey pieces from bean pot, cut meat into bite sized pieces and put back in bean pot. When rice is cooked, add it to garbanzo pot. Add chiles, parsley, more salt and pepper, oregano if needed to garbanzo pot. The BOWL should be like a sopa seca (thick soup) but juicy enough to eat with a spoon. It it's too thick, add some chicken bouillon cubes dissolved in hot water.

Peel the avocadoes and dice into ½-inch pieces. Dice Monterrey Jack cheese into ¼-inch pieces. Put avocado and cheese into side dishes so they can be added to individual servings of THE BOWL, as desired.

Elizabeth G. Miller, Louisiana

PUMPKIN BLACK BEAN TURKEY CHILI

2 tablespoons vegetable oil

1 medium onion, chopped

3 cloves garlic, minced

1 cup diced yellow bell pepper

1 small jalapeno pepper, seeded and diced

1½ teaspoons dried oregano leaves

1½ teaspoons ground cumin

1½ teaspoons chili powder

3 cups beef broth

1 (15-ounce) can black beans, drained

1 (14-ounce) can diced tomatoes, undrained

1 (16-ounce) can solid pack pumpkin

2½ cups chopped cooked turkey (1 pound)

½ cup cream sherry (optional)

¼ teaspoon salt

Dash ground pepper

Shredded Cheddar cheese

Sour cream

Heat oil in Dutch oven or large saucepan over medium heat. Add onion, garlic, bell pepper and jalapeno pepper, sauté until quite soft, about 8 minutes. Stir in oregano, cumin and chili powder and cook 1 minute. Add broth, beans, tomatoes, pumpkin, turkey, sherry, salt and pepper. Bring to a boil, stir occasionally. Simmer 45 minutes over low heat. Serve sprinkled with shredded cheese or topped with sour cream. Serves 6.

Jan Whittaker, California

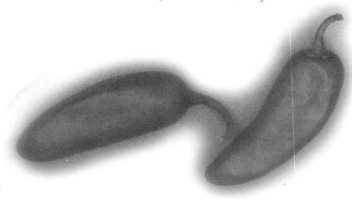

HAM AND TURKEY GALA

Wonderful and easy for company

4 pound all-white meat turkey roll

5 pound canned ham

½ cup peach preserves

¼ cup currant jelly

Early in day, roast turkey as label directs. Cover and refrigerate. About 1½ hours before serving, preheat oven to 350 degrees. Remove gelatin from ham. Slice turkey and ham in ¼-inch slices. Alternate slices in foil-lined shallow open pan. Roast 30 minutes. Warm jellies and generously glaze meat. Continue roasting 30 minutes.

Jan Watson, Illinois

FRUITED CORNISH HENS

This recipe was adapted from Eating Well Magazine. I submitted this recipe to the Austin American Statesman for their Holiday Cook Off Contest and it won first place in the entrée category.

2 (1¼ pound) Cornish hens

2 tablespoons curry powder

Vegetable cooking spray

½ cup mango chutney

¼ cup fresh lime juice

1 cup coarsely chopped Rome apple

¾ cup coarsely chopped Anjou pear

½ cup coarsely chopped peeled Kiwi fruit

¾ cup fresh or frozen cranberries

Remove and discard giblets from hens. Rinse hens under cold water and pat dry. Trim excess fat; using kitchen shears, split hens in half lengthwise and discard back bone. Rub hen halves with curry powder. Place hen halves, meaty side up, in a shallow roasting pan coated with vegetable cooking spray. Bake at 450 degrees for 25 minutes. Reduce temperature to 350 degrees. Combine chutney and lime juice; brush mixture over hen halves and arrange fruit and cranberries around them in pan. Bake for 35 minutes more or until hen juices run clear.

Gerry Lesseps, Louisiana

Seafood

SHRIMP SAUTE

36 medium-large shrimp, peeled

4 tablespoons unsalted butter

Salt and fresh ground pepper

¼ cup cognac

⅓ cup dry white wine or French vermouth

2 tablespoons minced shallots or scallions

Handful of fresh parsley, minced

Sprigs of fresh dill or tarragon, minced

⅔ cup heavy cream blended with 2 tablespoons cornstarch and 1½ tablespoons Dijon mustard

1 lemon, halved

Set wok over high heat. Add shrimp. Toss and turn for 1 minute, twirling and shaking pan to evaporate moisture. Add butter to coat shrimp; toss with sprinkling of salt and pepper. Continue cooking and tossing until shrimp turn pink. Pour cognac over shrimp. Add wine, toss with shallots and herbs. Stir in cream mixture. Spoon it over shrimp for 1 minute as it bubbles and cooks. Pierce the lemon with a fork and squeeze juice onto shrimp mixture. Serve over angel hair pasta. Serves 6.

Ralph and Jeanine Bowles, Washington

BACON WRAPPED SHRIMP

1/3 cup Pickapeppa sauce

2/3 cup honey

Bacon, partially cooked

Shrimp, raw, peeled

Mix Pickapeppa and honey in a small bowl. Set aside. Cut bacon strips in half and partially cook. Drain. Wrap shrimp in the half slice of bacon and secure with a bamboo skewer. After all shrimp have been wrapped with bacon and skewered, place in marinade for a couple of hours. Grill under broiler or in barbeque pit until shrimp are done.

Judy Boegler, Texas

SHRIMP WITH PINE NUTS

3 bunches broccoli, trimmed into 2-inch florets

1 tablespoons fresh lemon juice

2¼ sticks butter (18 tablespoons), room temperature

4 cups hot cooked brown rice (use some wild rice if desired)

8 cloves garlic, minced

2 red bell peppers, seeded and chopped

3 pounds large shrimp, peeled and deveined

¾ pound pine nuts

Steam broccoli in covered pot until crisp tender (about 6 minutes). Combine broccoli, lemon juice and 6 tablespoons butter in a large bowl. Add hot rice and 6 additional tablespoons butter. Toss lightly. Melt remaining butter in a large skillet over medium heat and sauté garlic and red pepper. Cover until pepper is soft. Add shrimp and pine nuts to garlic mixture and sauté until shrimp are pink and cooked through. Add rice mixture to the shrimp and toss lightly until heated through. Season with salt and pepper to taste. Serve hot.

Zina Versaggi Graalfs, Florida

OYSTER FRITTERS

30 stewing oysters

2 eggs

¼ teaspoon pepper

¼ teaspoon salt

¼ cup plus 1 tablespoon flour

1 teaspoon baking powder

¼ cup evaporated milk or Coffee Rich

Oil

Clean the oysters. Drain in strainer. Beat eggs. Add salt and pepper, flour, baking powder and milk or Coffee Rich. Beat with egg beater. Blend oysters into mixture.

Using a large non-stick skillet, pour in one inch of oil and heat and heat to 375 degrees. Drop mixture by tablespoons into hot oil, fry until brown, turning once. Takes approximately 6 minutes. Drain on paper towels.

Judy Ingram

LOBSTER THERMIDOR

Bake 12 lobster tails in uncovered shallow pan, in ½ inch of water at 350 degrees for 20 minutes. Cool enough to handle. Remove meat from shells and cut into bite sized pieces. To make roux, use a Dutch oven to melt one stick of butter; add 6 tablespoons flour and cook for a few minutes. (Don't brown). Beat 2 egg yolks in 2 pints of half and half and gradually add to roux. Add 1/2 cup dry sherry, 1/3 cup grated Gruyere cheese,1/3 cup Parmesan cheese, 1 teaspoon dry mustard, lemon pepper and salt to taste. Add lobster and heat. Replace meat in shells, sprinkle with Parmesan cheese and paprika. Broil 6 inches from heat for 4 to5 minutes. Serve hot.

Liz Offord, Texas

CRUNCHY WALNUT CRUSTED SALMON

1 cup chopped walnuts (or whole pine nuts)

2 tablespoons dry bread crumbs

2 tablespoons grated lemon rind

1 tablespoon olive oil

1 tablespoon chopped fresh dill

Salt and fresh ground pepper

4 salmon patties, skin on

2 teaspoons Dijon mustard

Lemon juice

In blender, combine nuts, bread crumbs, lemon rind, oil, dill, and salt and pepper to taste. (You can also just use a bowl and mix by hand). Set aside. Place salmon patties, skin side down and brush tops with mustard. Divide crust mixture evenly among fillets, press onto mustard. Cover with plastic wrap and refrigerate at least 15 minutes or up to 2 hours. Place salmon in baking pan. Bake at 350 degrees for about 20 minutes or until salmon flakes with a fork. Drizzle with a little lemon juice. Serves 4.

Lyn Gogis, California

GRILLED SALMON FILLET

1 pound salmon fillet

3 tablespoons red wine vinegar

2 teaspoons dried basil

1 tablespoon soy sauce

Dash pepper

3 tablespoons lemon juice

2 teaspoons grated lemon peel

1½ teaspoons garlic powder

Parmesan cheese

Place fish, skin side down, in a disposable foil pan. Combine all ingredients except Parmesan cheese and pour over fish. Sprinkle with Parmesan cheese. Place pan on grill. Lower cover on grill and cook over medium heat for 15 to 20 minutes or until fish flakes easily with fork.

Jeri-Lynn Sandusky, Utah

KATE'S SALMON BAKE WITH PECAN CRUNCH COATING

1 pound salmon fillet, or fillets, skin removed

⅛ teaspoon salt

⅛ teaspoon pepper

2 tablespoons Dijon mustard

2 tablespoons butter, melted

1 tablespoon honey

1 cup soft or fresh breadcrumbs

1 cup finely chopped pecans

2 teaspoons fresh chopped parsley

Sprinkle salmon with salt and pepper and place skin side down in a greased pan. Combine mustard, butter, and honey and brush on fillets. Combine bread crumbs, pecans and parsley and sprinkle on salmon. Bake in a 350 degree oven for a half hour or until salmon flakes easily. Top with fresh parsley and lemon. Serves 2.

Susan Barry, Texas

GLAZED SALMON STEAKS

2 tablespoons packed brown sugar (I use light)

2 tablespoons butter or margarine, melted

1 tablespoon soy sauce

1 tablespoon sherry (I just use Holland House cooking sherry)

2 salmon steaks (about 1 pound)

Combine sugar, butter, soy sauce and sherry, stirring until sugar dissolves. Place salmon steaks in a foil lined baking pan. Brush with half sugar mixture. Let sit for 15 minutes. Broil 5 minutes or until fish flakes easily when tested with a fork. Remove from oven and brush with remaining mixture. (I just use a spoon).

Eleanor Cowan, Texas

ZESTY SALMON BURGERS

1 (14¾-ounce) can salmon, drained, skin and bones removed

2 eggs

½ cup dry breadcrumbs

¼ cup finely chopped onion

¼ cup mayonnaise

1–2 tablespoons prepared horseradish

1 tablespoon diced pimentos (optional)

¼ teaspoon salt

⅛ teaspoon pepper

2 tablespoons butter or margarine

4 Kaiser rolls, split

Lettuce leaves

Combine salmon, eggs, breadcrumbs, onion, mayonnaise, horseradish, pimentos, salt and pepper. Shape into four patties. In a skillet over medium heat, cook patties in butter until browned, about 6 minutes on each side. Serve on rolls with lettuce. Serves 4.

Becky VanVraken, Washington, DC

GRILLED SALMON STEAKS

1 tablespoon crumbled dried sage

1/4 teaspoon pepper

2 tablespoons crumbled dried rosemary

2 tablespoons fresh lemon juice

2 tablespoons olive oil

2 salmon steaks

Mix together and coat salmon. Grill steaks approximately 6 minutes on each side.

Betty Ann Sheffloe, Nebraska

ORIENTAL HALIBUT SAUTE

Very, very easy

- 1 pound halibut, thawed
- 3 tablespoons oil, divided
- 1 cup each sliced carrots, green peppers, sliced green onions and broccoli florets
- 3 tablespoons teriyaki sauce
- 3 tablespoons water
- 2 teaspoons cornstarch
- Grated peel and juice of ½ fresh lemon
- 1 teaspoon grated fresh ginger root
- 1 clove garlic, minced

Cut halibut into 1-inch cubes. Satue in 2 tablespoons oil until barely cooked. Remove halibut from skillet. Saute vegetables in remaining oil until tender-crisp. Return halibut to skillet. In a small bowl, combine remaining ingredients and mix well. Add to fish mixture. Cook and stir until sauce is thickened and fish and vegetables are glazed. Serves 4.

If using the stir fry veggies from the freezer section of the grocery store, follow directions for cooking the vegetables, then add halibut and a little more stir fry sauce to the mixture.

Zina Versaggi Graalfs, Florida

Serve with cornbread and coleslaw.

BAKED CATFISH

⅔ cups Parmesan cheese

¼ cup all-purpose flour

½ teaspoon salt

¼ teaspoon pepper

1 teaspoon paprika

1 egg, beaten

¼ cup milk

2 pounds catfish (about 5-6 small fish)

¼ cup butter or margarine, melted

Combine cheese, flour, salt, pepper, and paprika. Set aside. In a small bowl, combine egg and milk. Stir well. Dip fish in egg mixture, then in flour mixture. Place on baking pan that has been lightly sprayed with non-stick vegetable coating. Drizzle with butter. Bake at 350 degrees for 35 to 40 minutes or until fish flakes easily when tested with a fork. Serves 4–6.

Jackie Brandmiller, Wisconsin

Also great grilled.

HAWAIIAN FISH FILETS

⅓ cup soy sauce

1 tablespoon packed brown sugar

2 tablespoons vegetable oil

1 tablespoon cider vinegar

½ teaspoon ground ginger

1 clove garlic, crushed

1½ pounds white fish fillets

1 tablespoon minced fresh parsley

Combine soy sauce, brown sugar, oil, vinegar, ginger and garlic. Marinate fish in sauce for 20 minutes, turning once. Reserve sauce. Broil fish 5 inches from heat for 4 minutes. Turn, baste with sauce and broil 4 minutes longer. Discard sauce. Just before serving, sprinkle with parsley. Serves 4.

Jan Whittaker, California

FISH FILLETS PARMESAN

- 1 pound fish fillets
- ½ cup sour cream
- 3 tablespoons grated Parmesan cheese
- 2 teaspoons lemon juice
- 1 small onion, diced
- 1 hard boiled egg, quartered
- ¼ teaspoon salt
- 2 drops Tabasco® sauce
- 1 teaspoon paprika (hold for sprinkling)

Grease a glass baking dish. Place fillets in dish in single layer. Blend remaining ingredients, except paprika, on high speed of electric mixer or blender. Spoon mixture over fish, then sprinkle with paprika. Bake 25 minutes in a 350 degree oven. Serves 4

Sandy Lester, Ohio

EASY FISH FILLETS

- 1 pound fish fillets
- ½ cup breadcrumbs
- ½ tablespoon vinegar
- ½ tablespoon Worcestershire sauce
- ½ tablespoon lemon juice
- ½ tablespoon prepared mustard
- ¼ cup melted butter
- ¼ teaspoon salt
- Pinch of pepper

Place fish in greased, shallow baking dish. Sprinkle with bread crumbs. Combine remaining ingredients and pour over fish. Bake for 20 minutes in a 400 degree oven. Serves 4.

Sandy Lester, Ohio

REMOULADE SAUCE FOR SEAFOOD

This is as close as you can get to Gaido's remoulade sauce. If you add a tablespoon of ketchup, it is a knock-off of Ralph & Kacoo's remoulade sauce.

- 1 cup mayonnaise
- 1/3 cup chopped onion
- 2 heaping teaspoons capers, drained
- 1 tablespoon chopped parsley (optional)
- 1 tablespoon Dijon-style mustard
- 2 teaspoon Cajun style whole grain mustard (Zatarain's is perfect)
- 1 teaspoon lemon juice
- Pinch of dried tarragon
- ¼ teaspoon Tabasco® sauce
- Salt and pepper to taste

Process all in blender until smooth. Chill well. Serve with cold boiled shrimp for dipping. Excellent for all other hot or cold seafood.

Bon appetit!

GRILLED SEAFOOD STUMBO (STEW-GUMBO COMBO)

1 can smoked salmon, optional

1 pound mahi mahi seasoned and grilled

1 pound cooked shrimp, seasoned

1 zucchini, quartered, seasoned and grilled

1 yellow squash, quartered, seasoned and grilled

½ purple onion, sliced, seasoned and grilled

½ yellow sweet onion, diced

2 stalks celery, diced

½ red sweet pepper, diced

2 tablespoons olive oil

1 can diced tomatoes

2 tablespoons flour

4 cloves garlic, crushed

1 tablespoons dried parsley

24 ounces chicken broth

Cajun seasoning to taste and for grilling vegetables

Black pepper to taste and for grilling vegetables

Grill fish and first three vegetables. Spray fish with non-stick vegetable spray while grilling. When fish is cooked, remove from grill and cut into small cube size pieces. Saute next three vegetables in olive oil until wilted. Add can of tomatoes and grilled vegetables to sauté mixture and stir for 3 to 5 minutes. Add flour, stirring constantly, cooking for about 5 more minutes. Add garlic and parsley and stir. Add chicken broth and cook for 10 minutes on low heat. Season to taste with Cajun seasoning and pepper. Add more broth if necessary,

Billy LeFrance, Louisiana

HAL'S FAVORITE BOUILLABAISSE MADE SIMPLE

2 tablespoons olive oil

2 cups chopped onion

1 tablespoon minced garlic

4 cups fish stock (you may substitute vegetable stock
  or a combination of both)

1 cup dry white wine

Juice of 1 lemon

2 cups chopped tomatoes, fresh or canned (not drained)

2 bay leaves

Several sprigs fresh thyme or ½ teaspoon dried

Sea salt and fresh ground black pepper to taste

Cayenne pepper to taste

1-1/2 pound red snapper, gutted, scaled, fins and gills
  removed

Minced fresh parsley for garnish

Heat the olive oil in a casserole. Add onions and cook
and stir over medium-high heat until they begin to
brown. Add garlic and cook 30 seconds. Add fish stock
and wine. Bring to a boil and simmer for 5 minutes. Add
lemon juice, tomatoes, herbs, salt, pepper, and cayenne. Simmer for 5 minutes.

Cut the fish into chunks. Place fish in broth and simmer for 5 minutes. Remove a chunk and cut in half. If
it is opaque throughout, turn off the heat. (If not,
return fish to broth and cook another 2 to 3 minutes).
Serve immediately in bowls garnished with parsley and
crusty bread.

This is an "everything goes" dish and you can combine
freely. I prefer to use shrimp, scallops, one lobster
tail, a few clams or mussels and a white fish like code
or sea bass.

Prep time is approximately 30 minutes. Serves 4.

Hal Jones

BACALHAU A PORTUGUESA (PORTUGUESE COD STEW)

1 pound boneless salted cod (or other salted fish) without skin

3 large potatoes, peeled and thinly sliced

3 large white onions, peeled and thinly sliced

3 large tomatoes, thinly sliced

3 large green bell peppers, thinly sliced as rings

½ cup olive oil

Freshly ground pepper

Soak codfish in several changes of water overnight. Drain and cut into bite-size pieces. In a large pot, alternate layers of fish, potatoes, onions, peppers and tomatoes. Pour the olive oil over all and sprinkle liberally with ground pepper. Cover and bring to simmer. Cook about 1½ hours or until veggies are fork tender. Do not stir. Ladle into bowls and serve with warm French bread and red wine.

Joe Miller, New York

CRAB PATTIES

4 medium potatoes, diced

1 small onion, finely chopped

½ stalk celery, finely chopped

¼ cup green onion, finely chopped

1 pound crabmeat

1 egg

1 pinch parsley, finely chopped

Salt, pepper, red pepper to taste

Boil potatoes, then smash them in a bowl. While potatoes are boiling, sauté onion, celery and green onion until wilted. Spread crabmeat in a bowl. Spread cooked seasonings over crabmeat. Add smashed potatoes, egg, parsley, salt, pepper and red pepper. Mix well. Form patties and dip in flour. Pan fry in oil until golden brown.

Zina Versaggi Graalfs, Florida

TUNA OR CRAB CASSEROLE

Saute green onion, celery and parsley in butter. When soft, add one can of drained albacore tuna (or crab), fresh or canned mushrooms, ½ cup milk or cream. Thicken with a heaping teaspoon of cornstarch. Season with ½ teaspoon soy sauce, dill week, beaumonde, celery salt, cayenne pepper, paprika and Tabasco®. Put mixture into casserole dish. Top with Monterrey Jack cheese. Bake until cheese is melted and bubbly.

Serve over broiled or baked large tomato halve or avocado. Serve with green veggie and fruit salad.

Fruit salad dressing: thin mayonnaise with orange juice. Add sugar to taste. Add orange peel, poppy seeds, and a tiny amount of vinegar and onion juice.

Josie Brummett, Kentucky

EASY OVERNIGHT TUNA CASSEROLE

Great dish to prepare the night before. Do not cook the pasta. This is low fat and good for you.

2 cups pasta, uncooked (rotini, elbow macaroni, gemelli or your choice)

2 cups frozen mixed vegetables, any variety

2 cans 98% fat free mushroom soup

1 cup shredded low fat Cheddar cheese

1 cup skim milk

1 large can solid white tuna, water packed, drained and flaked

2 tablespoons margarine

½ cup dry breadcrumbs

In a 2 quart casserole, combine all ingredients except margarine and bread crumbs. Mix well. Cover and refrigerate 12 hours or overnight.

When ready to bake combine melted margarine and breadcrumbs in a small bowl. Sprinkle over casserole. Bake uncovered in a 350 degree oven for 55 to 65 minutes or until hot and bubbly.

Janet LaCava, New York

Easy to fix and tastes so good.

QUICK SEAFOOD CASSEROLE

1 pound can or frozen crabmeat

1 pound cooked shrimp, peeled

¾ cup mayonnaise, light

½ cup chopped green pepper

½ cup finely chopped green onion

1 cup finely chopped celery

½ teaspoon salt

1 tablespoon Worcestershire sauce

2 cups coarsely crushed potato chips

Preheat oven to 400 degrees. Combine all ingredients, except potato chips in a buttered 2½-quart casserole dish. Top with potato chips and bake 20 to 25 minutes.

Bernadine Levy, Colorado

If you love eggplant, you'll really love this dish.

EGGPLANT WITH SEAFOOD CASSEROLE

1 medium eggplant

1 medium onion, chopped

½ punch green onions, chopped

½ bell pepper, chopped

2 coves of garlic, minced

½ cup butter

1 cup Italian breadcrumbs

1 (6½-ounce) can crabmeat, drained

1 egg, slightly beaten

1 teaspoon salt

Black pepper to taste

Red pepper to taste

Peel, dice and cook eggplant. Drain and mash. Saute onions, bell pepper and garlic in butter until soft; add to eggplant. Stir in breadcrumbs and crabmeat. Mix well and season to taste. Add egg by gently mixing. Pour mixture into greased casserole and bake 25 minutes at 325 degrees. Serves 2–4.

Optional: Cut eggplant in halves and parboil. Scoop out

the meat, saving the shells for stuffing. Place mixture in eggplant halves, sprinkle with bread crumbs and bake as above.

Bernadine Levy, Colorado

JO JO'S SHRIMP, MUSHROOM AND ARTICHOKE CASSEROLE

This recipe won a "blue ribbon" at a fund raising cook off. I proudly presented it to my Mom, my very best friend.

7 tablespoons butter, divided

1 pound fresh mushrooms, sliced

1½ pounds large shrimp, shelled and deveined

1 large can artichoke hearts, drained and cut in half

4½ tablespoons flour

¾ cup milk

¾ cup heavy cream

½ cup dry sherry

1 tablespoons Worcestershire sauce

½ cup Parmesan cheese

Salt, pepper, paprika

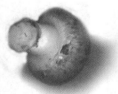

In a skillet, melt 2½ tablespoons butter and sauté the mushrooms. Set aside. Add shrimp to skillet and cook about 1 minute until shrimp starts to turn pink. In a 2-quart casserole dish, layer artichokes, shrimp and mushrooms. Set aside. In a saucepan, melt 4½ tablespoons of the butter. Add flour while stirring with a wire whisk. Gradually add milk and cream and stir until thick. Add sherry, Worcestershire, salt and pepper. Pour this mixture over the shrimp, mushrooms and artichokes. Sprinkle with the grated Parmesan cheese. Add paprika for a bit of color and bake at 375 degrees for about 25 minutes. Serve over rice.

Zina Versaggi Graalfs, Florida

NATIONAL

AVALON PG 7 PM   PREDATOR 2 R DEC 21   OPEN EVERY NIGHT
THE NUTCRACKER PRINCE G STARTS THUR DEC 20   549 2077

Bob Lilly

VEGGIES &

Veggie Casserole...

1 pound potatoes, thinly sliced
1 pound Crimini Mushrooms
2 medium onions, thinly sliced
1 pound yellow squash, thinly sliced
1 pound fresh tomatoes, sliced thick
2 ... peppers, sliced
... cheese, grated
... cheese, grated

BREAD AND BUTTER PICKLES

15 med. sized cucumbers   2 1/2 c. sugar
4 large white onions   1/4 t. tume...
1/4 c. salt   1 T. m...
1/4 t. clover

Wash cucumbers, peel...
Combline cucumb...
layers in...

POTATO BOATS

Prepare baked potatoes. Cut in half or slice
a piece from the surface. Scoop out contents.
Mash. Season pototoe mixture as
for mashed potatoes Whip until ... le.
Pile lightly into potato sh... le
with paprika, grated che... es of
bacon. Place in baking ... 375' until
lightly brown. Serve ...

Could mix grated che... re.

SIDES

BROCCOLI BAKE DU JOUR

1 (20-ounce) package frozen chopped broccoli

¼ cup chopped green onion

1 tablespoon butter

1 (3-ounce) package cream cheese, softened

1 can shrimp soup or Cheddar cheese soup

1 teaspoon lemon juice

⅛ teaspoon paprika

Cook broccoli according to package directions. Drain and set aside. Cook onion in butter until tender. Stir in softened cream cheese, soup and lemon juice. Put broccoli in a 2-quart casserole. Pour soup mixture over broccoli. Bake in a 350 degree oven until bubbly (about 10 to 15 minutes) or place in microwave, covered in waxed paper and cook 4 to 5 minutes on 80% power. Sprinkle with paprika before serving.

Beth Burt, Texas

JADE GREEN GINGERED BROCCOLI

6 cups sliced, trimmed broccoli pieces

⅓ cup chicken broth

2 cloves garlic, minced

1 teaspoon grated, fresh peeled ginger root

3 tablespoons reduced sodium (light) soy sauce

1 tablespoons brown sugar

1 teaspoon sesame oil

1 tablespoon corn starch

2 tablespoons cold water

Place broccoli in a large pan of boiling water. Return to boil and cook for 2 minutes. Drain and set aside. Heat chicken broth in a wok or large skillet over medium heat. Add garlic and ginger root stir for 1 minute. Add soy sauce, brown sugar and sesame oil. Combine cornstarch and cold water; add to skillet. Cook and stir until sauce thickens. Stir in broccoli. Ready to serve.

Betty Ann Sheffloe, Nebraska

PENNSYLVANIA RED CABBAGE

Melt in large frying pan:

>   2 tablespoons butter or bacon drippings

Add the following, cover, simmer for 20 minutes:

>   2 cups shredded red cabbage
>
>   1 cubed apple
>
>   2 tablespoons brown sugar
>
>   3 tablespoons vinegar
>
>   2 tablespoons water
>
>   ¾ teaspoon salt
>
>   ¼ teaspoon caraway seed

Serves 4.

Connie Timko, Illinois

LILLIE'S GLAZED CARROTS

>   2 pounds carrots
>
>   1 medium onion, diced
>
>   1 green pepper, diced
>
>   ¼ cup cooking oil
>
>   1 can tomato soup
>
>   ½ cup sugar
>
>   ½ cup vinegar
>
>   1 teaspoon prepared mustard
>
>   1 teaspoon Worcestershire sauce

A different taste, but so good! My aunt Lillie came up with this special carrot dish.

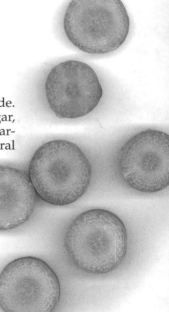

Cook carrots in salt water until tender; drain and set aside. Saute onion and pepper in oil. Add tomato soup, vinegar, mustard and Worcestershire sauce. Heat. Add cooked carrots and mix well. Serve hot or cold. May be made several days in advance and stored in refrigerator.

Bernadine R. Levy, Colorado

MARINATED CARROTS

1 small package of carrots, cooked

MARINADE:

1 can tomato soup

¾ cup sugar

1½ cups vegetable oil

¼ cup vinegar

You may add other spices as desired. This marinade is a good French dressing.

Combine marinade ingredients and pour over cooked carrots. Marinate for about 1 hour.

Marilyn Erlandson, Pennsylvania

HONEYED CARROTS

5 cups carrots, peeled and sliced ½ inch thick

¼ cup butter or margarine

¼ cup honey

2 tablespoons brown sugar

2 tablespoons fresh parsley, chopped or 1 teaspoon dry parsley

¼ teaspoon salt

⅛ teaspoon pepper

Cook carrots in boiling salted water until just tender. Drain. Melt butter; blend in remaining ingredients. Place carrots in a greased 1½-quart casserole; cover with sauce. Cover and bake for 20 to 30 minutes at 350 degrees.

Roberta Spurlock, Oklahoma

COPPER PENNIES

2 pounds carrots, peeled and sliced, cook until tender

Bell pepper, diced

Onion, diced

1 can tomato soup

1 cup sugar

½ cup oil

½ cup vinegar

1 teaspoon salt

1 teaspoon pepper

1 teaspoon dry mustard

Combine soup, sugar, oil, vinegar, salt, pepper and mustard and bring to a boil. Pour over vegetables. Serve hot or cold. Keeps indefinitely in refrigerator.

Jean Krest, Colorado
Anna Laura Doan, Indiana

CORN BAKE

1 (16-ounce) can whole kernel corn

1 (16-ounce) can creamed corn

1 box Jiffy corn bread mix

1 stick butter, softened

1 cup sour cream

1/4 cup water

Combine all ingredients and place in a 1½-quart casserole dish. Bake in a preheated 325 degree oven for 35—45 minutes.

Mary Ralston, Illinois
Betty Kuckles, Wisconsin

ted water
espoon of
prevent
te filling.
d baking
e are re-
25 to 30
d rest of

CHEESE FILLING

½ lb. Mozzarella cheese, diced
2 lbs. Ricotta cheese (or
    Pot cheese)
2 eggs
½ cup grated Parmesan cheese

MEAT FILLING

1½ lbs. chopped meat (beef or
    mixture of beef and pork)
1 egg
½ lb. Mozzarella cheese, diced
3 slices moist br___

BAKED CORN

1 can cream corn

1 egg, beaten

2 tablespoons corn meal

⅓ cup milk

1 tablespoon flour

Onion, finely chopped

Salt and pepper

Paprika for garnish (if desired)

Combine all ingredients, except paprika and pour into a greased baking dish. Can garnish with paprika, if desired Bake for 1 hour at 350 degrees.

Betty Sellers, Texas

MEXICAN CORN

2 cans cream style corn

4 eggs, beaten

1½ teaspoons garlic salt

2 cups grated cheese

1 cup oil

1 cup white corn meal

Salt

1 can diced green chiles

Combine and pour into a greased baking dish. Bake in a 350 degree oven for 30–35 minutes or until done.

Joyce Latta, Texas

APACHE CORN CAKES

2 cups prepared pancake mix

1 cup grated Longhorn cheese

2 tablespoons chopped green onion

1 (4-ounce) can chopped green chiles

1 can cream style corn

Preheat griddle or electric skillet. Mix all ingredients into batter. Fry as pancakes. Serve hot with syrup and sausage.   —Judy Cormany, Texas

CORN AND POTATO CAKES

> 1 pound russet potatoes, peeled and coarsely grated
> ¾ cups finely chopped green bell pepper
> 1½ cups fresh corn
> 4 to 5 green onions, thinly sliced
> 1½ teaspoons ground cumin
> 3 tablespoons flour
> Salt and pepper to taste
> 2 tablespoons olive oil, or butter, divided
> Sour cream, optional

Place potatoes and green peppers in a kitchen towel or several layers of paper towels; squeeze out excess moisture. Place in a large bowl; add corn, onions, cumin, flour, salt and pepper; toss to combine. In a sauté pan, heat 1 tablespoon oil; drop large spoonfuls of potato mixture into pan and flatten into 3- to 4-inch patties. Cook until patties are golden brown and crispy; turn and cook the other side, about 4 to 6 minutes per side. Remove and keep warm. Add the remaining tablespoon oil and repeat the process with remaining potato mixture. Serve warm with a dollop of sour cream, if desired.

Liz Hobbs, California

CORN PUDDING FOR 8

> ¼ cup butter
> ¼ cup flour
> 2 teaspoons salt
> 1½ tablespoons sugar
> 1¾ cups milk
> 3 cups fresh or frozen corn, chopped
> 3 eggs, beaten

Melt butter in saucepan; stir in flour, salt and sugar. Cook until bubbly. Add milk and cook until thick. Stir in corn. Stir in eggs that have been beaten until frothy. Pour into a well-buttered casserole. Bake in a hot water bath at 350 degrees for about 40 minutes. For smoother pudding, blend corn in a blender.

Fay Luker, Texas

SPANISH STRING BEANS

Saute 1 large onion and add 2 cans of drained green beans, 1 can whole tomatoes, 1 chopped green pepper, 1 clove garlic, 1 cup packed brown sugar, 2 tablespoons bacon fat and ½ cup ketchup.
  Cover and cook slowly for 20 minutes until well heated.

Betty Ann Sheffloe, Nebraska

SAVORY GREEN BEAN BAKE

2 (10.5-ounce) packages frozen French style green beans

1 (10 ¾ ounce) can cream of celery soup

½ cup bias cut celery

¼ cup chopped pimento, drained

¼ teaspoon Worcestershire sauce

5 drops hot pepper sauce

2 teaspoons instant minced onion

½ teaspoon salt

¼ teaspoon pepper

TOPPING:

⅓ cup bread crumbs

⅓ cup grated Parmesan cheese

2 tablespoons butter or margarine, melted

Thaw and drain green beans. Set aside. In a large bowl, combine all remaining ingredients, except topping. Mix well. Add green beans and stir gently; turn into a 1½-quart casserole. Combine topping ingredients, mixing well. Sprinkle over green bean mixture. Bake at 350 degrees for 45 to 50 minutes or until topping is browned and mixture is bubbly at edges. Serves 6.

MICROWAVE METHOD: Crumble frozen green beans into a 2-quart microwave save casserole. Stir in soup, celery, pimento and seasonings. Microwave on high power, covered with plastic wrap, for 10 minutes. Meanwhile, combine topping and mix well. Sprinkle topping over green bean mixture. Microwave on high power, uncovered for 1½ minutes.

Eleanor Cowan, Texas

GREEN BEANS WITH PECANS

Salt and freshly ground pepper

2 pounds green beans, trimmed and halved on the diagonal

5 tablespoons unsalted butter

1 cup chopped pecans

Fill a large pot with water and bring to a boil. Salt the water; add beans, and cook until crisp tender — 4 to 5 minutes. Drain, transfer immediately to a bowl of ice water, and let cool for 1 minute. Drain again and pat dry.

Melt butter in a large frying pan over medium heat. Add pecans and cook, stirring often, until nuts are lightly browned and fragrant, about 5 minutes. Add beans and toss to coat with butter. Add 4¾ teaspoons salt and 1¼ teaspoons pepper, cover and partially cook, tossing and stirring occasionally, until the beans are heated through, another 5 to 6 minutes. Taste and adjust the seasoning with salt and pepper. Serve hot. Serves 8–10.

Yvonne E. Constantino, Texas

I use this recipe a lot for company and even the young grandkids like it. Sometimes they pick out the pecans first, then eat the green beans then the pecans. You figure!

BEAN BAKE

1 can kidney beans, drained

1 can lima bean, drained

1 can butter beans, drained

1 cup packed brown sugar

4 large onions, chopped

1 teaspoon dry mustard

½ teaspoon garlic salt

1 teaspoon salt

½ cup vinegar

1 can (large) B & M baked beans, do not drain

Combine all ingredients except baked beans. Bring to a boil for 20 minutes. Add baked beans. Combine and top with bacon strips. Bake at 350 degrees for 1½ to 2 hours.

Jeanne Schroeder, Michigan

**My own recipe!
Freezes well.**

CREOLE RED BEANS AND RICE

1 pound red kidney beans

¾ cup vegetable oil or 6–8 slices bacon

⅔ cup flour (or 2 large cooking spoons full)

2 large white onions, chopped

4 cloves garlic, minced

8–10 cups water

1 pound Kielbasa sausage, sliced in 1-inch pieces

½ pound cubed ham

2 bay leaves

Pepper to taste

Pinch of sage

Salt to taste

Rinse beans in water and pick out any blemished beans; drain and put aside. Use a large heavy pot and brown bacon on low heat. Remove bacon from pot, leaving drippings or use ¾ cup oil in place of bacon drippings. To drippings, add flour, and stir constantly over very low heat until mixture turns light tan. Add onions and garlic; cook on low heat until limp (not brown). You may have to add a little oil if this gets too dry. Continue stirring while the vegetables cook to the limp stage. Remove from heat; add 8 cups water and 1 pound beans. Mix well. Return to low heat. Add sausage, ham, bay leaf, sage and pepper. Do not add salt until beans become tender (salt can cause the beans to become tough if added too soon). Bring mixture to a boil; turn down heat immediately after the mixture begins to boil. Lower temperature to simmer. Cover pot. Stir often to prevent sticking. Cook until beans are tender, about 3 hours. Serve over rice; add Tabasco® sauce to individual dishes for more spice.

Gerry Lesseps, Louisiana

CALICO BEANS

8 slices bacon, cut up

1 pound ground beef

1 cup chopped onion

1 can pork and beans

1 can small red beans

1 can small lima beans

½ cup packed brown sugar

½ cup granulated sugar

1 teaspoon prepared mustard

½ cup ketchup

1 tablespoon vinegar

Brown bacon, beef and onion. Drain. Add partially drained beans and remaining ingredients. Salt and pepper to taste. Bake for 45 minutes at 350 degrees.

Martha Trowbridge, Illinois

EGGPLANT CASSEROLE

Can be baked in microwave. Yellow squash is also good this way.

1 large eggplant, pared and cut into chunks

1 egg, slightly beaten

1 medium onion, chopped

1 stack of saltines, crushed

Margarine

Salt and pepper to taste

Cheddar cheese, grated

Peel and chunk eggplant and soak in water for 30 minutes. Drain salt water and cook eggplant in fresh water top of stove until tender. Drain. Mash eggplant. Add egg and onion and stir. Add margarine, salt and pepper. Add crushed saltines and stir well. Place in a casserole dish and top with lots of cheese. Bake for 30 minutes in a 350 degree oven.

Barbara Rhoades, Texas

MICROWAVE PORTOBELLO MUSHROOMS

- 2 large fresh Portobello mushroom caps, stems removed
- 2 tablespoons butter, divided between mushrooms
- 4 ounce cheese, shredded (Italian Three Cheeses suggested)
- 1 medium tomato, diced
- 2 tablespoons olive oil, divided between mushrooms

Place mushrooms upside down on microwave safe plate. Place 1 tablespoon of butter around each mushroom "fin". Microwave on high for 1 minute or until butter melts into mushrooms. Remove from microwave.

Evenly spread 2 ounces of cheese on each mushroom. Place mushrooms back in microwave and cook on high for abut 30 seconds or until cheese is melted and mushrooms are hot.

Place equal portions of tomato on the melted cheese surface. Pour olive oil over tomatoes. Serve immediately as an appetizer or side dish. This is also a tasty vegetarian entrée.

Jim Hester, Texas

...MUSHROOM-FETA-FILO

SWEET ONION PUDDING

2 cups whipping cream

3 ounces shredded Parmesan cheese

6 large eggs, lightly beaten

3 tablespoons all-purpose flour

2 tablespoons sugar

2 teaspoons baking powder

1 teaspoon salt

½ cup butter or margarine

6 medium sweet onions, thinly sliced

Combine whipping cream, cheese and eggs in a large bowl. In a separate bowl, combine flour, sugar, baking powder and salt. Gradually stir into egg mixture. Set aside.

Melt butter in a large skillet over medium heat; add onions and cook, stirring often, for 30 to 40 minutes or until onion is caramel colored. Remove from heat. Stir onions into egg mixture; spoon into a lightly greased 13 x 9-inch baking dish. Bake at 350 degrees for 30 minutes or until set. Serves 8.

Joyce Crane, Texas

Melt the butter. Mince
... Combine
... an
...and
...side.
...reserve
...me
...ay
2 inch
...red)
...ly
...at
...sheets

ONIONS AU GRATIN

An easy, tasty companion for beef.

2½ cups sliced onions

4 tablespoons butter

2½ cups grated Cheddar cheese, divided

⅓ cup packaged biscuit mix

¼ teaspoon salt

⅛ teaspoon pepper

3 tablespoons butter, melted

Saute onions in butter until tender. Mix onions with 2 cups grated cheese, biscuit mix, salt, pepper and melted butter. Pour into greased 1½-quart casserole dish. Sprinkle with remaining ½ cup cheese. Bake at 350 degrees for 30 minutes.

Judy Cormany, Tx

1015 ONION PIE

¼ cup plus 2 tablespoons butter, divided

3 medium 1015 onions, chopped

2 cups Swiss cheese, grated and divided

1 cup crushed saltine crackers, divided

2 eggs

¾ cup light cream or half and half or canned evaporated milk

Dash of salt

1 teaspoon freshly ground pepper

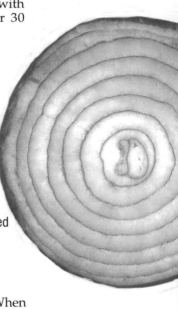

Melt ¼ cup butter in a large skillet over medium heat. When hot, add onions and sauté until tender. Place half of the onions in a 1½-inch deep pie pan. Sprinkle with half the cheese and half the cracker crumbs. Repeat layers of onions and cheese. In a medium bowl, beat eggs, cream, salt and pepper. Pour evenly over onion mixture. Melt 2 tablespoons butter in skillet over medium high heat, stir in remaining cracker crumbs. Lightly brown and then sprinkle crumbs over casserole. Bake at 350 degrees for 25 minutes. Serves 6–8.

Beverly Harrison, Texas

ROASTED RED PEPPERS

Cut desired number of red peppers in half, core and seed. Place upside down, skin side up, on tin foil under broiler for 10 minutes. Skins will blacken. Remove from under broiler, wrap tightly in foil to steam and cool. When cool, remove skins. Place peppers in a dish, add salt and fresh ground pepper to taste. Drizzle olive oil and balsamic vinegar over peppers to marinate.

Delicious served cold as an accompaniment to fish or fowl, or good in sandwiches. Can be made days ahead.

Lyn Gogis, California

ELVIS' FRIED PICKLE CHIPS

1 medium jar (10-12 ounces) of thin sliced hamburger dill chips

Cornmeal

Shake excess vinegar off the pickle chips and dredge them in cornmeal. Shake off excess meal and deep fry pickles in 360 degree oil until golden brown. Serve with Honey Dijon Sauce (recipe follows).

HONEY DIJON SAUCE

1 cup mayonnaise

Pinch cayenne pepper

1 tablespoon honey

1½ teaspoons cider vinegar

2 tablespoons Dijon mustard

Mix all ingredients together. Place dip in small bowl in center of serving plate and arrange fried pickles around the dip and serve.

Jeri-Lynn Sandusky, Utah

BUBBLE AND SQUEAK

1–2 cups potatoes, cooked and cold

½ head cabbage, cooked

1 cup parsnips, cooked

Vegetable shortening

1 onion, chopped

Salt and pepper to taste

Chop up desired amount of cooked vegetables (enough to fit your frying pan). In a large pan greased with vegetable shortening, fry the chopped onion until soft. Then add the chopped vegetables and mix together. Season with salt and pepper. Press down in the pan and fry until crisp on both sides. It may be necessary to slice to turn it over. When it is hot and crisped on the underneath, serve with cold meats or fried eggs.

Zina Versaggi Graalfs, Florida

My friend John Clarke's favorite using left overs from Sunday roast dinner.

Smaller patties can be made by mixing all ingredients together and then fying.

SINFUL POTATOES

2 (2-pound) bags frozen hash brown potatoes

2 pounds Velveeta cheese

1½ cups mayonnaise

Crumbled fried bacon

Salt and pepper to taste

Slightly defrost potatoes. Melt cheese and add to potatoes. Add mayonnaise, salt and pepper and toss together until well mixed. Bake in a greased 13 x 9-inch pan at 350 degrees for 30 minutes. Sprinkle bacon on top and bake for 30 minutes longer. Serves 24.

Shirley Thomas, Texas

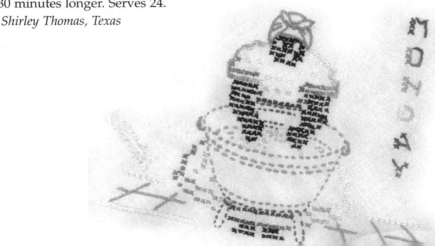

This is a popular dish! Many thanks to everyone who submitted their version!!

POTATOES DELUXE

1 cup margarine or butter, melted

1 (2 pound package) frozen hash brown or diced potatoes, thawed

½ cup chopped green onion

2 cups grated sharp Cheddar cheese

1 cup sour cream

1 can cream of chicken soup

2 cups crushed corn flakes

Melt half of the margarine or butter in an oven-proof baking dish in slow (300 degree) oven. In a large bowl, combine potatoes, onion, cheese, sour cream and soup and place in large oblong casserole. Bake at 350 degrees for 30 minutes. Meanwhile, mix corn flakes with remaining melted butter or margarine. Cover top of potatoes and bake 15 minutes longer. Serves 8–10.

Anna Laura (Loa) Doane, Indiana
Jan Whittaker, California
Loraine Franklin, Texas
Jeanine Bowles, Washington
Liz Offord, Texas
Sharon Odom, Texas

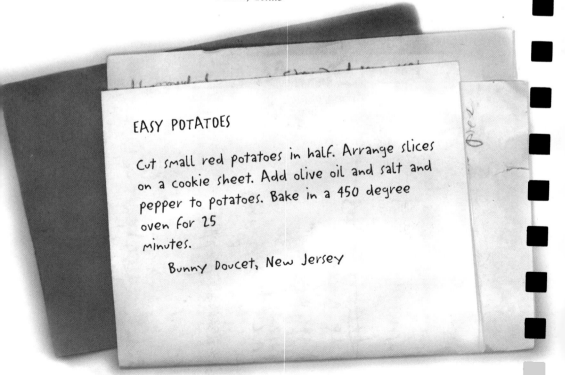

EASY POTATOES

Cut small red potatoes in half. Arrange slices on a cookie sheet. Add olive oil and salt and pepper to potatoes. Bake in a 450 degree oven for 25 minutes.

Bunny Doucet, New Jersey

LIGHT POTATO SALAD

    1 pound red potatoes
    ½ cup diced onion
    ½ cup diced celery
    ¼ cup chopped red pepper
    ¼ cup chopped green pepper
    ¼ cup grated carrots
    ¼ cup sweet pickle relish
    1 (2-ounce) jar chopped pimento, drained
    ¼ cup plain non-fat yogurt
    ¼ cup reduced calorie mayonnaise
    1 tablespoon each mustard, pepper, red pepper, Mrs. Dash
        Table blend

Cut potatoes (peeled or unpeeled) into cubes and boil for 8–10 minutes. Drain and cool. Combine cooled potatoes and onion, celery, red pepper, green pepper, carrots, relish and pimento; toss gently. Mix yogurt, mayonnaise and mustard in a cup. Stir well and pour over mixture. Add pepper and Mrs. Dash to taste.

Bernadine R. Levy, Colorado

DELUXE MASHED POTATOES

    5 to 6 medium potatoes
    ½ cup milk
    3 tablespoons butter
    1 egg, beaten
    1 teaspoon parsley
    ¼ teaspoon minced onion
    1 (3-ounce) package cream cheese, softened

This is one of those recipes that I just throw together without measuring, until it comes out the way that I want. Can also add garlic, chives, or chopped green onion, chopped basil or whatever herbs you like.

Peel potatoes and boil until tender. Mash. Add butter and milk. In a separate bowl, combine egg, parsley, egg and cream cheese. Add to potato mixture. Mix well. Bake in a buttered 2-quart casserole at 350 degrees for 20 minutes. Serves 6.

May be frozen. Thaw and bake for 30 minutes.

Liz Offord, Texas

POTATO LATKES

4 large potatoes

2 eggs

1 teaspoon salt

Dash of pepper

2 heaping tablespoons flour

1 teaspoon grated onion

½ teaspoon baking powder

Extra cinnamon if desired

Fat for frying

Peel potatoes and grate on a fine grater. Pour off half of the liquid. Beat eggs and add to the potatoes with remaining ingredients, except fat. Drop the mixture into a hot, well greased frying pan, turning to brown on both sides.

For a lighter texture, one cup of cooked and mashed potatoes may be substituted for the raw potatoes.

Serve hot with apple sauce, sour cream or sugar.

Jean Krest, Colorado

SWEET POTATO SOUFFLE

4 cups cooked yams

1 cup sugar

1 egg

½ cup milk

Use an electric mixer to combine well. Pour into a casserole dish.

TOPPING:

1 cup packed brown sugar

1 cup chopped pecans

½ cup flour

1 stick margarine

Melt margarine, crumble in other ingredients. Spread over potato mixture. Bake for 40 minutes in a 350 degree oven.

JoAnn Christal, Texas

SWEET POTATO-CRANBERRY-APPLE BAKE

1½ pounds sweet potatoes, peeled and cut into ¼-inch slices

2 Granny Smith or Golden Delicious apples, thinly sliced into rings

½ cup dried cranberries (you can use raisins as an alternative)

½ cup packed brown sugar

3 tablespoons butter or margarine, melted

½ teaspoon ground cinnamon

Preheat oven to 450 degrees. Generously butter a glass baking dish. Arrange sweet potatoes, apples and cranberries in dish. Sprinkle with brown sugar. Combine butter and cinnamon; drizzle over brown sugar. Bake in preheated oven for 25 to 30 minutes, until potatoes are tender.

Recipe can be doubled. Just adjust the baking time.

Robbin Roberts, Texas

SWEET POTATO-BANANA CASSEROLE

5 sweet potatoes

½ cup light brown sugar

3 bananas

1 cup orange juice

½ teaspoon grated orange rind

½ cup butter

1 teaspoon cinnamon

1 teaspoon vanilla extract

2 eggs, beaten

¾ cup cornflakes crushed

Cook sweet potatoes until tender. Peel and mash with bananas. Add remaining ingredients, except cornflakes. Sprinkle cornflakes on top. Bake at 350 degrees for 30 minutes.

Liz Offord, Texas

MERINGUE TOPPED SWEET POTATOES

4 cups cooked, pureed sweet potatoes

½ stick butter, softened

½ cup cream

2 eggs, separated, at room temperature

½ teaspoon cinnamon

¼ cup apricot or other brandy

¼ teaspoon salt

2 dashes pepper

1 tablespoon grated lemon (I always use more)

Blanched slivered almonds

3 tablespoons sugar

Puree sweet potatoes in a large mixing bowl. Add butter, cream, egg yolks, cinnamon, brandy, salt, pepper and lemon peel. Thoroughly beat until mixture is light and smooth. Evenly spread mixture into a buttered 8-inch square quart casserole. Bake at 400 degrees until heated through, 20 to 30 minutes. About 5 minutes before casserole is done, beat egg whites until stiff peaks form. Gradually add sugar, beating until very stiff. Spread meringue lightly over sweet potatoes. Sprinkle with almonds. Bake until meringue is lightly browned, about 10-20 minutes. Serves 8.

Leny Young, Ohio

SWEET POTATO CASSEROLE

3 cups mashed sweet potatoes

1½ cups granulated sugar (I use less)

¾ stick butter or margarine

1 cup evaporated milk

3 eggs, beaten

½ teaspoon nutmeg

½ teaspoon cinnamon

½ teaspoon salt

½ teaspoon vanilla extract

Combine all ingredients, mixing well. Pour into an 8-inch square pan and bake at 425 degrees for 15 to 25 minutes.

Remove from oven and reduce temperature to 400 degrees. Spread with topping. See below.

TOPPING:

- 1 cup crushed cornflakes
- ½ cup packed brown sugar
- ½ cup chopped pecans
- ¾ stick butter or margarine, melted

Spread over potato mixture and bake 15 minutes more at 400 degrees. Watch carefully after you put topping on — it burns easily.

Phyllis Kelso, Minnesota

LOW FAT MOROCCAN SPICED SWEET POTATO DISH

- 2 teaspoons olive oil
- 1 medium onion, chopped
- 2 garlic cloves, pressed
- 1½ teaspoons ground coriander
- 1½ teaspoons ground cumin
- 1 teaspoon salt (may be omitted or reduced)
- ¼ teaspoon ground red pepper (cayenne)
- 1½ pounds sweet potatoes (about 2 medium) peeled and cut into ¾ inch pieces
- 1 can 'no salt added' stewed tomatoes
- 1 cup bulgur
- 2½ cups water
- 1 can garbanzo beans, drained and rinsed
- ½ cup dark raisins
- 1 cup loosely packed fresh cilantro leaves, chopped

Cook onions in oil until tender. Add spices and garlic juice and cook 1 minute.

Add potatoes, tomatoes, bulgur and water, bring to a boil and simmer about 20 minutes, until potatoes are tender.

Finally, stir in beans, raisins and cilantro and heat through. Serve with a dab of low-fat yogurt.

Marilyn Sietsema, Illinois

Great for a holiday dish

SWEET POTATO PANCAKES

1 cup grated white potatoes

1 cup grated sweet potatoes, firmly packed

1 teaspoon salt

1 cup grated carrots, firmly packed

2 tablespoons grated onion

¼ cup chopped parsley

Dash of nutmeg

4 eggs, beaten

⅓ cup flour

Fresh black pepper

Juice of one half lemon

1 small clove, crushed (optional)

Place grated sweet and white potatoes in a colander over a bowl. Salt lightly and let stand 15 minutes. Rinse and squeeze out extra water. Combine all ingredients and mix well. Fry in butter until brown and crisp. Serve immediately topped with yogurt or sour cream and fresh chopped chives. Garnish with tomato wedges and lots of raw vegetable sticks.

Jean Krest, Colorado

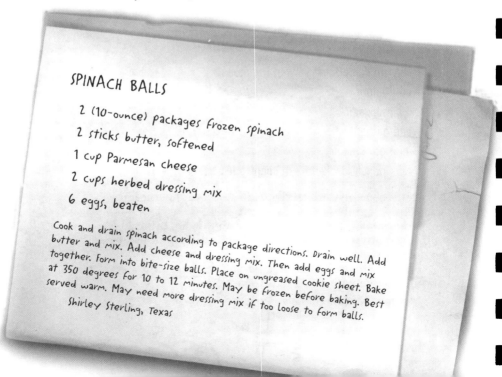

SPINACH BALLS

2 (10-ounce) packages frozen spinach

2 sticks butter, softened

1 cup Parmesan cheese

2 cups herbed dressing mix

6 eggs, beaten

Cook and drain spinach according to package directions. Drain well. Add butter and mix. Add cheese and dressing mix. Then add eggs and mix together. Form into bite-size balls. Place on ungreased cookie sheet. Bake at 350 degrees for 10 to 12 minutes. May be frozen before baking. Best served warm. May need more dressing mix if too loose to form balls.

Shirley Sterling, Texas

SPANAKOPITA (SPINACH PIE)

1 medium onion

2 green onions

2 tablespoons salad oil

1 (10-ounce) package frozen chopped spinach, thawed

1 (8-ounce) package low fat cottage cheese

1 (8-ounce) package light cream cheese, softened

½ cup crumbled feta cheese (about 2 ounces)

1 tablespoon minced fresh dill or ½ teaspoon dried
   dill weed

¼ teaspoon ground black pepper

1 (16-ounce) package frozen phyllo dough

½ cup margarine or butter, melted

Green onions for garnish

Chop onion and thinly slice green onions. In a 10-inch skillet, over medium heat, in hot salad oil, cook onion and green onion until tender and golden. Remove from heat.

Drain spinach and squeeze dry. Add spinach to onion mixture. Add cottage cheese, cream cheese, feta cheese, dill, pepper and egg. Mix well.

Remove half the phyllo dough sheets from the package, keeping the remaining sheets covered with plastic wrap to prevent drying out. Brush bottom and sides of a 13 x 9-inch glass baking dish with melted margarine. Place two phyllo sheets in the baking dish, pressing against sides of dish. Light brush phyllo with melted margarine. Top with two more phyllo sheets. Brush and continue process until all of the first half of the phyllo are in the baking dish.

Preheat oven to 350 degrees. Spread spinach mixture evenly over phyllo. Unwrap remaining phyllo and place two sheets over the spinach mixture, letting edges hang over sides of the dish. Brush with margarine, making sure to moisten the edges. Repeat layering with remaining phyllo and margarine.

Gently roll edges of phyllo that are hanging over the dish inward to provide an attractive border. Bake 45 minutes or until crust is golden and filling is hot. Remove from oven and let stand 10 minutes for easier serving. Garnish with green onion.

Jean Krest, Colorado

SPINACH AND ARTICHOKE CASSEROLE

3 (10-ounce) packages frozen chopped spinach

1 (8-ounce) package cream cheese, softened

½ cup butter, softened

Salt and pepper to taste

Dash Worcestershire sauce

2 (8.5-ounce) cans artichoke hearts

½ cup buttered bread crumbs or Italian bread crumbs

Cook spinach according to package directions. Drain and squeeze as much moisture as possible from spinach. While hot, mix with cream cheese, butter, and Worcestershire sauce. Season to taste. Place layer of spinach in a 2-quart casserole, then layer of artichokes. Repeat. Cover with bread crumbs. Bake at 350 degrees for 30 minutes. May be prepared early in the day and refrigerated or frozen until ready to bake.

Liz Offord, Texas

SPINACH SOUFFLE

2 tablespoons margarine

¼ cup flour

1 cup skim milk

1 package frozen chopped spinach, thaw and drain

3 eggs, separated

3 tablespoons minced green onion

¼ teaspoon salt

⅛ teaspoon pepper

⅛ teaspoon nutmeg

Melt margarine in a saucepan over medium heat. Stir in flour. Blend well. Slowly stir in milk. Cook and stir until mixture thickens and boils. Remove from heat. Stir in spinach, egg yolks, green onion, salt, pepper, and nutmeg. Beat egg white until stiff. Fold into spinach mixture. Pour into six greased ½-cup size soufflé dishes. Bake at 350 degrees for 20 minutes. Serve immediately as an appetizer or side dish. Serves 6.

Edith Ann Blood, Tennessee

SPINACH MADELEINE

2 packages frozen chopped spinach

2 tablespoons chopped onion

4 tablespoons butter

2 tablespoons flour

½ cup evaporated milk

½ cup liquid from spinach

¾ teaspoon garlic salt

½ teaspoon salt

1 teaspoon Worcestershire sauce

1 (6-ounce) roll jalapeno cheese*, cut into small pieces

Pepper to taste, if needed

Bread crumbs

Cook frozen spinach according to package directions and drain well, reserving ½ cup liquid. Satuee onions in butter until soft; add flour, stirring until smooth but do not brown. Add spinach liquid and milk, slowly stirring to avoid lumps. Add salts, Worcestershire sauce and cheese. Stir until cheese melts and combine with cooked drained spinach. Add pepper if desired. Pour into casserole and top with bread crumbs. Heat about 10 minutes at 325 degrees. Freezes well. Serves 6.

*Can use: 6 ounces of Velveeta cheese and 1 small jalapeno pepper, minced without seeds.

Bernadine R. Levy, Colorado

SQUASH CASSEROLE

5 to 6 small yellow squash, washed and sliced

3 beaten eggs

½ cup milk

2 tablespoons butter

6 crackers, crumbled

1 small onion, grated

1 cup grated cheese

Salt and pepper to taste

Boil in a small amount of water until tender. Drain. Mix remaining ingredients with squash and put in buttered 1½-quart casserole. Top with bread crumbs. Bake in 350 degree oven for 30 minutes.

Kathy Bratton, Texas

This is a beautiful side dish for any main course, or for pot luck. Delicious and flavorful.

POMODORI Y RISO

8 medium tomatoes, firm and ripe

½ cup risotto rice, uncooked

2 tablespoons finely chopped fresh Italian parsley

2 tablespoons finely chopped sweet basil

2 cloves garlic, minced

Salt and freshly ground black pepper

Olive oil

Preheat oven to 400 degrees. Trim about ¾-inch from the bottom of each tomato and set ends aside. Use a spoon to scoop out inner pulp and reserve. Put tomatoes open end up in a baking dish. Pulse pulp in food processor or blender to a chunky puree. Add rice, parsley, basil, garlic, and then season generously with salt and pepper. Mix well. Spoon into tomatoes and put the lid back on the tomatoes, drizzle a little olive oil over tops of the tomatoes and bake until rice is swollen and tender and tomatoes are soft and tender (about 50 minutes.)

Lyn Gogis, California

VEGETABLE CASSEROLE

2 cans Veg-all (mixed vegetables)

1 cup chopped celery

½ cup chopped onion

1 small can water chestnuts, sliced

1 cup grated sharp cheese

½ cup margarine

1½ cups Ritz cracker crumbs

¼ cup melted butter

Combine first six ingredients and place in greased casserole. Top with crumbs. Pour melted butter over all. Bake at 350 degrees or until casserole bubbles, about 45 minutes. Serves 6–8.

Lois Patterson, Wisconsin

VEGETABLE SAUTE

5 tablespoons margarine
1 medium onion, sliced
4 small zucchini, cut into strips
1 cup sliced mushrooms
10 cherry tomatoes, cut in half
½ teaspoon salt
¼ teaspoon oregano, dried
⅛ teaspoon pepper
1 teaspoon garlic powder

One of my favorite vegetable dishes. Everyone loves this casserole.

In a large skillet, melt margarine; add onion and cook over medium heat until tender. Add zucchini and mushrooms; cook 10 minutes. Add tomatoes and seasonings, cook 2 to 3 minutes. Sprinkle with Parmesan cheese and serve. Serves 2.

Terri Anderson, California

STUFFED ZUCCHINI

Saute garlic, onions, celery and bell pepper in butter until soft. Add chopped squash, scooped from large zucchini halves, and chopped plum tomatoes. Cook quickly over high heat to absorb liquid. Transfer to a bowl to cool.

In same skillet, brown ground beef or round steak with onions and seasonings such as fresh or dried thyme, rosemary and marjoram. Add salt and pepper to taste with each addition. When browned enough, drain fat and add to vegetables. Adjust seasonings. Add enough Parmesan cheese to make stuffing adhere.

Salt zucchini shells (parboil shells for 1 minute, if freezing) and fill with stuffing. Top with Monterrey Jack cheese and put into casserole dish and add enough tomato juice to cover bottom. Bake, covered, 45 minutes in a 350 degree oven until shells are soft. Remove cover during last 5-10 minutes of baking time.

OPTIONS: Hot sauce, small amounts of sugar, garlic salt can be added.

EGYPTIAN STUFFED ZUCCHINI, TOMATO, PEPPER OR CABBAGE LEAVES

1 pound ground meat

½ to ¾ cup uncooked rice

1 tablespoon dried parsley (if using fresh, add more)

1 teaspoon dried mint, optional (if using fresh, add more)

1 teaspoon cumin

½ teaspoon celery seeds

1 large onion, chopped very fine

Hint of garlic

Salt and pepper

1 medium sized can tomato sauce, divided

1 large can diced stewed tomatoes

1 tablespoon butter or margarine

8 to 9 medium to large zucchini or tomatoes or peppers (red or green) or 1 large head of cabbage

MEAT MIXTURE:

Combine ground meat, rice, spices and half the can of tomato sauce. Set aside.

VEGETABLES:

If you are stuffing zucchini, wash and cut each in half and then use a vegetable corer to remove pulp, leaving one end closed. Loosely fill each zucchini with meat mixture, stopping about a ¼-inch from the top. Stand upright in a pot (pack loosely together), with the closed end down. If you are stuffing tomatoes or peppers, clean out the seeds and stuff with meat mixture. Tomatoes and peppers can be cooked together, if you want to use both. Pour can of diced tomatoes and remaining tomato sauce over the top of vegetables. Add enough water to almost fill the pot. Add butter or margarine on top, along with some if not all of the reserved zucchini pulp. Cook covered on low heat until rice is done. If less sauce is desired, do not cover, but watch closely to prevent burning.

If stuffing cabbage leaves, boil them in a small amount of water until just limp. Save the water. Wrap a small amount of meat mixture in each leaf. Place leaves in a large pot. Pack tightly. If desired, pack leaves around a large onion that has been placed in the center of the pot. Mix a small amount of the saved cabbage water with the can of diced tomatoes and pour over the rolls. Top with butter or margarine. Leaves can be weighted down with a glass lid during cooking. Cook covered over very low heat until rice is almost done. More water or tomato sauce can be added if needed. If less sauce is desired, do not cover, but watch closely to prevent the bottom layer from burning.

QUICK METHOD: Slice zucchini lengthwise without coring. In a large buttered casserole dish, layer zucchini or cabbage leaves with meat mixture. Repeat several layers, ending with meat mixture. Do not fill dish. Leave room to add diced tomatoes and tomato sauce with water to cover. Bake at 300 degrees until rice is done. Check often and add additional water or tomato sauce if needed.

Maureen Vogl, Kansas

ROASTED VEGETABLES

Preheat oven to 350 degrees. Clean and prepare a variety of fresh vegetables of your choice. For example: peeled and sliced sweet potatoes, peeled and sliced beets, baby carrots, mushrooms, red bell pepper, zucchini, brussel sprouts, cauliflower, and/or sliced onions or leeks.

Put vegetables in bottom of a 13 x 9-inch baking pan and drizzle with olive oil. Sprinkle with fresh or dried herbs of your choice. For example rosemary, thyme, basil, and/or oregano. Use whatever combination you like. Sprinkle garlic powder over vegetables.

Cover with foil and bake in preheated oven for 30 minutes. Uncover and bake another 30 minutes.

Depending upon the number of vegetables, this makes approximately 6 or more delicious servings.

Nancy Wright, Arizona

Bob Lilly

Best Ever Carrot Cake

Cake:
2 cups flour
2 cups sugar
3 teaspoons cinnamon

Icing:
1 (8-ounce) package cheese cream
1 stick butter
1 (16-ounce) box of ...ar (4

...illa
...ecans
...ry

FUDGE

2 c. sugar   2 T. butter
2 or 3 sq. chocolate   1 t. vanilla
2 T. syrup   1/2 c. chopped nuts
2/3 c. milk   1/8 t. salt

Combine sugar, choclate, syrup, mil...
Cook until firm vall te...
Cool slightly th...
Beat...

LEMON PIE FILLING

1/2 c. flour   1 T. butter
1 c. sugar   2 egg yolks, beaten
2 c. boiling water   1/4 t. salt
rind of one lemon
juice of one lemon

Mix sugar, flour and salt add boiling water
and mix thoroughly. Cook until thick sti...
constantly. Add other ingredients and
at a simmer until beaten egg yolks th...
Cool, place in baked pie crust.
Top with meringue if desired.

...ter-
...',
...d
...st.
...d

...e.
W...
gr...
pa...
until cakes test done.

DESSERTS

Cakes

My mother, Ginnie Ricca, made this cake every December. It was our special holiday cake and still is! It is easy to make and is so delicious!

APPLESAUCE CAKE

2 cups sugar

1 cup butter

2 eggs

2 cups applesauce

3 cups all-purpose flour

1 teaspoon cinnamon

1 teaspoon nutmeg

2 level teaspoons baking soda

2 cups chopped pecans, dredged with a little flour

1 ½ to 2 cups raisins, dredged with a little flour

1 teaspoon vanilla extract

Icing (see below)

Preheat oven to 250 degrees. Grease and flour a 10 or 12 cup bundt or tube pan. Set aside. Cream sugar and butter together until light and fluffy. Add eggs, one at a time. Beat after each addition. Add applesauce and mix well. In a separate bowl, sift dry ingredients together. Add to creamed mixture. Mix well. Fold in pecans and raisins. Add vanilla and mix well. Pour into prepared pan. Bake 1 ½ to 2 hours, until cake tests clean. Let cake cook 25 to 30 minutes before icing.

ICING

1 pound ground pecans

1 pound box confectioners' sugar

2 egg whites, beaten fluffy but not dry

1 teaspoon vanilla extract

Whiskey to taste

Mix ground nuts and sugar. Add beating egg whites and vanilla. Mix and then add enough whiskey to make a spreading consistency. Frost the cooled cake. After cake has been frosted, sprinkle with a little whiskey.

Pecans may be very finely chopped instead of ground.

Bernadine Levy, Colorado

APPLE CAKE

Mix together:

> 1 cup sugar
> 1 cup flour
> 1 teaspoon soda
> Scant teaspoon nutmeg
> ½ teaspoon cinnamon
> Pinch of salt

Add:

> 1 egg, beaten
> ¼ cup melted margarine
> ½ cup nuts
> 3 medium diced apples

Pour mixture into a 9 x 9-inch pan. Bake 350 degrees for 30 minutes or until a toothpick inserted comes out clean. Add topping when ready to serve. Cake can be made ahead and frozen.

TOPPING:

> ½ cup butter
> ½ cup real whipping cream
> ½ cup brown sugar
> ½ cup white sugar

Bring to a rolling boil and add 1 teaspoon vanilla

NOTE: Can freeze.

Phyllis Kelso, Minnesota

CARROT CAKE

2 cup sugar

1½ cups salad oil

4 eggs

4 medium (2 cups) carrots shredded

2 cups flour

1½ teaspoon soda

2 teaspoons baking powder

2 teaspoons cinnamon

1 teaspoon salt

2 teaspoons vanilla extract

1 (8-ounce) can crushed pineapple, drained

CREAM CHEESE FROSTING

4 ounces cream cheese (I use a little more)

⅓ cup butter

1 teaspoon vanilla extract

1¾ cup confectioners' sugar

Mix sugar and oil, add one egg at a time, then add remaining ingredients. Bake at 350 degrees for 55 minutes in a 10-inch round springform pan. Cool, cut diagonally, put one half of cream cheese icing between layers, then the rest on top.

Asa Touba, Minnesota

PINEAPPLE CAKE

2 cups sugar

2 eggs

1 large can crushed pineapple

2½ cups flour

1½ teaspoons baking soda

½ teaspoon salt

Combine all ingredients and turn into two greased and floured cake pans. Bake for 25 minutes at 325 degrees. Remove cakes from oven and pour the following icing over the cakes. Return cakes to oven and continue to bake for an additional 20 to 25 minutes. If you like, eat one cake and freeze the other for later.

ICING

> 1 cup sugar
> ⅔ cup milk
> ¾ stick butter
> 1 teaspoon vanilla extract

Cook 3 minutes and pour over top of cakes.
> *Jeri Lynn Sandusky, Utah*

JOY'S GEM (MOM'S CAKE)

Preheat oven 350 degrees
Combine:
> 4 eggs
> ⅔ cup oil
> 1 cup water

Add:
> Dry cake mix (spice or carrot)

Mix as directed on cake box and add:
> 1 can of coconut and pecan icing

Mix thoroughly and pour into cake pan. Reduce oven to 325 degrees. Check cake mix for baking time; test cake; add 3 to 6 minutes until done. Cool on rack COMPLETELY before cutting
> *Carol Lazarus, Connecticut*

May want to try chocolate frosting with chocolate cake; caramel with white, etc.

POPPY SEED BUNDT CAKE

3 cups flour

1½ teaspoons salt

1½ teaspoons baking powder

3 eggs

1½ cups milk

1⅛ cup oil

2¼ cups sugar

1½ tablespoons poppy seeds

1½ teaspoons your favorite extract

Mix all ingredients in a large bowl for 2 minutes at medium speed. Pour into lightly greased Bundt pan. Bake 55–60 minutes at 325 degrees. Pour glaze over hot cake.

Jan Whittaker, California

ITALIAN CREAM CAKE

1 cup butter

2 cups sugar

3 egg yolks, beaten

2 cups sifted cake flour

1 teaspoon soda

1 cup buttermilk

1 teaspoon vanilla extract

1 (3½-ounce) can Baker's Coconut

5 stiffly beaten egg whites

1 recipe cream cheese frosting or one can store bought
     frosting

Mix together butter and sugar. Add beaten egg yolks, one at a time.

Add cake flour, soda, buttermilk, vanilla and coconut; fold in egg whites. Bake in three greased 8- or 9-inch cake pans at 350 degrees for 25 minutes. Frost with cream cheese frosting and decorate with ½ cup chopped pecans.

Jeri-Lynn Sandusky, Utah

EARTHQUAKE CAKE

1 cup chopped pecans

1 cup coconut

1 (18.25 ounce) box German chocolate cake mix

1 (8-ounce) package cream cheese, not fat free

1 stick margarine or butter

1 (16-ounce) box confectioners' sugar

Spray a 13 x 9-inch glass pan with non-stick cooking spray. Spread pecans and coconut in bottom of pan. Prepare cake mix according to package directions and pour over pecans and coconut. Combine cream cheese, butter and confectioners' sugar. Use a tablespoon and drop mixture over batter. Bake at 350 degrees for 45 to 50 minutes. Enjoy!

Chuck and Laverne Dawson, Kansas

WESTHAVEN CAKE

Great served warm.

1 cup hot water

1 package of dates, cut up

1 teaspoon baking soda

½ cup butter

1 cup sugar

2 eggs beaten

1¾ cups cake flour

1 teaspoon salt

1 heaping tablespoon cocoa powder

1 teaspoon vanilla extract

Pour hot water over dates, add soda. Cream butter, sugar and eggs. Sift flour, salt and cocoa together and add to creamed mixture. Add the dates and hot water. Add vanilla. Pour into 13 x 9-inch pan. Sprinkle German chocolate cut into small pieces and ½ cup nuts over top. Bake at 350 degrees for 25 minutes or until done. Serve with whipped cream.

Judy Cormany, Texas

CHOCOLATE CAKE

4 eggs

1¾ cups sugar

1½ sticks margarine

8 ounces chocolate chips

¾ cup strong coffee

1½ cup flour

2 teaspoons baking powder

Frosting (see below)

Beat eggs and sugar until fluffy. Set aside. In a medium saucepan, melt margarine, chocolate chips, and coffee. Cool. Add to egg mixture. Fold in flour and baking powder. Pour into cake pan and bake at 350 degrees for close to an hour. Frost cooled cake.

FROSTING

8 ounces chocolate chips

1¼ sticks margarine, melted

3 tablespoons coffee

3 to 4 cups confectioners' sugar

4 teaspoons vanilla extract

2 eggs

In a medium saucepan, melt chocolate chips, margarine, and coffee. Add confectioners' sugar, vanilla, and eggs. Stir until frosting reaches spreading consistency. Frost cooled cake.

Asa Touba, Minnesota

s

page 90

t, page 102

CAKE
at 53¢ each.

0 to 35 minutes.
utes.

1¼ sticks)
ter or

etened
ken into

ed
r

Vanilla ice cream *and a glass of milk*

GRANDMA HOWARD'S CHOCOLATE RUM CAKE

Combine the following ingredients and mix together well:

1 box yellow moist deluxe (Duncan Hines) cake mix

1 box instant chocolate pudding

1 cup sour cream

½ cup olive oil

4 eggs

2–4 tablespoons rum

1 teaspoon vanilla extract

Fold in:

1 cup chocolate chips

1 cup chopped nuts

Put ¼ cup olive oil into a bundt pan and coat the inside of the pan really well.

Pour batter into pan. Don't be concerned about the oil going over the mix. Bake at 325 degrees for 58 minutes. Allow finished cake to cool for 7 minutes, then turn it out of the pan. Sprinkle with confectioners' sugar (optional). This is a great cake to make, wrap tightly and freeze for a later occasion. Just remember to thaw it out completely before serving it!

Leona Howard Resteiner, Michigan

CRAZY CHOCOLATE CAKE   (Betty Kuckes, Wisconsin)

Sift together and sift again into 8 inch ungreased pan:

1-1/2 cups flour

1 cup sugar

1/2 teaspoon salt

3 tablespoons cocoa

1 teaspoon baking soda

Make 3 little "wells." In each well, pour:

1/3 cup salad oil

1 teaspoon vanilla extract

1 tablespoons vinegar

Add and mix with fork until well blended:

1 cup milk

Bake at 350 degrees for 30 minutes.

VIRGIL'S CHOCOLATE CAKE

1 stick butter, creamed

1 cup sugar

4 eggs (add one at a time)

1 (12-ounce) can Hershey's chocolate syrup

1 cup self-rising flour

2 teaspoons vanilla extract

Chocolate frosting (see below)

Combine all ingredients. Bake at 350 degrees for 20 to 25 minutes (2 layers). Frost cooled cake.

CHOCOLATE ICING:

12 large marshmallows

4 tablespoons cocoa powder

1 stick butter

1 package confectioners sugar

¼–½ cups milk

⅓ cup chopped pecans

Melt marshmallows, cocoa and butter. Beat in sugar and milk. Add pecans. Beat until well combined. Frost cooled cake.

Zina Versaggi Graalfs, Florida

KAY'S CHOCOLATE YEAST CAKE

This is my favorite cake. It doesn't require frosting. Add dollop of whip cream. Stays moist for several days in a cake tin.

Cream together:

1 cup butter or shortening

2 cups sugar

3 eggs, beaten

1 teaspoon vanilla extract

Stir in 2 squares bitter chocolate, melted

Add 3 cups flour alternating with 1 cup milk

1 package dry yeast in ¼ cup lukewarm water

1 teaspoon soda in 3 tablespoons boiling water

Combine all ingredients. Bake in a buttered angel food or Bundt pan in a cold oven with a temperature setting of 360 degrees for approximately 1 hour.

Nancy DeVries, Illinois

DEVIL'S FOOD CAKE

Clara Halden Nichols August 4, 1906 – December 9, 1997

2 squares unsweetened chocolate or ½ cup cocoa and
    1 teaspoon shortening

2 teaspoons baking soda

1 cup boiling water

3 cups sifted flour

1 teaspoon salt

½ teaspoon baking powder

½ teaspoon baking soda

⅓ cup shortening

1⅜ cups sugar

2 large eggs

1½ cups buttermilk

1 teaspoon vanilla extract

Several drops of red food coloring

Chocolate Frosting (see page 266)

Preheat the oven to 350 degrees. Grease and flour three round cake pans. Set aside. Melt the cocoa and shortening (or the unsweetened chocolate) in a medium (2-quart) pan. Stir in 2 teaspoons soda and the boiling water. It will foam up. Stir to mix, then set aside to cool. Stir the flour, salt, baking powder, and ½ teaspoon soda together in a small bowl. Cream the shortening well at high speed until fluffy. Add the sugar and cream well again. Add the eggs and cream well again, until pale and fluffy.

With mixer on lowest speed, add the flour mixture and the buttermilk alternately to the shortening mixture, making three divisions. Don't over-mix: pour in each addition when the preceding one is only partly mixed in, finishing mixing after the last addition.

With mixer on low, add the chocolate, vanilla, and food coloring and stir just until mixed.

Bake at 350 degrees for 30 minutes, or until a toothpick inserted in the center comes out clean.

This is my mother's favorite chocolate cake, one that won her a certain local fame at church potluck suppers in Cloudcroft, NM, and in Safford, Flagstaff, and Prescott, Arizona. The recipe came to her from her mother, Margaret Dama McNatt Halden (Dec 21, 1884 – May 19, 1974). Dama was born in Algerita and Clara was born in San Saba. Both towns are in San Saba County, Texas.

CHOCOLATE FROSTING

6 tablespoons cocoa plus 1 tablespoon shortening or 2 squares unsweetened chocolate

3 tablespoons shortening

About 2¾ cups confectioners' sugar

½ teaspoon (or more) vanilla extract

A few drops red food coloring

About 3 tablespoons milk

Melt the shortening with the cocoa plus shortening or the unsweetened chocolate. Stir in most of the confectioners' sugar. Add in the vanilla and food coloring. With mixer on lowest speed, add milk a spoonful at a time until it is the right consistency for spreading. If it is too thin, add more powered sugar.

Nancy Nichols Bryan, Arizona

NOTE: German Chocolate Cake mix can be substituted.

DEEP CHOCOLATE UPSIDE-DOWN CAKE

½ cup butter or margarine

¼ cup water

1 cup packed brown sugar

1 cup chopped nuts (pecans or walnuts)

1⅓ cups flaked coconut

1 box Deep Chocolate cake mix (using eggs and cooking oil and water according to package directions)

Preheat oven to 350 degrees. In a 13 x 9 x 2-inch metal cake pan, melt the butter by putting the pan in the oven. When melted, remove from oven and add the water. Sprinkle brown sugar evenly in pan.

Arrange nuts and coconut in sugar mixture.

Prepare cake mix in a large mixing bowl, according to package directions. Pour batter over mixture in pan. Bake at 350 degrees for 40 minutes or until cake tests done. Remove from oven and let stand for 5 minutes. Invert on a large platter. Yield: 12 servings.

Diane Watkins, Wisconsin

COCOA AND COLA CAKE

1 cup soft margarine or butter

1¾ cups sugar

1 teaspoon baking soda

2 eggs

2 cups flour, all purpose

3 tablespoons cocoa

1 teaspoon vanilla extract

½ cup buttermilk

1 cup carbonated cola

1½ cups miniature marshmallows

Preheat oven to 350 degrees. Combine all ingredients except cola and marshmallows in large bowl. Blend at low speed then beat one minute at medium speed. Add cola; blend well. Stir marshmallows in by hand. Pour batter into greased 13 x 9 x 2-inch pan. Bake 40 to 45 minutes or until wooden toothpick in center comes out clean. (I baked it for 35 minutes) Cool about 30 minutes. Spread with cola icing.

COLA ICING

½ cup softened margarine

⅓ cup carbonated cola

3 tablespoons cocoa

4 cups sifted confectioner's sugar

1 cup chopped toasted pecans

Combine everything except pecans in small bowl. Beat until smooth, stir in pecans. Spread on cooled cake.

JoAnn Christal, Texas

THREE MILK CAKE (TRES LECHES)

Beat:

> 6 eggs

Slowly add and mix together:

> 2 cups flour
>
> 1 cup sugar
>
> 3 teaspoons baking powder
>
> ½ cup milk
>
> 1 teaspoon vanilla extract

Bake for 20 minutes at 350 degrees. Once the cake is baked, mix the following:

> 2 cups condensed milk
>
> 2 cups evaporated milk
>
> 2 cups whipped cream.

Poke small holes in the cake and pour milk mixture over cake until all is absorbed.

> Finally, cover with whipped cream
>
> *Judy Boegler, Texas*

THE COCONUT CAKE

1 (18¼ ounce) box white cake mix with pudding

1 (8-ounce) can cream of coconut

1 can sweetened condensed milk

1 (8-ounce) carton whipped topping

1 (3-ounce) can coconut

Prepare cake mix according to directions, using whole eggs instead of white, if desired. Bake in a 13 x 9-inch cake pan until done. While cake is still warm, poke holes in cake and pour over the sweetened condensed milk and cream of coconut, which have been mixed together. Let cake cool and refrigerate overnight.

The next day spread whipped topping and sprinkle with coconut. Keep cake refrigerated. Will keep for a week covered.

JoAnn Christal, Texas

PUMPKIN CAKE ROLL

Confectioners' sugar

¾ cup all-purpose flour

½ teaspoon baking powder

½ teaspoon baking soda

½ teaspoon ground cinnamon

½ teaspoon ground cloves

¼ teaspoon salt

3 large eggs

1 cup granulated sugar

⅔ cup 100% pure pumpkin

1 cup chopped walnuts (optional)

FILLING:

1 package (8 ounce) cream cheese, softened

1 cup sifted powder sugar

6 tablespoons butter or margarine softened

1 teaspoon vanilla extract

Confectioners' sugar

Preheat oven to 375 degrees. Grease 15x10-inch jelly-roll pan; line with wax paper. Grease and flour paper. Sprinkle towel with confectioners' sugar. Combine flour, baking powder, cinnamon, cloves, and salt in small bowl. Beat eggs and sugar in large mixer bowl until thick. Beat in pumpkin. Stir in flour mixture. Spread evenly into pan. Sprinkle with nuts. Bake for 13 to 15 minutes or until top of cake springs back when touched. Immediately loosen and turn cake onto prepared towel. Carefully peel off paper. Roll up cake and towel together, starting with narrow end. Cool on wire rack.

Beat cream cheese, confectioners' sugar, butter, and vanilla in small mixer bowl until smooth. Carefully unroll cake; remove towel. Spread cream cheese mixture over cake. Reroll cake. Wrap and refrigerate at least one hour. Sprinkle with confectioners' sugar before serving. Garnish with and this is a beautiful dessert on the dish.

Yvonne E. Constantino, Texas

PUMPKIN GOOEY BUTTER CAKE

1 (18¼ ounce) package yellow cake mix

1 egg

8 tablespoons butter, melted

FILLING:

1 (8-ounce) package cream cheese, softened

1 (15-ounce) can pumpkin

3 eggs

1 teaspoon vanilla extract

8 tablespoons butter, melted

1 (16-ounce) box confectioners' sugar

1 teaspoon cinnamon

¼ teaspoon nutmeg

Preheat oven to 350 degrees. To make the cake: Combine all of the ingredients and mix well with an electric mixer. Pat the mixture into the bottom of a lightly greased 13 x 9-inch baking pan. Prepare filling.

To make the filling: In a large bowl, beat the cream cheese and pumpkin until smooth. Add the eggs, vanilla, and butter, and beat together. Next, add the confectioners' sugar, cinnamon, and nutmeg. Mix well. Spread pumpkin mixture over cake batter and bake for 40 to 50 minutes. Make sure not to over bake as the center should be a little gooey.

Serve with fresh whipped cream.

VARIATIONS:

For a Pineapple Gooey Cake: Instead of the pumpkin, add a drained 20 ounce can of crushed pineapple to the cream cheese filling. Proceed as directed above.

For a Banana Gooey Cake: Prepare cream cheese filling as directed, beating in 2 ripe bananas instead of the pumpkin. Proceed as directed above.

For a Peanut Butter Gooey Cake: Use a chocolate cake mix. Add 1 cup creamy peanut butter to the cream cheese filling instead of the pumpkin. Proceed as directed above.

Becky Van Vranken, Washington D.C.

PINEAPPLE NUT CAKE

- 2 cups flour
- 1 teaspoon vanilla extract
- 2 cups sugar
- 1 (20-ounce) can crushed pineapple juice and all
- 2 teaspoons soda
- 2 eggs
- 1 cup chopped nuts

Combine all the above — mix well. Pour into 9 x 13-inch pan greased and floured Bake at 350 degrees for 35 minutes or until done. Frost while slightly warm. 1 cup raisins can be added if liked.

FROSTING

- 8 ounce package creamed cheese
- ½ cup margarine or butter
- Whip together and add 1½ cup confectioners' sugar.
- 1 teaspoon vanilla extract

Whip until smooth — cover top of cake. Sprinkle with more chopped nuts.

Betty Lou O'Rourke, Michigan

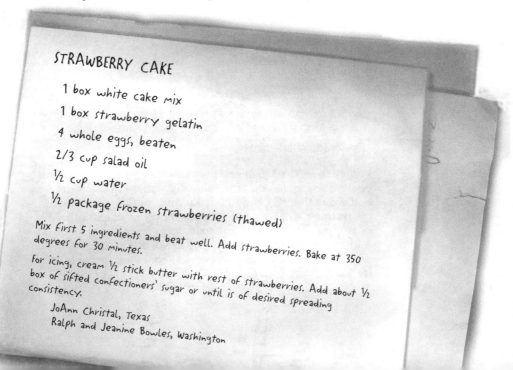

STRAWBERRY CAKE

- 1 box white cake mix
- 1 box strawberry gelatin
- 4 whole eggs, beaten
- 2/3 cup salad oil
- ½ cup water
- ½ package frozen strawberries (thawed)

Mix first 5 ingredients and beat well. Add strawberries. Bake at 350 degrees for 30 minutes.

For icing, cream ½ stick butter with rest of strawberries. Add about ½ box of sifted confectioners' sugar or until is of desired spreading consistency.

JoAnn Christal, Texas
Ralph and Jeanine Bowles, Washington

LOW FAT POPPY SEED CAKE

1 package yellow 97% fat free cake mix

1 cup sugar or Splenda™

⅓ cup oil

¼ cup water

1 cup plain low fat yogurt

1 cup egg substitute

3 tablespoons lemon juice (alternative: 1 teaspoon vanilla extract or ½ teaspoon almond extract)

2 tablespoons poppy seeds

Combine cake mix, sugar; add oil, water, yogurt, egg substitute. Beat at medium speed for 6 minutes. Stir in poppy seeds. Pour batter into a 10 cup bundt pan coated with cooking spray. Bake at 350 degrees for 40 minutes or until toothpick inserted comes out clean. Cool in pan or rack for 10 minutes, remove.

Andrea Martin, Texas

POPPY SEED AND WINE CAKE

1 box yellow cake mix (preferably super moist)

1 box Instant vanilla pudding mix (preferably French Vanilla)

4 eggs

¾ cup oil

¾ to 1 cup of cream sherry or tawny port

Dash of nutmeg

⅓ to ½ can of poppy seed filling (this is found in the kosher food section and the brand name is Solo)

Confectioners' sugar

Preheat oven to 375 degrees. Grease pan(s) and flour (or if you are using tins that the cake will remain in don't grease and flour them). Combine cake mix, pudding mix, eggs, oil, nutmeg, tawny port or cream sherry until smooth. Mix in poppy seed filling. Fill pans ½ to ⅔ full. Bake for 40 minutes or more, checking with toothpick. Do not over bake or you will burn off the alcohol. Let cool then sprinkle confectioners' sugar over top.

Terri Anderson, California

PRUNE CAKE

2 cups sugar

1 cup butter

1 teaspoon vanilla extract

3 eggs

1 cup buttermilk

3 cups flour

½ teaspoon salt

1 teaspoon baking soda

1 teaspoon cinnamon

1 teaspoon allspice

1 teaspoon cloves

2 cups cooked prunes, mashed (approx. 1½ pounds)

2 cups chopped pecans

Cream butter and sugar; add vanilla, then eggs one at a time. Sift dry ingredients. Add alternately with buttermilk. Fold in prunes and nuts. Pour into tube pan and bake at 300 degrees for approximately one hour and 30 minutes. Let cool, and remove from pan.

GLAZE

1 cup confectioners' sugar

1 good teaspoon lemon juice

1 good teaspoon orange juice

½ teaspoon vanilla extract

Mix ingredients well and drizzle over completely cooled cake.

Judy Krohn, Texas

PISTACHIO CAKE

1 box yellow cake mix (Duncan Hines)

4 eggs

¾ cup canola oil

¾ cup water

1 package instant pistachio pudding mix

½ teaspoon vanilla extract

½ cup chopped nuts

Mix and bake in greased and floured 13 x9 x 2-inch pan in preheated 350 degree oven 30 to 40 minutes. Cool.

FROSTING:

¾ cup milk

1 package pistachio instant pudding mix

1 (9-ounce) container whipped topping

Mix and spread on cooled cake. Refrigerate until ready to serve.

Anna Laura Doane, Indiana

HAWAIIAN CAKE

1 package yellow cake mix

1¼ cups cold milk

1 (3-ounce) package instant vanilla pudding mix

1 (20-ounce) can crushed pineapple, drained

1 envelope whipped topping mix

1 (3-ounce) package cream cheese, softened

¼ cup sugar

½ teaspoon vanilla extract

½ cup flaked coconut, toasted

Prepare and bake cake according to package directions. Use a 13 x 9-inch greased pan. Cool. In a bowl, whisk together milk and pudding mix. Let stand to thicken. Add pineapple. Spread over cake. Prepare whipped topping according to package directions. Set aside. In a mixing bowl, beat cream cheese, sugar, and vanilla until smooth.

Beat in 1 cup whipped topping. Fold in remaining topping. Spread over cake. Sprinkle with coconut. Cover and refrigerate 3 hours or overnight. Serves 12-15.

Sharon Odom, Texas

RUM CAKE

½ cup chopped pecans

1 Butter Recipe Golden Cake Mix (Betty Crocker)

1 (3-ounce) package vanilla instant pudding

½ cup rum (dark gives more intense flavor)

½ cup water

½ cup cooking oil

4 eggs

Prepare bundt pan and sprinkle nuts in bottom. Mix all ingredients and beat 2 minutes. Pour in pan and bake 50 minutes at 325 degrees.

GLAZE

1 cup sugar

1 stick butter

¼ cup rum

¼ cup water

Allow all ingredients to boil about 2 to 3 minutes. Immediately pour glaze over cake when you remove from oven and let sit one hour before turning out of pan. Cake will fall/settle from the glaze being put on but that's what makes it so good.

Liz Offord, Texas

LAZY DAISY OATMEAL CAKE

1¼ cups boiling water

1 cup Quaker or Mother's Oats (quick or old fashioned, uncooked)

½ cup butter or margarine, softened

1 cup granulated sugar

1 cup firmly-packed brown sugar

1 tsp vanilla extract

2 eggs

1½ cups sifted all purpose flour

1 teaspoon baking soda

½ teaspoon salt

¾ teaspoon cinnamon

¼ teaspoon nutmeg

LAZY DAISY FROSTING:

¼ cup butter or margarine, melted

½ cup firmly-packed brown sugar

3 tablespoons half and half

⅓ cup chopped nutmeats

¾ cup shredded or flaked coconut

For cake, pour boiling water over oats; cover and let stand 20 minutes. Beat butter until creamy; gradually add sugars and beat until fluffy. Blend in vanilla and eggs. Add oats mixture; mix well. Sift together flour, soda, salt, cinnamon and nutmeg. Add to creamed mixture. Mix well. Pour batter into well-greased and floured 9-inch square pan. Bake in preheated moderate oven, 350 degrees, for 50 to 55 minutes. Do not remove cake from pan. Makes one 9-inch square cake

For frosting, combine all ingredients. Spread evenly over cake. Broil until frosting becomes bubbly. Cake may be served warm or cold.

JoAnn Christal, Texas

OATMEAL CAKE

1¼ cups boiling water

1 cup rolled oats

1 tablespoon margarine

1 cup white sugar

1 cup brown sugar

2 eggs

1½ cups flour

1 teaspoon soda

1 teaspoon cinnamon

½ teaspoon salt

1 teaspoon vanilla extract

Pour water over oats and let stand for 20 minutes. Cream together margarine and sugars, add eggs, beating well. Add oat mixture and flour that has been sifted with soda, cinnamon, and salt. Mix in vanilla. Bake in 12 x 8-inch pan at 350 degrees for 25-30 minutes.

TOPPING

1 tablespoon margarine

¼ cup milk

1 cup brown sugar

1 cup coconut

1 cup chopped nuts

Let margarine, milk, and sugar boil a few minutes. Stir in coconut and chopped nuts. Spread on warm cake and put under broiler until golden brown.

Ralph & Jeannine Bowles, Washington
Betty Kuckes, Wisconsin
Pat Best, Colorado

JUDY DASHIELL'S KAHLUA CAKE

1 package Duncan Hines Golden Butter Cake Mix

4 eggs

1 cup sour cream

1 package instant vanilla pudding

¾ cup vegetable oil

1 teaspoon vanilla extract

⅓ cup packed brown sugar

¼ cup Kahlua

¾ cup chopped pecans

Combine all ingredients and pour into greased bundt pan. Bake 45 minutes at 325 degrees. Then quickly cover cake with "loose" tent of foil, then continue baking for another 25 minutes. Cool at least 15-30 minutes. Frost cooled cake.

THE FROSTING

2 cups confectioners' sugar

1 stick melted butter or margarine

⅓ cup of Kahlua

It's just supposed to drip down the cake like a glaze.

Judy Dashiell, Minnesota

THE CAKE

1 box yellow cake mix

1 (3-ounce) package instant vanilla pudding

4 eggs

¾ cup salad oil

¾ cup plus 1 teaspoon sherry

Combine all ingredients. Beat at medium speed for 5 minutes. Put into greased pan (bundt or 2 loaf pans). Bake 45 minutes at 350 until done.

Loraine Franklin, Texas

COMPANY CAKE

JIFFY white or yellow cake mix

Follow box instructions and bake cake mix in 13 x 9-inch pan. Cool to room temperature. Cut in half and put half of the cake on serving plate.

FROSTING

8 ounces of cream cheese, softened

2 cups milk

1 cup of crushed pineapple, drained

Whipped topping

Coconut

Slowly mix milk with cream cheese. Add pudding, beating carefully (don't whip). Spread over bottom half. Top with second layer.

Spread pineapple on top of cake. Cover with whipped topping and sprinkle with coconut. Keep in refrigerator until ready to serve.

Betty Ann Sheffloe, Nebraska

SURPRISE CAKE

1 yellow cake mix

1 (20-ounce) can crushed pineapple

2 packages instant vanilla pudding

3 cups milk

1 large container whipped topping

Bake cake as directed in 13 x 9-inch pan. Remove from oven and prick with fork. Pour crushed pineapple with juice over baked cake. Mix pudding with milk. When set, pour over pineapple. Spread whipped topping over pudding. Refrigerate until ready to serve.

JoAnn Christal, Texas

BUTTERSCOTCH ICING

Melt and bring to a boil, stirring constantly.

1 cup packed brown sugar

1 stick margarine

Add:

¼ cup milk

Boil slowly for 3 minutes. Let cool. Then add 1 ½ to 2 cups confectioners' sugar, stirring constantly until frosting reaches spreading consistency.

Mary Ralston, Illinois

**Appropriate
for ladies
parties, baby or
wedding showers,
luncheons.**

FESTIVE PARTY CAKE

1 package white cake plus pudding mix

Mix as directed adding 2 tablespoons creme de menthe. Bake in greased 13 x 9-inch pan. Cool. Spread with 1 jar chocolate sauce. Sprinkle on chopped walnuts or pecans. Spread with 9–12 ounces thawed regular or low fat whipped topping to which 2 tablespoons crème de menthe has been added. Refrigerate. Serves 12–15.

Sue Cardinal, Minnesota

MORAVIAN SUGAR CAKE

Mix in a large bowl:

1 cup instant mashed potatoes (dry)

1 cup sugar

1 teaspoon salt

3 cups flour

1 package Rapid Rise dry yeast

Mix together and add to the above:

1 cup hot water

½ cup cooking oil

Stir in:

2 eggs

1 additional cup flour

Cover with plastic wrap and towel, let rise at room temperature 4 to 5 hours or overnight. Spread evenly in greased jelly roll pan. Let rise in warm place until double (about 1 hour). Poke holes in dough. Pour over ½ cup melted butter. Sprinkle with topping: Serves 20

TOPPING MIX:

½ cup brown sugar

2 teaspoons cinnamon

½ cup chopped nuts (optional)

Bake at 350 degrees for 20 minutes

Jan Whittaker, California

TOTAL BRUNCH CAKE

1 cup Total Cereal
1 cup orange juice
1 cup canola oil
1 egg
2 small bananas, thinly sliced
1-1/2 cups flour
3/4 cup sugar
1/2 cup raisins
1 teaspoon baking soda
1 teaspoon cinnamon
1 teaspoon salt
Streusel Topping
1/2 cup packed brown sugar
1/2 cup chopped nuts
1/4 cup flour
1/4 cup butter
1/2 teaspoon cinnamon

Preheat oven to 350 degrees. Grease an 8-inch
square pan. Mix Total cereal and orange juice in
a large bowl and let stand for a few minutes.
Add oil, egg, and banana. Stir in remaining
ingredients. Pour batter into pan. Bake 45 minutes or until top springs back when lightly
touched. Remove from oven. Set oven to broil.
Sprinkle streusel topping over warm cake. Place
cake approximately 5 inches from broiler flame
and heat until top becomes bubbly. Watch carefully, as this happens quickly.

Judy Krohn, Texas

CJ'S BUNDT CAKE

½ cup sugar

½ cup chopped nuts

2 teaspoons cinnamon

1 box yellow cake mix

1 box instant vanilla pudding mix

¾ cup hot water

4 eggs

¼ cup vegetable oil

1 cup sour cream

1 teaspoon vanilla extract

1 teaspoon butter flavoring

Combine sugar, chopped nuts, and cinnamon and set aside. Dump cake mix, pudding mix, hot water, eggs, oil, sour cream, vanilla, and flavoring in a large bowl. Don't make cake or pudding mix, just use in powder form. Blend and beat with mixer.

Heavily grease a bundt pan, sprinkle bottom of pan with some of the sugar, nuts, and cinnamon mixture. Put layer of cake batter, then layer of sugar, nuts, and cinnamon mixture in top. Repeat. End with cake batter. Swirl batter with knife. Bake at 325 degrees for 1 hour and 5 minutes, or until toothpick comes out clean. Cool 10 minutes in pan. While still warm, drizzle with confectioners' sugar/milk frosting.

FROSTING

1 cup confectioners' sugar

2–3 tablespoons milk

½ teaspoon butter flavoring

Combine confectioners' sugar, milk and butter flavoring. Mix to spreading consistency.

Carol Ryan, Kansas

BUTTERSCOTCH COFFEE CAKE

2 cups flour

1 cup sugar

2 teaspoons baking powder

1 teaspoon salt

1 cup water

¾ cup oil

1 teaspoon vanilla extract

4 eggs

1 package instant butterscotch pudding

1 package instant vanilla pudding

1 cup packed brown sugar

2 teaspoon cinnamon

¾ cup chopped nuts

Preheat oven to 350 degrees. In a large bowl, combine flour, sugar, baking powder, salt, water, oil, vanilla, eggs, and puddings. Mix well, beating for 2 minutes on medium speed with an electric mixer. Pour into greased and floured 13 x 9-inch baking pan. Combine brown sugar, cinnamon and nuts and sprinkle over batter. Bake in preheated oven for 40 to 45 minutes.

Jeri-Lynn Sandusky, Utah

EASY COFFEE RING

20–24 frozen dinner rolls

Cinnamon and sugar

1 box butterscotch pudding

½ cup chopped nuts

½ cup packed brown sugar

½ cup butter

Recipe courtesy of Porch Swing Bed and Breakfast, Cheyenne, Wyoming

The night before baking, place frozen rolls in a well-greased bundt pan. Liberally sprinkle with sugar and cinnamon, then sprinkle with pudding. Add nuts and raisins if you like. Melt brown sugar and butter and pour over rolls. Let sit overnight. The next morning, bake 25 to 30 minutes in a 350 degree oven.

Myra Hill, Texas

JEANNE'S COFFEE CAKE

½ cup solid shortening

¾ cup sugar

1 teaspoon vanilla extract

3 eggs

2 cups sifted flour

1 teaspoon baking powder

1 teaspoon baking soda

½ pint sour cream

6 tablespoons butter

1 cup packed brown sugar

2 teaspoons cinnamon

1 cup chopped nuts

In a large bowl, combine cream shortening, sugar, and vanilla. Add eggs, one at a time, mixing after each addition. In a separate bowl, combine flour, baking powder, baking soda. Add to creamed mixture. Blend in sour cream. Pour half the batter into a greased and floured tube pan. Combine butter, brown sugar, cinnamon and nuts. Sprinkle half the mixture over the cake batter. Repeat with remaining batter and top with remaining nut mixture. Bake at 350 degrees for 50 minutes or until toothpick tests clean.

Jean Krest, Colorado

For non-fat cake, use egg substitute and omit coconut.

PINEAPPLE COFFEE CAKE

2 eggs, beaten (or ½ cup egg substitute)

2 cups flour

2 cups sugar

2 teaspoons baking soda

1 (20-ounce) can crushed pineapple, undrained

1 cup flaked coconut, optional

1 teaspoon vanilla extract

Mix all ingredients and pour into greased and floured 13 x 9-inch pan. Bake at 350 degrees for 40 to 45 minutes. If using a glass pan, reduce heat to 325 degrees.

Jan Whittaker, California

PRUNE AND APRICOT COFFEE CAKE

¾ cup dried prunes

¾ cup dried apricots

Boiling water

2 cups plus 1 tablespoon sifted flour, divided

2 teaspoons baking powder

½ teaspoon salt

⅔ cup packed brown sugar

1 tablespoon cinnamon

¼ pound plus 4 tablespoons butter, softened

¾ cup sugar

2 eggs

¾ cup milk

1 teaspoon vanilla extract

6 tablespoons melted butter

⅓ cup chopped walnuts

Cover prunes and apricots with boiling water. Let stand 5 minutes. Drain and finely chop. In a small bowl, sift 2 cups flour with baking powder and salt. In another small bowl combine brown sugar with remaining tablespoon flour and cinnamon. Set aside.

Cream butter until fluffy. Add ¾ cup sugar, mixing well. Add eggs, 1 at a time, beating until light. On low speed add flour mixture to butter mixture alternately with milk and vanilla until just blended. Fold in chopped fruit.

Pour one third of the batter into a greased 9-inch tube pan. Spread evenly and sprinkle with one third of the brown sugar mixture. Drizzle with one third of melted butter. Repeat for 2 additional layers. Top with chopped nuts.

Bake in a preheated 350 degree oven for 55 minutes or until inserted tester comes out clean. Cool on rack 10 minutes. Serves 12 to 15.

Joyce Crane, Texas

SOUR CREAM COFFEE CAKE

I have made this numerous times since 1975, and I continue to get positive reactions wherever I go!

½ cup butter

1 cup sugar

2 eggs

1 teaspoon vanilla extract

2 cups flour

1 teaspoon baking powder

1 teaspoon baking soda

¼ teaspoon salt

1 cup sour cream

TOPPING:

½ cup sugar

½ cup chopped pecans

2 teaspoons cinnamon

Cream butter and sugar. Add eggs and vanilla and mix well. In a separate bowl, combine flour, baking powder, baking soda, and salt. Alternately add flour mixture and sour cream to creamed mixture. Beat well. Combine topping ingredients. Set aside. Pour half of the cake batter into a greased 10-inch tube pan. Sprinkle three-fourths of the nut mixture over batter. Add remaining batter. Top with remaining nut mixture. Bake in a 350 degree oven for 40 to 45 minutes, or until a toothpick inserted in the center comes out clean.

Leny Young, Ohio

Pies

APPLE PANDOWDY

- 2 ready made piecrusts
- 4 tablespoons melted butter
- ½ cup sugar
- ½ teaspoon ground cinnamon
- ¼ teaspoon ground nutmeg
- Dash salt
- 10 cups thinly sliced apples, pared
- ½ cup light molasses
- ¼ cup water
- 3 tablespoons melted butter

Roll out pie crusts to 15 x 11-inch rectangle. Brush with 4 tablespoons melted butter. Fold in half. Brush with butter and fold again. Seal edges. Repeat rolling again, brushing with butter and folding. Chill pastry.

Combine sugar, spices, and salt. Toss with apple slices. Place in a 13 x 9 x 2-inch baking pan. Combine molasses, water and 3 tablespoons melted butter. Pour over apples. Roll pastry into a 15 x 11 -inch rectangle. Place over apples. Turn edges and flute. Bake in 400 degree oven for 10 minutes. Reduce heat to 325 degrees; bake 30 minutes more. Remove from oven. "Dowdy" the crust by cutting through the crust and apples with a sharp knife. Return pandowdy to oven for 10 minutes more. Serve warm. Serves 6-8.

PAT-A-PIE PASTRY

- 2 cups sifted flour
- 2 teaspoons sugar
- ¾ teaspoon salt, or less
- 2/3 cup salad oil
- 3 tablespoons milk

Into a pie plate, sift flour, sugar, and salt. Using a fork, whip salad oil into the milk; pour over flour mixture. Mix with fork until flour is all dampened. Reserve 1/3 of the dough to crumble over filling for top crust. Press rest of dough to evenly line bottom and sides of pie pan. Crimp edges; add fillings; crumble reserved dough over filling. Bake at time and temperature required for filling. Makes 1 8-9 inch double crust pie

Winola VanArtsdalen, Kansas

COUNTRY APPLE PIE

2 (9-inch) piecrusts

5 or 6 tart apples

1 tablespoon lemon juice

¼ to ½ teaspoon lemon peel, optional

¾ cup sugar

2 tablespoons enriched flour

1 teaspoon cinnamon

¼ teaspoon nutmeg

Dash salt

Scrub, but do not peel, 5 or 6 tasty, tart apples and slice into thin slices to make approximately 5 cups. Mix lemon juice and grated peel with apples, adding more lemon if the apples are not tart. Combine sugar, flour, cinnamon, nutmeg and a dash of salt. Mix with apples. Pour into bottom crust. Adjust top crust. Bake in a hot oven (400 degrees) for 50 minutes or until done.

Winela VanArtsdalen, Kansas

JERI-LYNN'S CHERRY NECTARINE PIE

1 (9- or 10-inch) unbaked pastry shell

6 medium nectarines

4½ tablespoons flour

1 tablespoon lemon juice

1 can sour cherries, drain reserving ½ cup juice

1 cup sugar

1 teaspoon cinnamon

Crumbled topping, see below

Slice nectarines and toss with all ingredients. Spoon into pie shell. Sprinkle nectarines with Crumble Topping. Bake in 375 degree oven for 50-60 minutes.

CRUMBLE TOPPING

Combine ½ cup sugar, ½ cup flour, ½ teaspoon cinnamon, ¼ teaspoon ginger, and ⅓ teaspoon ground cloves. Cut in ¼ cup butter until mixture is crumbly.

Jeri-Lynn Sandusky, Utah

OUT OF THIS WORLD PIE

2 (9-inch) piecrusts, baked

1 can cherry pie filling

1 can crushed pineapple

¾ cup sugar

2 tablespoons cornstarch

1 box raspberry gelatin

6 bananas, sliced

dash of red food coloring (optional)

1 cup chopped pecans

Mix first four ingredients and cook until thick. Remove from heat. Add gelatin and food coloring. Cool. Add nuts and cut up bananas. Put in two piecrusts. Refrigerate. Top with whipped topping.

Phyllis Kelso, Minnesota

PINEAPPLE PIE

2 prepared Pillsbury Piecrusts (in a box)

1 cup sugar

2 heaping tablespoons flour

¼ stick butter, cut into small pieces

2 eggs, beaten with a fork

1 (20 ounce) can crushed pineapple, (undrained)

This delicious pineapple pie recipe was given to me by a friend in Houston. It is easy to make.

CRUST TOPPING:

1 tablespoon milk

About 2 tablespoons sugar

Preheat oven to 350 degrees. In a large bowl or pitcher, mix together all the ingredients. Place one piecrust in a large pie plate. Pour the mixture into the crust. Cover with remaining crust and seal the edges and crimp them. Slice the top of the crust with a sharp knife to let out the steam. Using a pastry brush, brush milk over the crust. Sprinkle with sugar. Bake at 350 degrees for 1 hour.

Diane Watkins, Wisconsin

QUICK AND EASY COCONUT PIE

2 cups milk

¾ cup sugar

½ cup biscuit mix

¼ cup butter

1½ teaspoons vanilla extract

1 cup coconut

Mix all ingredients, except coconut, in a blender and blend on low speed for three minutes. Pour into greased 9- or 10-inch pie pan. Let stand for about 5 minutes, then sprinkle with coconut. Bake at 350 degrees for about 40 minutes. Cool and then refrigerate.

Jeri-Lynn Sandusky, Utah

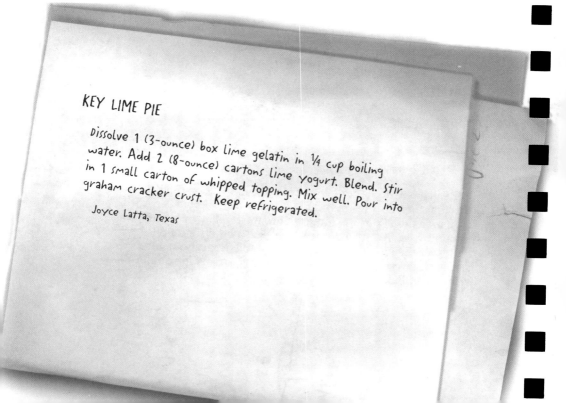

KEY LIME PIE

Dissolve 1 (3-ounce) box lime gelatin in ¼ cup boiling water. Add 2 (8-ounce) cartons lime yogurt. Blend. Stir in 1 small carton of whipped topping. Mix well. Pour into graham cracker crust. Keep refrigerated.

Joyce Latta, Texas

COCONUT MERINGUE PIE

1 (9-inch) piecrust, baked

2 cups milk, divided

2 egg yolks

⅔ or ¾ cup sugar

Dash salt

3 tablespoons cornstarch

1 teaspoon vanilla extract

1 tablespoon butter

2 cups flaked coconut

MERINGUE:

3 egg whites

6 tablespoons sugar

¼ teaspoon cream of tartar

In a small bowl, mix ½ cup of the milk, egg yolks, sugar, salt, and cornstarch. Set aside. Put 1½ cups of the milk and the coconut into a saucepan, then add egg-sugar mixtures from bowl and mix well. Heat on low medium heat, stirring constantly. When thick, turn off heat. Add vanilla and butter. Stir well. Pour into baked pie shell, let cool slightly.

FOR MERINGUE: Preheat oven to 400 degrees. With electric mixer on high speed, beat egg whites until soft peaks form. Gradually add sugar and then cream of tartar. Continue to beat on high speed to form stiff, glossy peaks. Spread meringue over filling, carefully sealing entire edge of crust to prevent shrinking.

Bake for 8 to 10 minutes or until golden. Cool on cake rack away from draft for 2 hours. Serve warm or refrigerate and serve cold.

Judy Boegler, Texas

KEY LIME PIE/TARTS

1 (9-inch) graham cracker piecrust or 10 graham cracker tart shells

1 (14 ounce) can sweetened condensed milk

1 cup non-dairy topping

½ cup key lime juice (adjust to taste)

8 drops green food coloring

Grated rind or zest of one lime, juice also if desired

In a medium bowl, place sweetened condensed milk, non-dairy topping, key lime juice, and food coloring. Beat until blended. Taste for flavor. Add additional key lime juice if needed. Mix in grated rind. Spoon into piecrust or tart shells. Refrigerate for 3 hours before serving. Can be topped with whipped cream or non-dairy topping and lime slices for garnish. Enjoy!

Judy Krohn, Texas

FRENCH LEMON PIE

1 (9-inch) pie shell, unbaked

1 cup sugar

3 tablespoons flour

3 eggs

1 cup light corn syrup

¼ cup butter

2 teaspoons grated lemon rind

3 tablespoons lemon juice

1 lemon, thinly sliced

Prepare pastry in a 9-inch fluted, springform pan with removable bottom. Chill. Mix sugar and flour in a large bowl. Add eggs, syrup, and butter. Beat with rotary beater until well mixed. Stir in lemon rind and juice. Pour mixture into unbaked pastry shell. Arrange lemon slices around edge. Bake in a 375 degree oven for 45 minutes. (Bottom will turn brown).

Betty Ann Sheffloe, Nebraska

BESSIE'S LEMON CAKE PIE

1 (9-inch) piecrust, unbaked

2 egg yolks

1 cup sugar

4 tablespoons flour

1 cup milk

2 tablespoons butter

1 lemon rind and juice of 1 lemon

2 egg whites, beaten with 4 tablespoons sugar

Beat egg yolks, sugar, and flour together in mixer. Heat milk and butter together. Cool. Add to egg mixture. Add lemon rind and lemon juice. Fold in stiffly beaten egg whites and sugar. Bake in uncooked piecrust. Bake in a 350 degree oven for 35 to 40 minutes.

Addalie McMinn, Texas

CHEESE CAKE PIE

Graham cracker crust (see below)

1 (8-ounce) package cream cheese

2 tablespoons butter

½ cup sugar

1 egg

2 tablespoons flour

⅔ cup milk

Preheat oven to 350 degrees. Combine cream cheese and butter until smooth. Add sugar and egg. Mix well. Add flour and milk, mixing well. Pour into unbaked graham cracker pie shell. Bake for 35 minutes.

GRAHAM CRACKER CRUST

⅓ cup margarine

1¼ cup graham cracker crumbs

¼ cup sugar

Melt margarine. Combine graham cracker crumbs and sugar with melted margarine. Press into an 8 or 9 -inch pie pan.

Betty Kuckes, Wisconsin

MANGO CREAM PIE

GRAHAM CRACKER CRUST:

> 1¼ cups graham cracker crumbs, about 11 crackers
> 4 tablespoons melted butter
> 1 tablespoon sugar
> ¼ teaspoon cinnamon

Preheat oven to 375 degrees. In a 9-inch pie plate, mix all the ingredients until evenly moistened. Press into plate and bake 10 minutes. Cool.

FILLING:

> 1 (8-ounce package) light cream cheese
> ⅔ cup confectioners' sugar, sifted
> 1 cup heavy cream, whipped stiff

In a bowl, beat cream cheese and powdered sugar together with an electric mixer on medium speed until well blended. Fold in whipped cream and spread into cooled pie shell.

TOPPING:

> 3 cups thinly sliced mangoes (papaya is good, too)

Arrange fruit slices over cheese filling in an overlapping pattern. Save a few slices for garnish.

GLAZE:

> 4 teaspoons cornstarch
> 1 teaspoon finely shredded orange peel, optional
> ⅓ cup sugar
> ¾ cup mango nectar
> 1 teaspoon lemon juice

In a saucepan, mix cornstarch with orange peel and sugar. Add mango nectar and lemon juice. Cook until thick, bubbly and clear. Cool completely. Spoon over mango slices, top with remaining mango slices for garnish. Cover loosely with plastic wrap and refrigerate 3-6 hours or overnight. Serves 8–10 (more like 6-8!)

Darlene Davasligil, Wisconsin

NEW SOUTH STRAWBERRY PIE

1 (10-inch) piecrust, baked

1 cup sugar

2 tablespoons cornstarch

1½ cups water

1 tablespoon margarine

1 (3-ounce) package strawberry gelatin

1 tablespoon lemon juice

2 cups fresh strawberries, sliced

Whipped cream or whipped topping

Combine sugar, cornstarch, and water in a small pan. Boil until thickened. Remove from heat and add margarine, gelatin, and lemon juice. Stir until dissolved. Chill until partially set. Add sliced strawberries and pour into baked crust. Chill at least 1 hour. Serve with whipped cream.

Jeri-Lynn Sandusky, Utah

STREUSEL CREAM PEACH PIE

1 (9-inch) piecrust

4 cups quartered, peeled peaches (8-10)

½ teaspoon nutmeg, if desired

2 tablespoons cream

½ cup flour

½ cup sugar

1 egg

¼ cup packed brown sugar

¼ cup butter, softened

Preheat oven to 425 degrees. Arrange peaches in piecrust. Sprinkle sugar and nutmeg over peaches. Beat egg and cream together, then pour over peaches and sugar. Mix brown sugar, flour and butter until crumbly. Sprinkle crumb mixture over peaches. Baked 35-45 minutes or until browned. Serve slightly warm. For a special garnish, add whipped cream or commercial sour cream.

Joan Elsea, Colorado

PIROUETTE PIE

1 (9-inch) pie crust, baked
½ cup butter, softened
¾ cup sugar
2 eggs
2 ounces Hershey sweet chocolate, melted
½ cup chopped pecans
1 (4 ounce) package instant vanilla pudding
Whipped cream
Shaved chocolate

Cream butter and sugar in a mixer bowl until fluffy. Add eggs, one at a time, beating well after each addition. Stir in melted chocolate. Add pecans, mixing well. Pour into pie shell. Chill. Prepare pudding according to package directions. Spread over chocolate layer. Top with whipped cream and chocolate sprinkles or shaved chocolate. Serves 8.

Liz Offord, Texas

My son ate this pie in high school and 10 years later still loves this recipe. Nancy Stine, a teacher cohort of mine, gave it to me. Nancy and husband Bob now live in Sun City, Texas

WHITE HOUSE PECAN PIE

1 (9-inch) piecrust, unbaked
1 stick butter, softened
1 cup dark Karo corn syrup
½ teaspoon salt
1 cup sugar
1½ teaspoons vanilla extract (Mexican is best)
3 eggs
2 cups pecans

Combine butter, syrup, salt, sugar, and vanilla to softened butter. Add eggs and pecans and beat gently until just blended. Bake at 375 degrees on lower rack for 40-45 minutes.

Bunny Petty, Texas

PECAN PIE

    1 (9-inch) pie shell, unbaked

    3 eggs

    ⅔ cup sugar

    1 tablespoon flour

    ⅓ teaspoon salt

    ⅓ cup butter, melted

    1 cup dark corn syrup

    1½ tablespoons dark rum

    1 cup pecan halves

Prick unbaked pie shell three times. Combine all ingredients and pour into pie shell. Shield crust with foil. Bake at 375 degrees for 40-50 minutes.

Liz Offord, Texas

TINY PECAN TARTS

    1 (8-ounce) package cream cheese, softened

    1 cup butter, softened

    2 cups all-purpose flour

    2 eggs, slightly beaten

    1½ cups packed light brown sugar

    2 teaspoons vanilla extract

    ½ teaspoon salt

    2 cups chopped pecans

Blend together softened butter and cream cheese. Stir in flour to make pastry dough. Divide into 48 balls. Press each ball into tiny muffin pans to make shells.

    Combine eggs, sugar, vanilla, and salt. Fold in nuts. Fill pastry shells and bake 25-30 minutes, or until filling is set in a 325 degree oven. Yield: 48 tarts.

Judy Ingram

PECAN TARTS

Packaged pastry cups, 24 plus minis or 12 full size

2 eggs, beaten

1 cup packed brown sugar

4 tablespoons butter

1 cup chopped pecans

1 cup raisins

1 teaspoon vanilla extract

Beat eggs slightly, add brown sugar and butter. Mix thoroughly. Then add pecans, raisins and vanilla. Line muffin pans with pastry. Fill each cup half full with filling and bake in 425 degree oven, for approximately 15 minutes for mini tarts. Watch carefully so they do not burn. You may want to lower oven temperature for last 5 minutes of baking so top will not burn. If you make full size pastry cups, they will need approximately 20 minutes to bake with temperature lowered to 350 degrees the last 10 minutes.

Winola Van Artsdalen, Kansas

These ingredients sound strange, but never fear! You will be amazed at the results. You would never guess it has Ritz™ crackers in it.

RITZ™ CRACKER PIE

3 egg whites, stiffly beaten

1 cup sugar

22 Ritz™ crackers, crushed fine

1 cup pecans, chopped

1 teaspoon vanilla extract

Beat egg whites. Beat in sugar. Fold in Ritz™ cracker crumbs and pecans. Add vanilla. Place in buttered Pyrex™ pie pan. Bake at 325 degrees for 25-30 minutes. Chill. Top with whipped cream.

Jan Schmidt, Texas

LENY'S PUMPKIN CHIFFON PIE

This recipe is well worth the effort and please do not cheat on the ingredients. Enjoy!

CRUST:

> 2 cups vanilla wafers, crushed
>
> 6 tablespoons butter, melted
>
> ¼ cup sugar

Mix all ingredients and press into bottom of pie pan. Bake at 400 degrees for 10 minutes. Cool.

FILLING:

> 1 can pumpkin
>
> ½ cup heavy cream
>
> ½ cup sugar
>
> 3 egg yolks, lightly beaten
>
> ¾ teaspoon cinnamon
>
> ½ teaspoon ground ginger
>
> ¼ teaspoon nutmeg
>
> ½ teaspoon allspice

In a medium saucepan, combine all ingredients. Cook over low heat, stirring constantly with a wooden spoon until mixture thickens. Transfer mixture to a bowl. Mix 1 ounce Knox gelatin with ¼ cup Drambuie in top of double boiler. Add to pumpkin mixture. In a large bowl, beat 4 egg whites with a pinch of cream of tartar until soft peaks form. Beat in ¼ cup sugar, 2 tablespoons at a time, beating until stiff peaks form. Fold egg mixture into cooked pumpkin mixture. Pour into cooled shell. Cover and chill for 6 hours. The next day, whip a small carton of whipping cream and spread over pie. (I always add 1 tablespoon cognac to my whipping cream for added flavor).

Leny Young, Ohio

PEANUT BUTTER PIE

Cream together:

>   1 (8-ounce) package cream cheese, not low fat
>
>   1 cup confectioners' sugar

Add and beat until smooth:

>   ½ cup milk
>
>   ¾ cup peanut butter

Beat in:

>   6 to 8-ounces whipped topping.

Pour mixture into a 10-inch graham cracker crust. Chill. Serve with chocolate syrup.

Connie Timko, Illinois

FUDGE PIE

>   1 cup hot water
>
>   1½ ounces bitter chocolate squares
>
>   1 (5.33 ounce) can evaporated milk
>
>   ½ stick margarine or butter

Place all ingredients in a microwave safe bowl and heat chocolate and butter melt.

Add to chocolate mixture:

>   1¾ cup sugar
>
>   ½ cup flour
>
>   ⅛ teaspoon salt
>
>   1 teaspoon vanilla extract

Beat with electric mixer until lumps are dissolved. And all is mixed well. Pour into unbaked pie shell. Sprinkle with chopped pecans, if desired. Bake in a 375 degree oven for 40 minutes or until center is set. Be sure to shield crust edges with foil or protectors so as not to burn too much. If you use a frozen shell, use deep dish.

Jan Schmidt, Texas

SHOOFLY PIE (PENNSYLVANIA DUTCH)

1 (8-inch) pastry shell, unbaked
1½ cups flour
½ cup sugar
½ teaspoon baking soda, divided
4 tablespoons butter
½ cup light molasses
½ cup hot water

Thoroughly mix together flour, sugar, and ¼ teaspoon baking soda. Cut in butter or margarine until crumbly. Set aside. Combine molasses, remaining ¼ teaspoon baking soda and water. Pour ⅓ of the liquid into unbaked pastry shell; sprinkle with ⅓ of the flour mixture. Repeat layers, ending with flour mixture. Bake in 375 degree oven for 40 minutes. Cool.

Betty Ann Sheffloe, Nebraska

CARAMEL CHIFFON PIE

1 (9-inch) piecrust, baked
23 light Kraft caramels
¾ cup water, divided
½ envelope unflavored gelatin
½ teaspoon vanilla extract
1 cup heavy cream, whipped
1 cup chopped pecans, divided

Melt caramels with ½ cup of the water over low heat in a double boiler, stirring until smooth. Soften the gelatin in ¼ cup of the water, then add vanilla. Chill until slightly thickened. Fold in cream and ¾ cup of the pecans. Pour into pie shell. Sprinkle remaining pecans on top. Chill until firm.

Dean Ingram

Desserts

EASY YUMMY CHEESECAKE

1 (9-inch) graham cracker crust

Cream together:
2/3 cup sugar

2 (8-ounce) packages cream cheese

Add:
2 eggs (beaten one at a time)

Beat slightly. I use a wire whisk. Add:
1 teaspoon vanilla extract

Pour mixture into graham cracker crust. Bake for 25 minutes in a 350 degree oven.
Prepare topping while cheesecake bottom is cooking. Combine:

1 cup sour cream

3 tablespoons sugar

1 teaspoon vanilla extract

Spread over crust when it comes out of oven. Continue to bake for 15 minutes. Cool completely. Freeze. Serve with or without topping.

Lou Magel, Michigan

PUMPKIN LAYER CHEESECAKE

2 (8-ounce) packages cream cheese, softened

½ cup sugar

½ teaspoon vanilla extract

2 eggs

½ cup canned pumpkin

½ teaspoon ground cinnamon

Dash each ground cloves and nutmeg

1 ready to use graham cracker crust

In a large bowl, mix cream cheese, sugar, and vanilla using an electric mixer on medium speed until well blended. Add eggs, mixing until blended. In a small bowl, mix pumpkin and spices into one cup of batter. Pour remaining plain batter into crust. Top with pumpkin batter. Bake in a 350 degree oven for 35-40 minutes until center is almost set. Cool. Refrigerate 3 hours or overnight. Serves 6-8.

Mary Lee Whipple, Texas

FAST AND EASY CARAMEL PECAN CHEESECAKE

2 (8-ounce) packages cream cheese, softened

½ cup sugar

½ teaspoon vanilla extract

2 eggs

20 caramel candies

2 tablespoons milk

½ cup chopped pecans

½ cup caramel ice cream topping (optional)

Whole pecans (optional)

1 graham cracker crust

Mix cream cheese, sugar, and vanilla with an electric mixer until well blended. Add eggs and blend. Melt caramels with milk over low heat, stirring until smooth. Stir in pecans. Pour caramel/pecan mixture into crust. Top with cream cheese mixture. Bake in 350 degree oven for 40 minutes, or until center of cheesecake is almost set. Cool. Refrigerate 3 hours or overnight. Garnish with whole pecans and drizzle with melted caramel ice cream topping.

Jeri-Lynn Sandusky, Utah

NO BAKE CHEESECAKE

GRAHAM CRACKER CRUST

Combine:

- ⅓ cup melted margarine
- ¼ cup sugar and 1 ¼ cups graham crackers

Press into 8-inch square pan.

FILLING

Use an electric mixer on medium speed and combine:

- 1 (8-ounce) package cream cheese and 1/3 cup sugar

Gently stir in:

- 1 (8-ounce) tub whipped topping

Pour into graham cracker crust. Refrigerate until ready to serve.

Betty Kuckes, Wisconsin

COBBLER DU JOUR

A brand new dessert each time you use a different pie filling. Quick and easy!

- 1 can prepared pie filling (cherry, apple, blueberry, or peach)
- 1 (8-ounce) can fruit cocktail, drained
- 1 (9-ounce) box Jiffy yellow cake mix
- ⅓ cup chopped nuts
- ⅓ cup butter, melted
- Nutmeg

Combine pie filling and fruit cocktail in 2-quart casserole. Cover with dry cake mix. Sprinkle nuts on top. Drizzle melted butter, particularly around edges. Microwave uncovered on high until bubbly (10 to 12 minutes). Rotate dish once during cooking. Serve warm or cold.

Beth Burt, Texas

FRUIT COBBLER

½ cup butter

1 cup flour

1 cup sugar

1 tablespoon baking powder

½ cup milk

8 cups sliced fresh fruit

½ cup packed brown sugar

½ cup chopped pecans

Brown butter and pour into a 9 x 12 x 2-inch pan. Combine flour, sugar, baking powder, and milk. Pour or drop evenly into pan. Combine fruit and brown sugar and spoon into pan. Bake at 350 degrees for 1 hour. Batter will rise and be beautifully brown.

Jan Whittaker, California

BLACKBERRY COBBLER

Recipe works well for peaches, too.

½ cup butter or margarine

1 cup flour

1 cup sugar

2 teaspoons baking powder

¾ cup milk

Cinnamon

1 cup blackberries

Put the butter in an 8 x 10 x 2-inch dish and melt in the oven. Sift together flour, sugar, baking powder, and salt. Stir in milk and blend until smooth. Put blackberries into baking dish with melted butter. Sprinkle with cinnamon. Pour batter over the blackberries. Bake at 375 degrees for 40 minutes or until topping is brown and crisp.

Lynda Rowan, Texas
Mary Genenwein, Texas

A clipping from years ago that we have used many times. Quick and easy.

APPLE NUT DESSERT (OZARK PUDDING)

1 egg

½ to ¾ cup sugar

2 tablespoons flour

1¼ teaspoons baking powder

¼ teaspoon salt

1 cup diced, peeled apples

½ cup chopped nuts

1 teaspoon vanilla extract

In a medium bowl, beat egg until fluffy. In another bowl, combine sugar, flour, baking powder, and salt. Stir gradually into egg. Fold in apples, nuts, and vanilla. Turn mixture into greased Pyrex pie plate. Bake at 350 degrees about 20 minutes or until dessert puffs and falls, becomes semi-set and is browned on top. Serve warm or cold, topped with ice cream or whipped topping. Makes 4-6 servings.

Ghita Carter, Texas

APPLE CRISP

1 quart sliced apples, peeled and sweetened to taste

⅔ cup packed brown sugar

½ cup flour

½ cup oats

¾ teaspoon cinnamon

¾ teaspoon nutmeg

½ cup butter

Pour the sweetened apples into an 8 x 8-inch pan. Mix remaining ingredients together and spread over apples. Baked about 30-35 minutes in a 375 degree oven. Serve warm with ice cream.

Zina Versaggi Graalfs, Florida

CRANBERRY APPLE CASSEROLE

3 cups chopped, peeled apples

2 cups fresh cranberries, washed

2 tablespoons flour

1 cup sugar

3 (1.5 pounce) packages instant oatmeal with cinnamon and spice

¾ cups chopped pecans

½ cup flour

½ cup packed brown sugar

1 stick butter or margarine, melted

Combine apples, cranberries, and 2 tablespoons flour. Toss to coat. Add sugar and mix well. Place in 2 quart casserole. In a large bowl, combine oatmeal, chopped pecans, ½ cup flour, and brown sugar. Add butter. Mix to crumb stage. Spoon over fruit mixture. Bake uncovered in a 350 degree oven for 45 minutes. Garnish with pecan halves and cranberries (optional).

Lola Russell

FRUIT PIZZA

1 package (about 1 pound) slice and bake sugar cookie dough

1 (8-ounce) package cream cheese, softened

⅓ cup sugar

½ teaspoon vanilla extract

Fresh or thoroughly drained canned fruit of your choice*

1 jar apricot preserves

*Half pints fresh halved strawberries, sliced bananas, 1 pound can of mandarin oranges, 1 pound can pineapple chunks make a nice combination

Cut cookie dough into ⅛-inch slices and line the bottom of a 12-inch pizza pan with the dough. Press dough together with finger tips as evenly as possible to make a crust. Bake in a preheated 375 degree oven for about 12 minutes, or until golden brown. Cool crust to room temperature and then refrigerate until chilled.

Beat together cream cheese, milk, and vanilla. Spread mixture over crust. Arrange fruit in a circle on top. Mix together apricot preserves and enough water to make them of spreading consistency. Carefully drizzle preserves over top of the fruit to glaze it. Refrigerate until chilled.

Jean Krest, Colorado

SNAILS

Use as a dessert or appetizer.
Wonderful for a coffee or brunch

Combine and mix well:
    1 pound butter or margarine, softened
    1 pint sour cream
    4 cups all-purpose flour

Chill mixture for at least 1 hour. While dough is chilling, mix:
    2 cups finely chopped pecans
    1½ cups sugar
    2 tablespoons cinnamon

Form 6 balls from dough. On floured board, roll each ball thin like a pie crust. Sprinkle generously with one-sixth of the sugar mixture. Roll mixture into dough with a rolling pin. Cut into 12 slices like tiny pie slices. Roll as crescent rolls. Repeat with each ball. Bake on ungreased cookie sheets at 400 degrees for 15 minutes. Frost while still warm.

FROSTING:

Combine:
    2 cups confectioners' sugar, sifted
    ¼ teaspoon maple flavoring

Add enough milk to make spreading consistency.
Shirley Thomas, Texas
Gold Diggers Investment Club

Delicious!

QUICK APPLE DESSERT

• 4 Granny Smith apples

Leave apples intact but remove core. Stuff apples with pecans or walnuts, sugar and cinnamon. Bake in 300 degree oven for 30 — 40 minutes. Slice and serve.

Bunny Doucet, New Jersey

HOT CURRIED FRUIT

- 1 can black cherries
- 1 can apricot halves
- 1 can pear halves
- 1 can grapefruit sections
- 1 can peach halves
- 2 bananas, sliced
- 1 tablespoon cinnamon
- 1 tablespoon curry
- 1 tablespoon cornstarch
- 1 cup packed brown sugar
- 1 stick butter
- ¼ cup liqueur, (Grand Marnier, Amaretto, or cognac)

Put all fruit into a baking dish. Toss with cinnamon, curry cornstarch, and brown sugar. Melt butter; add liqueur and pour over the fruit. Toss lightly. Bake at 325 degrees for 30 minutes. Serve warm as a side dish with lamb/poultry/ pork or as a dessert with ice cream.

Zina Versaggi Graalfs, Florida

MELON GLORY DESSERT

- 1 cup cubed watermelon
- 1 cup cubed cantaloupe
- 1 sliced banana
- ½ cup sliced strawberries
- 1 cup fresh blueberries or raspberries, or any combination

Place in a crystal bowl and cover with:
- 2 tablespoons confectioners' sugar
- ½ cup Marsala wine
- 1 jigger cherry brandy

Cover and refrigerate until ready to serve.

Fay Luker, Texas

PEAR MINCE

7½ cups ground pears

1 orange, ground with peel

1 lemon, ground with peel

1 apple, ground with peel

3 pounds sugar

1 small or large can crushed pineapple

1 cup pear juice

1 tablespoon cinnamon

1 tablespoon allspice

1 tablespoon cloves

1 pound raisins

1 cup vinegar

1 teaspoon salt

Simmer for 15 minutes. Can while hot. Makes 8 pints.

When ready for a pie, open and add ½ cup sugar and ½ cup water. Add 2 ½ tablespoons flour or cornstarch and cook until thick. Pour into unbaked pie crust and put a criss-cross top of pie dough on top. Bake at 350 degrees until crust is golden brown – approximately 35 to 40 minutes. This is absolutely the best mince ever.

Addalie McMinn, Texas

CHOCOLATE CHIP CHEESE BALL

1 (8-ounce) package cream cheese, softened

1/2 cup butter softened

1/4 teaspoon vanilla

3/4 cup confectioners' sugar

2 tablespoons sugar

3/4 cup miniature semi-sweet chocolate chips

3/4 cup finely chopped pecans

Graham crackers

In a mixing bowl, beat the cream cheese, butter, and vanilla until fluffy. Gradually add sugars; beat just until combined. Stir in chocolate chips. Cover and refrigerate 2 hours. Place cream cheese mixture on a large piece of plastic wrap. Shape into a ball. Refrigerate for at least 1 hour. Optional: Just before serving, roll cheese ball in pecans. Serve with graham crackers.

Donna Hixon, Illinois

PEACH ALMOND CREAM TART

1 (9- or 10-inch) unbaked pastry shell
1 (14-ounce) can sweetened condensed milk
1 (8-ounce) container sour cream
2 tablespoons lemon juice
1 teaspoon almond extract
1 (21-ounce) can peach filling
Sliced almonds, lightly toasted

Preheat oven to 375 degrees. Bake pastry shell 15 minutes. Meanwhile, in a medium bowl, combined sweetened condensed milk, sour cream, lemon juice, and almond extract. Mix well. Reserving 6 peach slices, spread remaining peach filling on bottom of prepared pastry shell. Top with sour cream mixture. Top with reserved peach slices and almonds. Bake 30 minutes or until set. Cool and chill before serving.

Jeri-Lynn Sandusky, Utah

LENY'S POTLUCK TRIFLE

1 (.75-ounce) package fat free instant vanilla pudding
1 (10-ounce) package fat free pound cake, cut into ½-inch slices
1 (10-ounce) jar all-fruit raspberry preserves
¼ cup orange juice
3 ripe bananas, sliced
At least ¾ cup Triple Sec

When I prepare this dessert, I make it the night before the party because it tastes even better the second day.

Prepare pudding according to package directions, using skim milk. Arrange a single layer of cake in the bottom of a deep trifle bowl. Spread with one-third of the preserves and sprinkle with a generous tablespoon of orange juice and a quarter of the triple sec. Top with one third of the sliced bananas and one third of the pudding. Continue layering two more times, ending with pudding. Cover with plastic wrap and refrigerate at least 6 (or more) hours.

Leny Young, Ohio

PUMPKIN TORTE

1½ cups crushed graham crackers

⅓ cup sugar

½ cup butter

2 eggs, beaten

¾ cup sugar

1 (8-ounce) package cream cheese, softened

2 cups pumpkin

3 eggs, separated

½ cup sugar

½ cup milk

½ teaspoon salt

1 tablespoon cinnamon

1 envelope plain gelatin

¼ cup cold water

1 cup heavy cream, whipped

Mix crushed graham crackers, sugar, and butter and press into a 13 x 9-inch pan. Mix 2 beaten eggs, sugar, and cream cheese and pour over crust. Bake for 20 minutes at 350 degrees. Beat 3 egg yolks with pumpkin, sugar, milk, salt, and cinnamon. Cook until thickened. Remove from heat. Dissolve gelatin in cold water. Add to pumpkin mixture. Cool. Beat 3 egg whites to soft peaks. Add ½ cup sugar gradually and beat until stiff. Fold into pumpkin mixture. Pour over crust and chill. Serve topped with whipped cream. Serves 10 to 12.

Grace Arledge DuBose, Texas

TRICKY TORTE

1 Sara Lee Pound Cake, cooled but not frozen

1 (6-ounce) package chocolate chips

½ pint sour cream

1 cup slivered almonds, sauteed

While cake is cool, slice into five layers. Melt chocolate chips and stir in sour cream. Evenly frost all layers, including top. Top with sauteed almonds, pressing lightly. Refrigerate. Let stand at room temperature before serving.

Marilyn Erlandson, Pennsylvania

LEMON RASPBERRY TIRAMISU

2 (8-ounce) packages fat-free cream cheese, softened

6 packages artificial sweetener (Splenda™) or equivalent of
¼ cup sugar

1 teaspoon vanilla extract

⅓ cup water

1 (3-ounce) package sugar-free lemon flavored gelatin

2 cups fat-free nondairy whipped topping, thawed

½ cup all-fruit red raspberry preserves (or a sugar free
variety)

¼ cup water

2 tablespoons Marsala wine

2 (3-ounce) packages ladyfingers or pound cake cut into
the size and thickness of ladyfingers

2 pints fresh raspberries (or frozen unsweetened raspberries, thawed)

Combine cream cheese, sweetener, and vanilla in a large
bowl. Beat with electric mixer on high speed until smooth.
Set aside. Combine water and gelatin in a microwave safe
bowl. Microwave on HIGH for 30 to 60 seconds or until
water is boiling and gelatin is dissolved. Cool slightly. Add
gelatin mixture to cheese mixture; beat 1 minute. Add
whipped topping; beat 1 minute more, scraping side of
bowl. Set aside.

Whisk together the preserves, water and wine in small
bowl until well blended. Reserve 2 tablespoons of preserves
mixture. Set aside. Spread ⅓ cup preserves mixture evenly
over bottom of an 11 x 7-inch glass baking dish. Split ladyfingers in half, place half in bottom of the baking dish.
Spread half of the cheese mixture evenly over ladyfingers;
then spread ⅓ cup of the preserve mixture; and then
sprinkle 1 cup raspberries evenly over cheese mixture. Top
with remaining ladyfingers; spread remaining preserves
mixture over ladyfingers. Top with remaining cheese mixture. Cover and refrigerate for at least 2 hours. Sprinkle
with remaining raspberries and drizzle with reserved 2
tablespoons of preserve mixture before serving.

Zina Versaggi Graalfs, Florida

Recipe can be doubled for a big trifle dish

TIRAMISU

1 (3-ounce) package vanilla pudding mix

2 cups skim milk

1 cup mascarpone cheese, or (1 (8-ounce) package reduced fat cream cheese, 3 tablespoons sour cream and 2 tablespoons milk)

2¾ cups reduced fat whipped topping, thawed and divided

1 angle food cake loaf

1½ teaspoons instant coffee granules (I use espresso)

½ cup hot water

¼ cup brandy

1 cup Kahlua

Combine pudding mix and milk. Cook and cool. Add cheese. Beat on low speed until smooth. Fold in 1 ¾ cups whipped topping. Set aside. Slice angel food cake lengthwise, then cut each layer into 16 equal rectangles. Dissolve instant coffee in hot water. Add brandy and Kahlua. Brush coffee mixture over tops and bottom of cake. Line bottom and sides of trifle bowl with cake. Cover with half of the pudding mix, repeat. Spread 1 cup whipped topping over all. Garnish with cocoa powder.

Liz Offord, Texas

CHOCOLATE ÉCLAIR CAKE

1 (16 ounce) package graham crackers

2 (3-ounce) packages instant vanilla pudding

3½ cups milk

1 (8 ounce) container whipped topping

2 squares unsweetened baking chocolate

1 teaspoon vanilla extract

1½ cups confectioners' sugar

3 tablespoons light corn syrup

3 tablespoons melted butter

3 tablespoons milk

Line a 13 x 9-inch dish with graham crackers. Prepare pudding mix according to package directions, using 3½ cups milk. Fold in whipped topping. Spread half the pudding mixture over crackers. Repeat layers, ending with crackers. Melt chocolate in saucepan over low heat. Add vanilla, confectioners' sugar, corn syrup, butter and 3 tablespoons milk. Mix well. Spread over graham crackers. Best if chilled for 3 days, but can be eaten sooner. Yield 15 to 18 servings.

Liz Offord, Texas

CHOCOLATE ECLAIRS

DOUGH:

> 1 cup water
> ½ cup butter
> 4 eggs

Heat water to boiling. Stir in flour over low heat. Beat with electric mixer until ball is formed. Add eggs, one at a time. Spoon batter onto cookie sheet. Bake at 400 degrees for 30 minutes. Cool. Split in half. Spoon out excess dough to form a pocket or a shell for the custard filling.

FILLING:

> 2 (3-ounce) packages French vanilla pudding
> 2½ cups milk
> 1 teaspoon vanilla extract
> 1 (8-ounce) container whipped topping

Mix pudding and milk until thick. Add vanilla and whipped topping. Beat until blended. Fill shells.

CHOCOLATE TOPPING:

> ¼ cup semi-sweet chocolate chips, melted
> 2 tablespoons margarine
> 1 teaspoon vanilla extract
> 2 tablespoons milk
> 1 cup confectioners' sugar

Melt chocolate chips. Add margarine, vanilla, and milk. Beat in confectioners' sugar until smooth. Add more milk if needed. Drizzle over eclairs.

Betty Kuckes, Wisconsin

PECAN TASSIES

CRUST:

> ½ cup butter
>
> 3 ounces cream cheese
>
> 1 cup flour

Mix with pastry blender. Wrap in wax paper and refrigerate for 1 hour. Pinch off or slice into 24 slices and pat in mini muffin pans, lining the bottom and sides.

FILLING:

> 1 egg
>
> 1 tablespoon butter
>
> ¾ cup packed brown sugar
>
> 1 teaspoon vanilla extract
>
> ⅔ – 1 cup pecans

Divide pecans in half. Put half of the pecans in the bottom of muffin cups. Add filling and top with rest of pecans. Bake at 350 degrees for 20 minutes. Cool on wire racks. Gingerly swirl a knife blade around crust of each tassie to remove from pan. Yield: 24.

Anna Laura Doane, Indiana

BANANA PUDDING

> 1 (8-ounce) package cream cheese, room temperature
>
> 1 (14-ounce) can Eagle brand condensed milk
>
> 1 large box instant vanilla pudding
>
> 3 cups milk
>
> 1 (12-ounce) container whipped topping
>
> 4-6 bananas, sliced
>
> Vanilla wafers

Mix cream cheese and condensed milk. Add pudding mix and milk. Beat until smooth. Fold in half of the whipped topping. Line a 13 x 9-inch pan with vanilla wafers and sliced bananas. Pour pudding mixture over bananas. Top with remaining whipped topping. Refrigerate.

Jean Beall, North Carolina
Jeanne Schroeder, Michigan

BANANA SPLIT

2 cups low fat buttermilk

2 cups fat free whipped topping

1 small package sugar free vanilla pudding

3 bananas, split lengthwise

Combine buttermilk and pudding. Fold in whipped topping. Chill. Before serving, slice bananas and put into individual serving cups. Spoon in chilled mixture. Serve. May top with chocolate sauce if desired.

Nancy DeVries, Illinois

EGG CREAM DESSERT

3 egg yolks

½ cup sugar

¼ cup rum

½ cup coffee

1 (8-ounce) block cream cheese, softened

Combine in a medium bowl. Using an electric mixer on medium speed, beat for 5 minutes. Use a glass trifle bowl. Layer mixture with pound cake slices. Top with grated chocolate.

Bunny Doucet, New Jersey

MEXICAN ROMPOPE

1 quart milk

1½ cups sugar

1 teaspoon vanilla extract or 1 stick cinnamon

10 egg yolks

1 cup white rum

Bring milk to a boil, cool to lukewarm and add sugar. Bring to a boil and simmer for 20 minutes. Add vanilla and cool. Beat egg yolks until very thick and ribbony. Gradually beat in milk and rum. Stir, strain and chill. Makes 15 servings.

Pat Simpson, Iowa

My children and grandchildren love this dessert. It really is easy and can be made in the morning of serving.

FLAN

1 cup sugar, divided

2 tablespoons water

4 eggs

1 cup milk

1 (14-ounce) can sweetened condensed milk

1 teaspoon vanilla extract

⅛ teaspoon salt

In a small heavy skillet over medium heat, stir ½ cup sugar and the water until sugar melts and turns to syrup and is golden in color. Immediately pour into a one quart casserole. Using a potholder, tilt the casserole in all directions to coat bottom and sides until syrup stops running. Set aside. In bowl or blender, beat remaining ingredients until smooth. Pour into prepared casserole. Set casserole in baking pan. Place in bottom third of preheated 350 degree oven. Pour hot water into pan to come halfway up sides of casserole. Bake 1 hour or until knife inserted near center comes out clean. Remove casserole from water. Cool. Refrigerate at least 3 hours. To serve, run a knife around edge; invert onto serving plate.

Yvonne E. Constantino, Texas

BLUEBERRY SOUFFLE

12 slices white bread, crusts removed

1 (8-ounce) package cream cheese

1 cup fresh or frozen blueberries

12 eggs

2 cups milk

⅓ cup maple syrup

Cut bread into cubes and put half in a 13 x 9-inch baking pan that has been coated with non-stick cooking spray. Cut cream cheese into cubes and place on top of bread. Top with 1 cup of the blueberries and reaming bread. In a large bowl, combine eggs, milk, and syrup, mixing well. Pour over bread. Cover and chill overnight. Remove from refrigerator 30 minutes before baking. Cover and bake at

350 degrees for 30 minutes. Uncover and continue to bake for 30 minutes until golden brown and center is set. When 20 minutes is left on the cooking time, prepare the sauce.

SAUCE

1 cup sugar

2 tablespoons cornstarch

1 cup cold water

1 cup blueberries

Combine sugar and cornstarch in saucepan. Add water and bring to boil over medium heat. Boil for 3 minutes, stirring constantly. Stir in blueberries and simmer for 8 to 10 minutes. Pour the sauce over the souffle to serve.

Pat Simpson, Iowa

HEATH™ BAR DESSERT

Mix together and pat into a 13 x 9-inch pan. Bake at 350 degrees for 10 minutes. Cool.

1 cup crushed graham crackers

1 cup crushed saltine crackers

⅓ cup butter, melted

3 tablespoons sugar

Mix pudding mix with milk and beat until thick, about 3–5 minutes. Mix in ice cream. Pour over crust and refrigerate for 1 hour.

2 small boxes instant vanilla pudding

2 cups whole milk

1 quart butter pecan ice cream, softened

Beat cream, add a little confectioners' sugar to taste and vanilla extract. Spread this over pudding mix layer. Sprinkle crushed bars over top. Refrigerate. Serves 12-18.

1 cup whipping cream

confectioner's sugar

1 teaspoon vanilla extract

3 or 4 large Heath™ or Skor™ bars, crushed

Lois Patterson, Wisconsin

CHOCOLATE COCONUT DELIGHT

My all-time favorite military dessert from early years. This is a nice make ahead dish. It can be frozen and you just take it out to thaw a little ahead of when you want to serve.

FILLING:

> 1 cup butter (2 sticks)
> 1½ cups confectioners' sugar
> 4 squares chocolate, melted
> 4 eggs
> 2 teaspoons vanilla extract
> 1½ cups whipping cream, whipped

Combine butter, sugar, and chocolate. Add eggs, one at a time, beating well after each addition. Add vanilla. Beat mixture until fluffy. Add whipped cream. Set aside.

CRUST:

> 1 cup coconut (sometimes I leave the coconut out – your preference)
> 1 cup chopped nuts, or more to suite your taste (I like pecans)
> Crushed vanilla wafers to fit into a 10 x 6-inch dish
> Butter for bottom of dish

Place crushed vanilla wafers into the bottom of buttered pan. Pour filling over cookies. Chill overnight.

Ruth H. Jones, Kentucky

CHOCOLATE DELIGHT

> 1½ cups all-purpose flour
> 1½ sticks margarine, softened
> 1 cup chopped pecans
> 1 (8-ounce) package cream cheese, softened
> 1 cup confectioners' sugar
> 1 (12-ounce) container frozen whipped topping, divided
> 2 (3-ounce) packages instant chocolate pudding mix
> 4½ cups milk

Mix together flour, margarine and pecans and pat down into a 13 x 9-inch baking pan. Bake at 350 degrees for 20 minutes. Cool completely. Set aside. Blend together cream cheese, confectioners' sugar, and 2 cups of the frozen whipped topping and spread on cooled crust. Using an electric mixer, place pudding mix and milk in bowl and beat until thick. Spread on top of cream cheese mixture. Top with remaining whipped topping. Refrigerate 24 hours before serving. Cut into squares for serving.

Christine Smart, Texas

CHOCOLATE TORTE — FROZEN

It is so delicious.

3 egg whites

½ teaspoon cream of tartar

¾ cup sugar

¾ cup finely chopped hazelnuts or pecans

FILLING:

2 cups whipping cream

¾ cup chocolate syrup

1 teaspoon vanilla extract

Milk chocolate, shaved

Beat egg whites until frothy. Add cream of tartar and beat until soft peaks form. Add sugar, one tablespoon at a time and beat until very stiff peaks form. Do not let them become dry. Fold in nuts. Draw two 9-inch circles on a brown paper sack. Spread mixture evenly divided within the circles. Bake in a preheated 275 degree oven, for 45 minutes. Turn off oven and leave door closed for 45 additional minutes. Remove to rack and cool.

Prepare filling. Whip cream until firm. Stir in chocolate syrup and vanilla. Divide between two layers. Sprinkle with shaved chocolate. Freeze until firm. Slip a knife under the layer to release from paper when ready to stack.

Marian Butcher, Pennsylvania

GINA'S PHONY SPUMONI

1 large can fruit cocktail, drained overnight

½ cup Jamaican rum

3 flavors of ice cream – vanilla, strawberry and chocolate

Cinnamon

Chopped pecans or pistachios

Soak fruit cocktail overnight with rum. Let ice cream become spreading consistency but not too soft. Using a spring form pan, spread a layer of each kind of ice cream, then a sprinkling of rum soaked fruit, a dash of cinnamon and chopped nuts. Continue layering ingredients until the pan is filled. Freeze until ready to serve.

Zina Versaggi Graalfs, Florida

CREAMY CAPPUCCINO FROZEN DESSERT

1 (8-ounce) package cream cheese

1 (14-ounce) can sweetened condensed milk

½ cup chocolate flavored syrup

1 tablespoon instant coffee powder (espresso is best)

1 tablespoon hot water

1 ½ cups frozen whipped topping, thawed

1 (6-ounce) prepared chocolate crumb crust

½ cup chopped pecans, toasted

Additional chocolate syrup for topping

In a large bowl, using an electric mixer on medium speed, beat cream cheese for 2 to 3 minutes or until fluffy. Add condensed milk and syrup. Beat on low speed until well blended. In a small bowl, dissolve coffee powder in water. Cool slightly. Add to cream mixture. Fold in whipped topping. Spoon mixture into piecrust. Sprinkle with pecans. Cover and freeze overnight. Let dessert stand in refrigerator 10 to 15 minutes before serving. Cut into wedges. Drizzle with additional chocolate syrup.

Zina Versaggi Graalfs, Florida

PERRY'S FRUIT CUPS

1 (15.5-ounce) can of crushed pineapple

1 (11-ounce) can mandarin oranges, drained

1 (16-ounce) can frozen orange juice, thawed

1 (10-ounce) carton frozen sliced strawberries, thawed

3 bananas, sliced

½ lemon, squeezed over bananas

This was served at Bay Breeze Bed and Breakfast, Corpus Christi, Texas

Mix all fruit together and spoon into individual, ½ cup cocktail size, plastic cups. Freeze. Thaw 1 hour before serving.

OPTIONS: Add blueberries, raspberries and/or blackberries in season.

Perry Tompkins, Texas

PUMPKIN SQUARES

Toast 1 cup pecans in oven and set aside.

In a large chilled bowl, combine 2 cups pumpkin, 1 cup sugar, 1 teaspoon salt, 1 teaspoon cinnamon, 1 teaspoon ginger, 1 teaspoon nutmeg. Fold in softened vanilla ice cream.

Line the bottom of a 13 x 9-inch pan with 18 gingersnaps. Layer half of ice cream/pumpkin mixture, another layer of gingersnaps, and top with ice cream/pumpkin mixture.

Sprinkle toasted pecans on top and freeze for 5 hours until firm. Garnish with a dollop of whipped topping.

Betty Ann Sheffloe, Nebraska

CINNAMON ICE CREAM

1 quart vanilla ice cream, slightly softened

1 – 2 teaspoons ground cinnamon

In a large bowl, combine ice cream and cinnamon. Refreeze, if desired. Serve by itself or over warm apple or peach pie.

Jeri-Lynn Sandusky, Utah

CHOCOLATE ICE CREAM CAKE

10 oat biscuits

6 chocolate biscuits

4½ ounces butter

5 egg yolks

1 egg

5 tablespoons caster sugar*

2¼ cups cream

½ cup chocolate sauce

¼ cup Kahlua

4 tablespoons shredded chocolate

1 cake mold

Melt butter. Crush oat biscuits and chocolate biscuits and mix with butter. Press into mold. Cool. Whip egg yolks and egg with the caster sugar to a fluffy mixture. Whip the cream. Set aside. In a separate bowl, combine chocolate sauce, Kahlua, and shredded chocolate with eggs and then fold in whipped cream. Pour into mold. Freeze for at least 6 hours. Serve with chocolate sauce and whipped cream.

*Caster sugar is refined white sugar

Marian Butcher, Pennsylvania

Cookies, Bars & Squares

GINGER COOKIE STICKS

1¾ cups all-purpose flour

½ cup cornstarch

2 tablespoons ground ginger

½ teaspoon cinnamon

¼ teaspoon ground cloves

¼ teaspoon salt

2 sticks butter, softened

⅔ cup packed brown sugar

¼ cup molasses

2 tablespoons crystallized ginger, finely chopped

2 tablespoons coarse decorating sugar

Preheat oven to 350 degrees. Line a 13 x 9-inch baking pan or dish with foil. Slightly overhang the foil. Coat foil with cooking spray.

In a large bowl, sift together flour, cornstarch, ginger, cinnamon, cloves and salt. In a separate bowl, beat butter until creamy. Add sugar and molasses; beat until smooth. On low speed, beat flour mixture into butter mixture until blended. Spread in prepared pan. Sprinkle with crystallized ginger.

Bake in preheated oven for 15 minutes. Remove from oven and sprinkle with coarse sugar. Bake an additional 10 minutes or until center is set. Cool in pan on rack.

Use foil to lift mixture to cutting board. Cut into thirds lengthwise; cut crosswise into twelve 1-inch strips to make 36 rectangles. Makes 3 dozen cookies.

Jeri-Lynn Sandusky, Utah

BESSIE'S SOFT MOLASSES COOKIES

Preheat oven to 350 degrees. Have all ingredients at room temperature. Sift into a large bowl:

2 cups all-purpose flour

1 teaspoon baking soda

½ teaspoon salt

1½ teaspoons ginger

½ teaspoon cinnamon

½ teaspoon cloves

Add remaining ingredients to flour mixture:

½ cup packed brown sugar

1 egg, unbeaten

⅓ cup molasses

⅓ cup buttermilk

½ cup soft vegetable shortening

Beat at speed 3 with an electric mixer for 3 minutes. Drop by teaspoonful onto an ungreased cookie sheet. Bake in preheated oven for 15–18 minutes.

Addalie McMinn, Texas
Martha Trowbridge, Illinois

ORANGE GUMDROP COOKIES

These are easy to make and store. At Christmas, I make these cookies with red and green gumdrops. Looks great. These squares make great finger desserts.

1 pound orange gumdrops

4 eggs

1 pound light brown sugar

Pinch of salt

2 cups all-purpose flour

1 cup chopped nuts

1 teaspoon vanilla extract

Cut gumdrops in pieces and lightly flour. Beat eggs. Add sugar, salt, flour, nuts and vanilla. Mix well. Bake in an 8-inch square pan at 350 degrees for 1 hour. Cut into squares. Makes 30.

Yvonne E. Constantino, Texas

NUT DIAMOND COOKIES

CRUST:

    2 sticks butter, softened
    ¾ cup sugar
    1 large egg
    1 teaspoon vanilla extract
    ¼ teaspoon salt
    3 cups all-purpose flour

TOPPING:

    1 stick butter, cut up
    1½ cups packed light brown sugar
    ⅔ cup honey
    ½ cup heavy cream
    3 cups chopped nuts (can use mixed nuts)

Preheat oven to 350 degrees. Line a 15 x 10 x 1-inch jelly roll pan with foil, extending over the sides.

FOR TOPPING: Melt butter and sugar together. Remove from heat. Add honey and heavy cream. When blended, add chopped pecans. Set aside.

FOR CRUST: In a large bowl, beat butter, sugar, egg, vanilla and salt for 2 minutes. Beat in flour. With floured hands, press dough into prepared pan. Pour topping over dough. Bake in preheated oven for 25 minutes until bubbly. Let cool in pan. Lift cookie from pan. Cut 6 lengthwise strips 1 ½ inches wide. To make diamond shape, cut diagonally at 2-inch intervals. Makes 4 ½ dozen.

Jeri-Lynn Sandusky, Utah

HELEN McKERN'S OVERNIGHT COOKIES

2 cups packed brown sugar

1 cup butter

3 eggs

1 teaspoon vanilla extract

1 teaspoon cream of tartar

1½ teaspoons baking soda

Pinch of salt

3–4 cups all-purpose flour (enough to make a stiff dough)

½ cup black walnuts

Cream together sugar and butter. Add eggs and vanilla. Add dry ingredients and nuts. Form into a roll and refrigerate overnight. Slice and bake at 375 degrees for 15 minutes.

Henry Graalfs
Jan Dargin, Iowa

These are great to make ahead and have on hand for a quick snack for company.

BROWN SUGAR COOKIES

⅔ cup shortening

⅔ cup butter or margarine, softened

1 cup granulated sugar

1 cup packed brown sugar

2 eggs

2 teaspoons vanilla extract

3¼ cups all-purpose flour

1 teaspoon baking soda

1 teaspoon salt

Mix shortening, butter, sugars, eggs and vanilla thoroughly. Stir in remaining ingredients. Turn dough onto a lightly floured board. Lightly flour your hands and then shape dough into a ball, pressing to make dough compact. Cut dough in half. Shape each half into a roll that is 2 inches in diameter and about 8 inches long. Roll dough onto plastic wrap; wrap and twist ends tightly. Dough can be refrigerated up to 1 month of frozen up to 3 months.

Heat oven to 375 degrees. Cut roll into ¼-inch slices. It isn't necessary to thaw frozen dough before slicing. Place cookies about 2 inches apart on an ungreased baking sheet. Bake for 9 to 11 minutes. Immediately remove cookies from baking sheet onto wire rack. Makes 5½ dozen cookies.

VARIATIONS:

CHOCOLATE CHIP: Add 1 cup mini semi-sweet chocolate chips and 1 cup chopped nuts with the flour.

OATMEAL-COCONUT: Reduce flour to 2¾ cups. Add 1 cup flaked coconut and 1 cup quick-cooking oats with the flour.

PEANUT BUTTER: Add 1 cup creamy or chunky peanut butter with the shortening.

CHOCOLATE-NUT: Add 1 cup chopped nuts and ½ cup cocoa powder with the flour.

FRUIT SLICES: Add 1 cup whole candied cherries, ½ cup chopped nuts and ½ cup chopped mixed candied fruit with the flour.

Yvonne E. Constantino, Texas

KANSAS COOKIES

1 cup margarine, softened

1 cup packed brown sugar

1 cup granulated sugar

2 eggs

1 teaspoon vanilla extract

1¾ cups all-purpose flour

1 teaspoon baking soda

3 cups rolled oats

1 cup salted, shelled, sunflower seeds

Preheat oven to 350 degrees. Cream margarine and sugars. Beat in eggs and vanilla. Stir in flour, baking soda and oats. Add sunflower seeds. Mix well. Drop by teaspoons onto an ungreased cookie sheet. Bake in preheated oven for 10 minutes. Cool on racks.

Carol Ryan, Kansas

RANGER COOKIES

1 cup solid vegetable shortening or margarine

1 cup granulated sugar

1 cup packed brown sugar

2 eggs

1 teaspoon vanilla extract

Mix all the above ingredients together. Then, add the following:

2 cups all-purpose flour

1 teaspoon baking soda

1 teaspoon baking powder

½ teaspoon salt (omit if using margarine)

Stir in:

2 cups quick oats

2 cups Rick Krispies®

1 cup coconut

Drop by spoonful onto cookie sheet and bake for 10 minutes in preheated oven.

Martha Trowbridge, Illinois

NEIMAN MARCUS COOKIES

Recipe may be halved

5 cups blended oatmeal

2 cups butter

2 cups packed brown sugar

2 cups sugar

4 eggs

2 teaspoons vanilla extract

4 cups all-purpose flour

1 teaspoon salt

2 teaspoons baking powder

2 teaspoons baking soda

2 (12-ounce) bags chocolate chips

1 (8-ounce) Hershey Bar, grated

3 cups chopped nuts, your choice

Preheat oven to 375 degrees. Measure oatmeal and blend in a blender to fine powder. Set aside. Cream butter and sugars. Add eggs and vanilla. Mix with flour, oatmeal, salt, baking powder and soda. Add chocolate chips, Hershey Bar, and nuts. Roll into balls and place two inches apart on a cookie sheet. Bake for 10 minutes in preheated oven. Makes 112 cookies.

Mary Q. Smith, Texas
Betty Wilkins, California

JUMBO PEANUT BUTTER OATMEAL COOKIES

2⅔ cups rolled oats

1½ cups all-purpose flour

2–3 teaspoons grated orange peel

1 teaspoon baking soda

1 teaspoon baking powder

¾ teaspoon salt

1¼ sticks butter

½ cup chunky peanut butter

⅔ cup packed brown sugar

1⅓ cups granulated sugar

2 eggs (or egg product)

1 teaspoon vanilla extract

Preheat oven to 325 degrees. Spread oats on a baking sheet. Toast until pale golden brown — about 10 to 12 minutes. Set aside and cool. Increase oven temperature to 350 degrees. In a medium bowl, whisk flour, orange peel, baking soda, baking powder and salt to blend. In a large bowl, cream butter and peanut butter until light. Beat in brown sugar. Beat in granulated sugar. Beat in eggs, one at a time. Add vanilla. Fold in flour mixture. Gently fold in oats.

Drop batter onto baking sheets by mounded spoonful (or scoop) about 3 inches apart. Bake until cookies are barely golden brown around the edges — about 10 to 12 minutes. Cool on baking sheet about 5 minutes. Transfer to racks and cool. To maintain softness, store cookies in airtight container with a slice of two of bread. These cookies can be frozen if tightly wrapped. Enjoy!

VARIATIONS: Margarine would make this cookie puffier. Butter makes it flatter and crisper. Smooth peanut butter changes the texture, but works well. To make it more peanuty — add some ground peanuts. Substitute orange extract for the vanilla, if you don't have any orange peel. Low or reduced fat peanut butter does not work well. Toasting the oats will work with other oatmeal cookie recipes as well as this one. The toasted oats impart a richer, more earthy flavor.

Judy Krohn, Texas

PEANUT BLOSSOMS

Sift together and set aside:

    1¾ cups all-purpose flour

    1 teaspoon baking powder

    ½ teaspoon salt

Cream:

    ½ cup solid vegetable shortening

    ½ cup peanut butter

Add:

    ½ cup granulated sugar

    ½ cup packed brown sugar

Blend in:

    1 egg, unbeaten

    1 teaspoon vanilla extract

Add dry ingredients and mix thoroughly. Shape by rounded spoonfuls into balls. Roll in granulated sugar. Place on greased baking sheets. Bake at 325 degrees for 10 minutes. Top each baked cookie with a solid milk chocolate candy kiss — pressing down firmly so cookies crack around edges. Return to oven and bake 2 minutes longer.

Phyllis Rademacher, Iowa

EASY PEANUT BUTTER COOKIES

    1 cup peanut butter, chunky or creamy

    1 cup light or dark brown sugar

    1 egg, slightly beaten

    1 (6-ounce) package semi-sweet chocolate chips

Preheat oven to 350 degrees. Mix all ingredients. Drop dough by spoonful onto cookie sheet. Bake in preheated oven for about 10 minutes. Enjoy!

Joan Miller, Texas

TASTIEST AND EASIEST PEANUT BUTTER COOKIES

Mix together:
1 cup sugar
1 egg
1 cup peanut butter.

Wet hands and roll into walnut-sized balls. Place
on ungreased cookie sheet. Press with fork and
bake for 8 to 10 minutes in a 350 degree oven.

Betty Ann Sheffloe, Nebraska

PERSIMMON COOKIES BY MIG BEELARD

Mig was my best friend ever. She died at the age of 97. I loved her!

1 cup persimmon pulp

1 cup sugar

1 egg

1 cup salad oil

1 teaspoon baking soda

½ teaspoon baking powder

½ teaspoon salt

½ teaspoon nutmeg

½ teaspoon cloves

½ teaspoon cinnamon

In a large bowl, combine all ingredients. Then add, in the
order listed:

2 cups sifted all-purpose flour

1 cup chopped nuts

1 cup raisins

Mix well. Drop by teaspoon on a greased cookie sheet. Bake
at 350 degrees for 12 minutes.

Ann L. Anderson, Pennsylvania

CHOCOLATE RUM BALLS

2 cups vanilla wafer crumbs (crush cookies with a
   rolling pin)

2 cups confectioners' sugar

4 tablespoons cocoa powder

6 tablespoons white corn syrup

2 cups finely chopped nuts

¼ to ⅓ cup rum

Mix above in a bowl. Roll into 1½-inch balls. And roll in
confectioners' sugar. No cooking.

The entire box of vanilla wafers is exactly what is
needed to make 1½ batches of 4½ to 5 dozen large balls

Lou Magel, Michigan

SNICKERDOODLES

½ cup butter or margarine, softened

½ cup solid vegetable shortening

1½ cups sugar

2 eggs

2¾ cups all-purpose flour

2 teaspoons cream of tartar

1 teaspoon baking soda

¼ teaspoon salt

2 tablespoons sugar

2 tablespoons cinnamon

Preheat oven to 400 degrees. In a large bowl, combine
margarine, shortening, sugar and eggs. Blend in flour,
cream of tartar, soda and salt. In a separate bowl, combine
sugar and cinnamon. Set aside. Shape dough by rounded
teaspoons into balls. Roll each ball in the sugar mixture.
Place two inches apart on an ungreased cookie sheet. Bake
in preheated oven for 8 to 10 minutes. Immediately remove
from cookie sheet and cool on rack. Makes 6 dozen.

Jeri-Lynn Sandusky, Utah

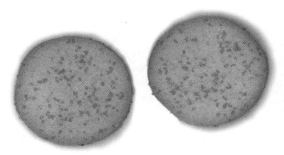

SUGAR COOKIES

½ cup shortening

½ cup margarine or butter

1 teaspoon vanilla extract

1½ cups sugar

2 eggs

2⅔ cup all-purpose flour

2 teaspoons cream of tartar

½ teaspoon baking soda

⅛ teaspoon salt

Preheat oven to 400 degrees. In a large bowl, combine short-ening and butter until soft. Add vanilla, sugar and eggs and mix well. Sift remaining ingredients together and stir into margarine mixture, a little at a time. Roll dough into small balls. Dip top of cookie into a mixture of 2 table-spoons sugar and 2 teaspoon cinnamon. Place cookies 2 inches apart on an ungreased cookie sheet. Bake 8 to 10 minutes in a preheated oven, until lightly browned but still soft. Cookies will puff and then flatten out. Cool on racks. Makes 5 dozen.

Betty Wilkins, California

FORGOTTEN COOKIES

2 egg whites

¾ cup sugar

1 (6-ounce) package miniature chocolate chips

Preheat oven to 375 degrees. With an electric mixer, beat egg whites until soft peaks form. Slowly add sugar. Beat until stiff. Fold in chocolate chips.

Drop by teaspoons onto cookie sheets that have been lightly coated with non-stick cooking spray. Cookies can be placed close together on the sheet because they don't expand while baking. Place cookie sheets in oven and turn off the heat. Leave in the oven for two hours. Makes 2½ dozen.

Diane Watkins, Wisconsin

At holiday time, these cookies can be decorated with different types of sprinkles before baking. This is a recipe I've had for many years.

BUTTERFINGER™ COOKIES

½ cup butter, softened

¾ cup sugar

⅔ cup packed brown sugar

2 egg whites

1¼ cup chunky peanut butter

1½ teaspoons vanilla extract

1 cup all-purpose flour

½ teaspoon baking soda

¼ teaspoon salt

5 (2.1-ounce) Butterfinger™ candy bars, chopped

Preheat oven to 350 degrees. In a large bowl, cream butter and sugars. Add egg whites; beat well. Blend in peanut butter and vanilla. Combine flour, baking soda and salt. Add to creamed mixture and mix well. Stir in chopped candy bars. Shape into 1½-inch balls, and place on greased cookie sheets. Bake in preheated oven for 10 to 12 minutes, or until golden brown. Cool on wire racks. Makes 4 dozen.

Becky Van Vranken, Washington, DC

GRAHAM CRACKER TOFFEE

1 cup butter

1 cup margarine

½ cup sugar

48 graham crackers

¼ cup finely chopped pecans

Preheat oven to 350 degrees. Place crackers on a cookie sheet (with sides). Boil butter, margarine and sugar for 2 minutes. Add nuts and mix well. Pour hot mixture over crackers. Be sure to cover all of the crackers with syrup mixture. Bake in preheated oven for 8 to 11 minutes. Cool for 1 minute on the cookie sheet, then transfer to wire racks to cool. Makes 48.

Anna Laura (Loa) Doane, Indiana

COCONUT CRANBERRY CHEWS

About 1½ cups butter or margarine, room temperature

2 cups sugar

1 tablespoon grated orange peel

2 teaspoons vanilla extract

3¼ cups all-purpose flour

1 teaspoon baking powder

¼ teaspoon salt

1½ cups dried cranberries

1½ cups sweetened, flaked, dried coconut

Preheat oven to 350 degrees. Butter 12 x 15-inch cookie sheets and set aside. In a large bowl, use an electric mixer on medium speed to combine butter, sugar, orange peel and vanilla until smooth. In a separate bowl, combine flour, baking powder and salt. Add to butter mixture, then beat on low speed until dough comes together (about 5 minutes). Add cranberries and coconut. Shape dough into 1-inch balls and place about 2 inches apart on prepared cookie sheets. Bake for 8 to 11 minutes in preheated oven. A shorter baking time gives you chewy cookies and a long baking time gives you crispy cookies. Cool on cookie sheet for 5 minutes, then cool on wire racks.

Betty Wilkins, California

ALMOND BARK COOKIES

Very popular!

1 package chocolate almond bark

1 cup chunky peanut butter

4 cups Rice Krispies™

2 cups mini marshmallows

1 teaspoon vanilla extract

Melt almond bark in the top of a double boiler. Add remaining ingredients. Drop by spoonful onto waxed paper.

Joyce Latta, Texas

BENA GAGLIANO'S ITALIAN COOKIES

We make these cookies every Christmas. My grandmother worked hard at this recipe and I watched carefully to write down the correct amounts, as she had no written recipes.

1 cup solid vegetable shortening

1½ cups sugar

3 eggs

2 teaspoons vanilla extract

¾ cup milk

7 cups all-purpose flour

1 teaspoon cocoa powder

1 teaspoon cloves*

7 teaspoons baking powder

1 teaspoon cinnamon*

1 cup finely chopped nuts

GLAZE:

1 cup confectioners' sugar

2 tablespoons milk

Preheat oven to 350 degrees. Cream shortening and sugar until light and fluffy. Beat in eggs. Add vanilla and milk. Sift dry ingredients (flour, cocoa, cloves, baking powder and cinnamon) and add to creamed mixture. Mix well. Roll into small balls. Place on ungreased cookie sheet and bake in preheated oven for 15 to 20 minutes. Mix confectioners' sugar with milk and pour over cookies, turning to coat.

*May substitute 2 teaspoons of clove instead of cloves and cinnamon

Bernadine R. Levy, Colorado

THING-A-MA-JIGS

2 eggs, Beaten

1 cup sugar

¼ cup butter

8-ounce package of dates

Cook until thick. Add:

2 ½ cups Rice Krispies

1 cup chopped nuts

Form into small balls and roll in coconut.

Joyce Latta, Texas

CINNAMON CHEESE ROLL UPS

This freezes well before baking.

2 sticks butter

1½ cups sugar

2 teaspoons cinnamon (add a little more if you want)

1 (8-ounce) package cream cheese, softened

1 egg

⅓ cup sugar

1½ loaves thin sandwich bread

Preheat oven to 350 degrees. Melt butter in a small pie plate. Combine sugar and cinnamon in another pie plate. Use an electric mixer to combine cream cheese, egg, and sugar together until creamy. Remove crust from bread. Spread each slice of bread with cream cheese mixture. Roll jelly-roll style, then dip in butter and roll in cinnamon/sugar mixture. Bake for 18-20 minutes in preheated oven.

Bev Tackett, Missouri

CATHEDRAL COOKIES

Melt in top of a double boiler:

12 ounces milk chocolate chips

6 ounces of semi-sweet chocolate chips

4 tablespoons margarine

Add:

1 cup chopped pecans

2 beaten eggs

10-ounce bag of colored marshmallows.

Sprinkle coconut on waxed paper and pour mixture over coconut. Roll into a log. Freeze and slice as needed.

Joyce Latta, Texas

LEMON DREAM MERINGUES

MERINGUE

4 egg whites

2 teaspoons lemon juice

½ teaspoon cream of tartar

1⅓ cups sugar

1½ cups whipping cream

LEMON FILLING

½ cup butter

1 teaspoon grated lemon peel

½ cup lemon juice

⅛ teaspoon salt

1½ cups sugar

3 egg yolks, beaten

3 whole eggs, beaten

½ cup whipping cream

To Make Individual Meringues: Let egg whites stand at room temperature in a large mixing bowl for about 30 minutes. Meanwhile line a baking sheet with parchment paper. Using a pencil, draw eight 3-inch circles about 1 inch apart on the parchment paper. Turn paper pencil side down on baking sheet; set aside. Preheat oven to 300 degrees.

Add lemon juice and cream of tartar to egg whites. Beat with an electric mixer set on medium speed until soft peaks form (tips curl). Add sugar, 1 tablespoon at a time, beating on high speed about 7 minutes or until very stiff peaks form (tips stand straight) and sugar is almost dissolved.

You can either use a pastry decorator to make a base in the circles and build up sides or you can use the back of a large spoon to spread meringue over the bottom of circles, building up sides to form shells.

Bake 30 minutes. Turn off oven. Let meringues dry in oven, with door closed, at least 1 hour. Remove from paper. Place in an airtight container. Store in a cool, dry place for up to 1 week. At least 5 hours before serving (can be done the night before) whip cream with confectioners' sugar and vanilla to taste. Spread it around the sides and bottom of the shells, saving some for the top.

Spoon some of the lemon filling into each meringue and put a dab of sweetened whipped cream on top. Garnish with a lemon curl.

To make lemon filling: In a medium saucepan, melt butter; add lemon peel, lemon juice, salt and sugar. Stir in beaten egg yolks and whole eggs. Cook over very low heat, beating constantly with a whisk, until mixture is shiny and thick. Cool. Whip cream. Fold whipped cream into lemon mixture.

Pat Fenno, Iowa

BISCOTTI

Cut butter into flour mixture.

2¼ cups unsifted flour

1 cup sugar

½ teaspoon baking powder

½ teaspoon salt

6 tablespoons butter, cut into small pieces

Add, one at a time:

2 large eggs

Then Add:

1 teaspoon vanilla extract

1 cup unsalted, coarsely chopped pistachios

Mix well. Divide dough in half and shape each half into a 12 x 2-inch log. Cover with plastic wrap and refrigerate for 30 minutes.

Lightly grease baking sheets and set aside. Preheat oven to 375 degrees. Transfer logs to cutting board. Cut crosswise, diagonally into ½ inch thick slices. Place slices in a single layer on prepared baking sheet. Bake for 20–25 minutes, turning once, until light golden brown on both sides. Cool completely on wire racks. Store in airtight container.

VARIATIONS:

½ cup coarsely chopped maraschino cherries, drained

½ cup dried cranberries

Jean Krest, Colorado

CHOCOLATE BROWNIE BISCOTTI

2½ cups all-purpose flour

¾ cup unsweetened cocoa powder

1½ cups sugar

2 teaspoon baking powder

½ teaspoon baking soda

½ teaspoon salt

½ cup butter or margarine, melted

5 large eggs

2 teaspoons vanilla extract

1 tablespoon water

1 cup almonds, toasted and coarsely chopped

4 ounces semi-sweet chocolate, coarsely chopped

Preheat oven to 325 degrees. In a medium bowl, mix flour, cocoa powder, sugar, baking powder, baking soda and salt. Set aside. In a large bowl, with mixer on medium speed, beat butter, eggs and vanilla until mixed. Reduce speed to low; gradually add flour mixture and beat until blended. With floured hands, knead in almonds and chocolate until combined. Divide dough in half. On ungreased cookie sheet, shape each half into 12 x 3-inch log, and place about 3 inches apart. Bake for 30 minutes. Cool on wire rack for 15 minutes. Place logs on cutting board. With serrated knife, cut each log crosswise.

CRANBERRY NUT BISCOTTI

1⅓ cups hazelnuts

3¼ cups all-purpose flour

2 cups sugar

1 teaspoon baking powder

½ teaspoon salt

5 large eggs

2 teaspoons vanilla extract

½ cup dried cranberries or currants

Preheat oven to 350 degrees. Toast nuts about 20 minutes. Wrap nuts in a clean cloth towel, roll back and forth to remove skins; coarsely chop. Grease and flour 2 large cookie sheets. Set aside. In a large bowl, combine flour, sugar, baking powder and salt. In a small bowl, with fork or whisk, beat 4 whole eggs and 1 egg yolk, reserving 1 egg white, vanilla, and water. Pour egg mixture into flour mixture; stir with wooden spoon. Use hands to knead dough together. Dough will be very stiff. Knead in nuts and berries. Divide dough into 4 equal pieces. On lightly floured surface, with floured hands, roll into 11 x 2-inch logs. Place logs about four inches apart on each cookie sheet. Beat reserved egg white and brush on top. Bake 35 to 40 minutes, until toothpick inserted comes out clean. Cool 10 minutes on wire rack. Cut diagonally and bake about 10 to 15 minutes longer. Store in tightly covered container. Makes 4½ dozen biscotti.

APPLE BROWNIES

   ½ cup margarine, melted

   1 cup sugar

   1 egg

   3 medium unpeeled apples, cored and diced

   ½ cup coarsely chopped walnuts or pecans

   1 cup all-purpose flour

   ½ teaspoon baking powder

   ½ teaspoon baking soda

   ½ teaspoon salt

   1 teaspoon cinnamon

Preheat oven to 350 degrees. Cream margarine and sugar. Add egg, beating well. Stir in apples and nuts. Combine dry ingredients in a separate bowl and add to apple mixture. Coat a 9-inch square pan with non-stick cooking spray. Pour batter into prepared pan. Bake for 45 to 50 minutes in preheated oven. Cool and cut into squares.

   Doris Feldman, Arizona

BOURBON BROWNIES

¾ cup all-purpose flour

1 teaspoon baking soda

¼ teaspoon salt

½ cup sugar

⅓ cup margarine

2 tablespoons water

1 cup chocolate chips

1 teaspoon vanilla extract

2 eggs

1½ cups chopped pecans or walnut pieces

¼ cup bourbon

White Bourbon Frosting (see below)

1 cup chocolate chips, melted

Preheat oven to 325 degrees. Sift flour, baking soda and salt into a bowl. Set aside. Combine sugar, margarine and water in a saucepan. Bring to a boil over low heat, stirring constantly. Remove from heat. Add 1 cup chocolate chips and vanilla and stir until smooth. Add eggs and beat well. Add chocolate mixture to flour mixture and mix well. Stir in walnuts or pecans. Spoon batter into a greased, 9-inch baking pan. Bake in preheated oven for 30 to 35 minutes or until edges pull back from the side of the pan. Remove from oven and pierce holes in the brownies using wooden toothpicks. Pour bourbon over the top. Let stand until cool. Spread White Bourbon Frosting over brownies. Spread melted chocolate chips over top to glaze. Yield: 12 servings.

WHITE BOURBON FROSTING

½ stick butter, softened

2 cups confectioners' sugar

2 tablespoons bourbon

1 tablespoon water

Beat all ingredients together until smooth.

Lois Patterson, Wisconsin

BROWNIES WITHOUT SATURATED FAT OR SALT

6 tablespoons cocoa powder (use 7 if you are addicted to chocolate)

2 cups sugar

½ cup canola oil

2 teaspoons vanilla extract

4 jumbo egg whites

1 cup unbleached flour

½ cup frozen pecans

Preheat oven to 350 degrees. Whisk together the cocoa and sugar until smoothly mixed. Add canola oil and vanilla and mix thoroughly with a spoon. Add egg whites and beat until incorporated into mixture. Add flour and mix until all flour disappears. Pour batter into a 13 x 9-inch baking dish that has been lightly coated with peanut or olive oil. Place frozen pecans on top of batter, so they will toast while the brownies are baking. Bake in preheated oven for 25 minutes or until top springs back. This will be a chewy brownie.

SPONGE CAKE BROWNIES: For a more sponge-cake like brownie, use two whole jumbo eggs and 4 egg whites. Then proceed as directed above.

OPTIONAL CHOCOLATE FROSTING: Place 3 cups of icing sugar and 2 tablespoons of cocoa in a mixing bowl. Whisk until smooth and add 2 teaspoons vanilla extract and enough milk to make a mixture that will drizzle off the spoon. The mixture can be beaten by hand with a spoon or with a mixer. When brownies come out of the oven, drizzle over the top while they are still warm.

Marilyn Sietsema, Illinois

CHOCOLATE CHIP BROWNIES

2 (8-ounce) packages cream cheese

3 eggs

1 teaspoon vanilla extract

¾ cup sugar

2 packages slice and bake chocolate chip cookies

Preheat oven to 350 degrees. Use a mixer and blend cream cheese, eggs, vanilla and sugar. It will be lumpy. Set aside. Slice one package of cookie dough and place in bottom of a 13 x 9-inch pan. Pour cream cheese mixture over cookies. Slice other package of cookies and place on top of cream cheese mixture. Bake for 45 minutes in preheated oven.

Can sprinkle with confectioners' sugar while still warm, if desired.

Bev Tackett, Missouri

EASY BROWNIES

2 cans Eagle brand condensed milk

1 (12-ounce) package semi-sweet chocolate chips

1 box graham cracker crumbs

Mix milk and crumbs together thoroughly. Add chips and mix well. Mixture will be thick and hard to stir. Heavily coat (with margarine and non-stick vegetable spray) a 9-inch square metal baking pan. Spoon mixture into pan and press to evenly distribute. Bake at 350 degrees for 30 to 35 minutes. Cool completely before cutting into squares.

These brownies freeze well, can be mailed easily and appeal to everyone. Had to double the recipe for family camping trips, to feed hungry hikers and tired fishermen.

Mary Lee Whipple, Texas

MAPLE BROWNIES

½ cup margarine, melted

1 ½ cups packed brown sugar

1 ½ teaspoons maple flavoring

2 eggs

1 ½ cups all-purpose flour

1 teaspoon baking powder

1 cup chopped walnuts (optional)

Combine margarine, brown sugar and maple flavoring, mixing well. Add eggs, one at a time, beating after each addition. Add flour, baking powder and walnuts, mixing well. Bake in a greased 9-inch square pan at 350 degrees for 30 minutes. Dust with confectioners' sugar when cool. Recipe can be doubled.

Betty Kuckes, Wisconsin

NEW YORK SLICES

½ cup butter

¼ cup granulated sugar

3 tablespoons cocoa powder

1 egg, beaten

1 teaspoon vanilla extract

2 cups graham cracker crumbs

1 cup coconut

½ cup chopped nuts

¼ cup butter

2 cups confectioners' sugar

2 tablespoons custard powder

2 tablespoons milk

2 squares semi-sweet chocolate

1 teaspoon butter

Heat butter, granulated sugar and cocoa in the top of a double boiler; stirring until smooth. Add egg and vanilla. Beat lightly. Remove from heat and add graham cracker crumbs, coconuts and chopped nuts. Spread mixture in an 8-inch square pan. Place in refrigerator to set. Cream butter. Stir in confectioners' sugar, custard powder and milk. Spread over first mixture. Return to refrigerator to set. Melt semi-sweet chocolate and 1 teaspoon butter together in top of double boiler. Spread thinly on top. Refrigerate 30 minutes. Cut into 30 rectangles. Freezes well.

Pat Fenno, Iowa

LENY'S APRICOT SQUARES

I have made these so often and they are always very popular at any occasion. Bon Appetit!

¾ cup dried apricots

¼ cup warm water

1 stick butter

1⅓ cups flour, divided

¼ cup confectioners' sugar

½ cup chopped nuts

1 cup packed brown sugar

¾ teaspoon baking powder

2 eggs

1 teaspoon vanilla extract

Add warm water to apricots. Set aside.

Preheat oven to 325 degrees. Place steel blade in food processor. Cut butter into 8 slices. Place butter, 1 cup of the flour and confectioners' sugar in machine. Pulse 8 times, just to blend. Pat dough evenly into an 8-inch square glass pan. Bake 25 minutes at 325 degrees. Do not wash bowl.

Combine remaining ⅓ cup flour with nuts. Set aside.

Still using steel blade, add brown sugar, apricots, baking powder, eggs, and vanilla. Pulse 5 times to see if apricots are cut evenly. Add flour and nut mixture and pulse 3 times. Pour over baked crust, then bake at 325 degrees for 35 minutes. Sprinkle with confectioners' sugar and cut into squares.

Leny Young, Ohio

TOFFEE SQUARES (Phyllis Rademacher, Iowa)

1 cup butter, softened

1 cup packed brown sugar

1 egg yolk

1 teaspoon vanilla extract

2 cups all-purpose flour, sifted

½ pound milk chocolate

1 cup chopped nuts

Cream butter and sugar until light. Add beaten egg yolk, vanilla, and flour. Spread thinly and smoothly in an 8-inch square pan. Bake in a preheated 350 degree oven for 10-15 minutes. Melt chocolate and spread over cookie surface while warm. Sprinkle with nuts and cut into squares.

BROWN SUGAR BARS

½ cup oil

1¾ cups packed brown sugar

2 eggs

1½ teaspoons vanilla extract

1 teaspoon salt

1½ cups all-purpose flour

2 teaspoons baking powder

½ cup chopped nuts

Preheat oven to 350 degrees. Grease and flour a 13 x 9-inch baking pan and set aside. Combine all ingredients and pour batter into pan. Bake for 20 to 25 minutes. Cool and cut into squares.

Betty Ann Sheffloe, Nebraska

LEMON BARS

Sift flour and sugar. Cut in butter until crumbly. Pat this mixture into a greased 13 x 9-inch pan. Bake 20 minutes at 350 degrees.

1½ cups all-purpose flour

⅔ cups confectioners' sugar

1 cup butter

While crust is baking, beat together until light and fluffy:

4 extra large or jumbo eggs

2 cups sugar

½ teaspoon baking powder mixed with ¼ cup all-purpose flour

½ cup lemon juice

Dash of salt

Pour mixture over baked crust. Bake for 22 to 25 minutes. Edges will begin to brown. Cool. Cut into one-inch squares.

Cordelia L. Razek, Louisiana

OAT BARS

- 2 sticks margarine or butter
- ½ cup packed brown sugar
- 1 (17.4-ounce) package cinnamon swirl bread and coffee cake mix
- ¼ cup orange juice
- 1 egg
- 1 teaspoon vanilla extract
- 1½ cups uncooked quick cooking Quaker Oats
- ½ cup coarsely chopped pistachios (walnuts or pecans can be substituted)
- ½ to ¾ cup dried cranberries

Preheat oven to 375 degrees. Spray a 13 x 9-inch pan with non-stick cooking spray.

In a large bowl, using an electric mixer, beat butter and sugar on medium speed until creamy. Add quick bread mix and the clear packet of cinnamon swirl (reserve foil glaze packet for later use), orange juice, egg and vanilla. Beat just until blended. Add oats, nuts and cranberries. Mix at low speed just until combined. Spread evenly into prepared pan.

Bake for 30 to 35 minutes or until edges are golden brown and wooden tooth pick inserted in center comes out with a few moist crumbs sticking to it. Cool completely in pan on wire rack.

Knead reserved foil packet from mix about 10 times, cut tip off one corner of packet; squeeze glaze decoratively over cookies in pan. Cut into squares or bars. Makes 2 dozen.

Janice Konetchy, Massachusetts

DATE OATMEAL BARS

½ cup sugar

1 package dates

½ cup water

½ pound butter

½ teaspoon salt

1 cup packed brown sugar

½ teaspoon baking soda

½ teaspoon baking powder

1½ cups oatmeal

1½ cups flour

Combine sugar, dates and water in a saucepan and cook to a thick paste. Cool. Mix butter, salt, brown sugar, baking soda, baking powder, oatmeal and flour and press half of the mixture in the bottom of a 13 x 9-inch pan. Spread date filling over batter, press remaining crumble mixture over dates. Bake at 275 degrees for 40 to 45 minutes. Cool and cut into 2-inch squares.

Lou Magel, Michigan

DANISH PASTRY APPLE BARS

Combine 2-1/2 cups flour and 1 teaspoon salt. Cut in 1 cup shortening. Beat 1 egg yolk (reserving the white) in a measuring cup and add enough milk to make 2/3 cup liquid. Mix well and stir into flour mixture.

On a floured surface, roll half the dough into a 17 x 12-inch rectangle. Fit into and up sides of 15 x 11 x 2-inch jelly roll pan. Sprinkle with 1 cup cornflakes.

Peel and slice 8 cups of apples. Spread over cornflakes.

Sprinkle 1 cup sugar and 1 teaspoon cinnamon over apples and cover with remaining dough that has been rolled out into a rectangle. Seal edges and cut slits in top.

Beat egg white until frothy, brush on top of crust. Bake at 350 degrees for 50 minutes.

If desired, frost with 1 cup sifted confectioners' sugar and 3-4 teaspoons milk and drizzle over warm pastry.

Betty Ann Sheffloe, Nebraska

This is a sweet dessert and usually one piece is plenty to satisfy anyone's sweet tooth.

PECAN SQUARES

2 cups all-purpose flour

¼ teaspoon salt

¼ cup sugar

1 cup butter or margarine

Combine and spread into a 15 x 11-inch jelly roll pan, shaping up the sides.

FILLING:

1½ cups packed brown sugar

½ cup sugar

2 tablespoons all-purpose flour

½ teaspoon salt

2 eggs, beaten

¾ cup evaporated milk

¼ teaspoon vanilla extract

2½ cups chopped pecans

Pour filling into the crust and bake at 350 degrees for 30 to 35 minutes. Cut into squares and serve with whipped topping or whipped cream. Makes 18.

Mary Baker, Washington

PEANUT BUTTER GRANOLA BARS

Mix and bring to a boil:

2 cups sugar

1 1/3 cups corn syrup

Remove from heat and add:

2 cups peanut butter

3 tablespoons vanilla extract

Mix well and pour over:

8 cups rolled oats combined with 1 cup coconut

Mix well. Press into waxed paper lined jelly roll pan. May add nuts, dried fruit. Let set. Cut into squares.

Jan Whittaker, California

PUMPKIN BARS

Mix the following ingredients and set aside:

> 4 eggs
>
> 2 cups sugar
>
> 1 cup vegetable oil
>
> 1 (15-ounce) can pumpkin

Combine:

> 2 cups flour
>
> 2 teaspoons baking powder
>
> 1 teaspoon baking soda
>
> ½ teaspoon salt
>
> 2 teaspoons cinnamon
>
> ½ teaspoon ginger
>
> ½ teaspoon cloves
>
> ½ teaspoon nutmeg

Add to pumpkin mixture. Pour into a greased and floured 18 x 12 x 1-inch pan. Bake at 350 degrees for 25-30 minutes. Cool completely and frost. Cut and serve.

FROSTING:

> 1 (6-ounce) package cream cheese
>
> ¾ stick margarine
>
> 1 teaspoon vanilla extract
>
> 1 tablespoon milk

Combine and mix until mixture reaches spreading consistency. Frost cooled bars.

Adrienne Padfield, Texas

FROSTED PUMPKIN BARS

4 eggs

1⅔ cups sugar

1 cup oil

1 (16-ounce) can pumpkin

2 cups all-purpose flour

2 teaspoons baking powder

2 teaspoons cinnamon

1 teaspoon salt

1 teaspoon baking soda

Cream Cheese Frosting (see below)

Preheat oven to 350 degrees. Beat eggs, sugar, oil and pumpkin until light and fluffy. Add flour, baking powder, cinnamon, salt and baking soda, mixing thoroughly. Spread batter in an ungreased 15 x 10-inch jelly roll pan. Bake for 25 to 30 minutes. Cool completely before frosting.

CREAM CHEESE FROSTING

1 (3-ounce) package cream cheese, softened

½ cup margarine

1 teaspoon vanilla extract

2 cups confectioners' sugar

Combine cream cheese and margarine, and cream until fluffy. Add vanilla and confectioners' sugar. Mix until smooth. Frost cooled lemon bars. Add a few chopped nuts on top.

Betty Kuckes, Wisconsin

JUDY'S PUMPKIN BARS

  2 eggs

  1⅔ cups sugar

  1 cup vegetable oil

  1 (16-ounce) can pumpkin

  2 teaspoons baking powder

  1 teaspoon salt

  2 cups all-purpose flour, sifted

  2 teaspoons cinnamon

  1 teaspoon baking soda

  Cream Cheese Frosting (see recipe on opposite page)

Cream eggs, sugar, oil and pumpkin. Add dry ingredients until well blended. Spread mixture in a greased jelly roll pan. Bake at 350 degrees for 25 to 30 minutes. Cool completely before frosting

  Judy Dashiell, Minnesota

HOLIDAY GIFT GRANOLA

  Cooking oil spray

  ½ cup oil

  ½ cup pure maple syrup

  1½ cups lightly packed light brown sugar

  6 cups quick-cooking or old-fashioned oats

  1 cup chopped walnuts

  1 cup wheat germ

  1 cup sweetened, shredded coconut

  1 cup raisins

  1 cup sweetened dried cranberries or dried cherries

Place the oven racks in center positions. Preheat oven to 350 degrees. Spray two 11 x 7-inch jelly roll pans with cooking oil spray. Set aside.

  In a 1-quart microwave safe dish, combine the oil, maple syrup, and brown sugar. Microwave uncovered on HIGH for 3 minutes, or until sugar starts to melt. Remove from microwave and whisk until any limps disappear.

  In a 3-quart or larger bowl, combine oats, walnuts, wheat germ and coconut. Toss to mix well. Pour syrup mixture over oat mixture and stir until well mixed. Spread evenly onto prepared jellyroll pans. Place a pan on each oven rack for 10 minutes, taking note of which pan was on top rack. Remove the pans from the oven and stir granola. Return pans to oven, rotating to the opposite rack. Bake for 8 to 10 minutes more taking care not to over brown. Remove form oven. Cool in pans for 1 hour or until granola reaches room temperature.

Leny Young, Ohio

Candy

LOW FAT MICROWAVE FUDGE

1 pound confectioners' sugar

⅔ cup cocoa powder

¼ teaspoon salt

¼ cup milk

2 teaspoons vanilla extract

2 tablespoons margarine

¼ cup finely chopped nuts (optional)

Combine ingredients in large microwave safe bowl. Cook on HIGH for 1 minute and stir. Cook 1 more minute or until smooth. Beat well and spread in foil-lined 8-inch square pan. Chill 1hour and cut into squares.

Jan Whittaker, California

CROCK POT CANDY

2 (16-ounce) jars unsalted roasted peanuts

1 (4-ounce) bar German chocolate

12 ounces chocolate chips

24 ounces white almond bark

Layer ingredients in a large crock pot in the order given. Do not mix or stir. Heat on low for two hours without lifting the lid. After two hours, stir well and drop by teaspoon onto waxed paper. Cool until firm before lifting from paper.

Brenda Martinez, Alabama

PECAN PRALINES

3 cups sugar

1 teaspoon baking soda

⅛ teaspoon salt

1 cup buttermilk

¾ cup light corn syrup

2 tablespoons butter

2 cups pecans

Combine sugar, baking soda and salt. Add buttermilk and syrup. Cook and stir and bring to a boil over medium heat. Cook and stir to softball stage (234 degrees). Remove from heat. Add butter. Stir in pecans. Beat until mixture is thick enough to drop from spoon onto waxed paper. If mixture gets too thick, add 1 teaspoon hot water. Makes 45 pralines.

EASY AND SCRUMPTIOUS PRALINES

1 cup whipping cream

1 (16-ounce) box light brown sugar

2 cups pecans

2 tablespoons butter, at room temperature

1 overflowing teaspoon vanilla extract

Water

Mix whipping cream and brown sugar in a microwave safe 2 quart glass bowl, preferably with a handle. Microwave on HIGH for 11 minutes in a 1000 watt oven or 13 minutes in a 750 watt oven. It is not necessary to stir. Remove very carefully. The mixture will be extremely hot.

Add pecans, butter and vanilla to hot mixture, stirring until mixture is stiff. Add 2 to 3 teaspoons water and stir until mixed. Immediately begin to drop by teaspoonfuls onto foil. Use another teaspoon to release mixture if it sticks to the spoon, because mixture is very hot. Allow to cool before removing from foil. Makes about 3 dozen.

Marilyn Hamner, Texas

PECAN ROLL

1 jar Hippolite (same as marshmallow crème)

1 (16-ounce) box confectioners' sugar

1 teaspoon vanilla extract

3 tablespoons cream

29 caramels

Chopped nuts

Combine Hippolite, confectioners' sugar, vanilla, and cream. If a little too stiff, add a little more milk, be careful not to add too much for mixture must be hard and firm. When it's creamed together good, roll into a long roll and place in refrigerator to harden.

Melt the caramels over hot water. When you think the refrigerated candy is hard enough, cut into small lengths. Roll each piece in melted caramel, then quickly roll in finely chopped nuts. Return candy to refrigerator to harden.

Addalie McMinn, Texas

A delicious pecan treat, especially for parties

GLAZED PECANS

1 cup packed brown sugar

⅛ teaspoon cream of tartar

½ teaspoon cinnamon

¼ cup water

1 teaspoon vanilla extract

2 cups pecan halves

In a saucepan, combine sugar, cream of tartar, cinnamon and water. Heat to about 250 degrees; stirring constantly. This takes about 8 to 10 minutes. Add vanilla and pecans. Remove from heat and spread on waxed paper to dry.

Bernadine Levy, Colorado

ORANGE PECANS

2 cups sugar

¾ cup orange juice

1 tablespoon grated orange rind

3 cups pecan halves

In a large, heavy saucepan (Dutch oven size) cook sugar and orange juice to soft ball stage (236 to 240 degrees). Mixture will boil and bubble up. Turn off heat; add orange rind and pecans. Stir with wooden spoon until mixture turns cream color, about 5 to 7 minutes. Remove from heat. Pour and spread onto a cookie sheet. When cool, break apart.

Judy Krohn, Texas

SUGAR PECANS

1 cup sugar

1 teaspoon cinnamon

½ cup milk

1 teaspoon vanilla extract

3 cups pecan halves

In a large, heavy saucepan (Dutch oven size) cook sugar, cinnamon and milk to soft ball stage (236 to 240 degrees). Mixture will boil and bubble up. Turn off heat; add vanilla and pecans. Stir with wooden spoon until mixture is well coated. Remove from heat. Pour and spread onto a cookie sheet. When cool, break apart.

Judy Krohn, Texas

PECAN BRITTLE

Cook 1 cup sugar with 1 cup white Karo syrup to 280 degrees on candy thermometer.

Add 2 cups pecans. Cook and stir to hard crack stage (290 degrees). Remove and add 1 teaspoon baking soda. Mix well. Pour on greased cookie sheet. Spread. Cool Break in small pieces.

Joyce Latta, Texas

PEANUT BUTTER CRUNCH

Mix and bring to a full boil over medium heat:
   2 cups sugar
   1½ cups dark syrup

Remove from heat and add:
   1 (18-ounce) jar peanut butter (2 cups)
   3 tablespoons vanilla extract

Mix well and pour over:
   10 cups Rice Krispies cereal

Drop by tablespoon on waxed paper to cool.
   Jan Whittaker, California

PEANUT BUTTER AND CHOCOLATE BARK

   20 ounces light almond bark or one pound white chocolate
   ½ cup creamy peanut butter (for variety, chunky can be
      used)
   1 cup peanut butter chips
   1 (6-ounce) bag semi-sweet chocolate chips

Mix almond bark, peanut butter, and peanut butter chips in a microwave safe bowl. Place in microwave for about 3-5 minutes at 50% power. Check at about 3 minutes and stir. Continue checking and stirring every 45 seconds until all ingredients are melted and smooth. Do not let the ingredients burn. Spread almond bark mixture on aluminum foil.

   Melt semi-sweet chocolate chips in a separate microwave safe bowl. Begin checking and stirring after about 1 minute in microwave on 50% power. Drizzle melted chocolate over almond bark mixture and use a knife to swirl into a patterns.

   Chill and break apart into pieces. Store in the refrigerator in a baggie or sealed container. Can be refrigerated for up to a month.

   Judy Krohn, Texas

BUTTERY ALMOND CRUNCH

1 tablespoon butter
½ cup butter (no substitutes)
½ cup sugar
1 tablespoon light corn syrup
1 cup sliced almonds
2 chocolate bark squares, melted

Line an 8-inch square pan with foil; butter the foil with ½ tablespoon butter. Set aside. Spread the sides of a heavy saucepan with ½ tablespoon butter. Add ½ cup butter, sugar and corn syrup. Bring to a boil over medium-high heat, stirring constantly. Cook and stir until mixture is golden brown, about 4 minutes. Stir in almonds. Quickly pour into prepared pan. Chill until firm. Invert pan and remove foil. Break candy into pieces. Melt chocolate bark on power 5 in microwave. Dip part of each piece in chocolate bark.

Pat Fenno, Iowa

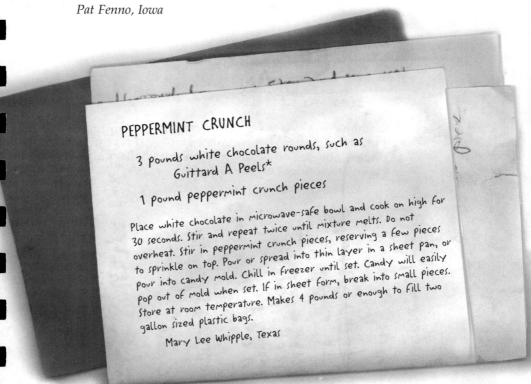

PEPPERMINT CRUNCH

3 pounds white chocolate rounds, such as Guittard A Peels*

1 pound peppermint crunch pieces

Place white chocolate in microwave-safe bowl and cook on high for 30 seconds. Stir and repeat twice until mixture melts. Do not overheat. Stir in peppermint crunch pieces, reserving a few pieces to sprinkle on top. Pour or spread into thin layer in a sheet pan, or pour into candy mold. Chill in freezer until set. Candy will easily pop out of mold when set. If in sheet form, break into small pieces. Store at room temperature. Makes 4 pounds or enough to fill two gallon sized plastic bags.

Mary Lee Whipple, Texas

TEXAS WHITE TRASH

Melt in microwave:

> 7 squares white almond bark

Stir in:

> 2 cups Honey Graham Cereal
>
> 2 cups pretzels (snap or small)
>
> 2 cups mixed nuts

Spread on waxed paper lined cookie sheet. Chill. Break into small pieces.

Joyce Latta, Texas

BON BONS

> 2 sticks margarine, melted
>
> 2 cups crushed graham crackers
>
> 1 cup packed coconut
>
> 1 cup crunchy peanut butter
>
> 1 (16-ounce) box confectioners' sugar
>
> 1 (12-ounce) package chocolate chips
>
> ½ inch wax, cut from block

Combine margarine, graham crackers, coconut, peanut butter and sugar. Melt chocolate chips and wax in top of double boiler. Roll candy mixture into balls and dip in chocolate. Refrigerate 15 minutes.

Marilyn Erlandson, Pennsylvania

GRANDMOM'S KISSES

2 egg whites

2 heaping cups confectioners' sugar

Juice of ½ lemon

Chopped nuts

Combine egg whites and confectioners' sugar with a spoon, then beat at high speed until mixture forms peaks. Add lemon juice. Beat again to peak. Add more confectioners' sugar if not stiff enough. Fold in chopped nuts. Drop by teaspoons onto a greased and floured cookie sheet. Bake at 325 degrees for 10 minutes.

Jean Krest, Colorado

JUDY'S CARAMEL CANDIES

    1 pound butter
    2 pounds brown sugar
    2 cups white or light corn syrup
    2 (14-ounce) cans sweetened condensed milk
    2 teaspoons vanilla extract

Melt butter, add sugar and syrup. Slowly stir in milk. Cook over medium heat, stirring until your arm falls off or it reaches 245 degrees. Add vanilla. Pour into buttered pan. Cool, cut and wrap.

Judy Dashiell, Minnesota

CARAMEL CORN

Combine and boil 5 minutes:
    1 cup margarine
    2 cups packed brown sugar
    ½ cup dark brown syrup
    1 teaspoon salt

Remove from heat and add:
    ½ teaspoon baking soda.

Pour over:
    5 quarts popped corn (1 cup unpopped popcorn)

Bake 1 hour, stirring every 15 minutes. Remove from oven and continue stirring while cooling to keep popcorn from sticking together. Store in tightly covered container. Freezes well.

Betty Kuckes, Wisconsin

CONTRIBUTORS

Kay Alexander
Lydia Alexander, Texas
Ann L. Anderson, Pennsylvania
Mary Beth Anderson, Texas
Terri Anderson, California
Kay Atkins, Texas
Mary Baker, Washington
Susan Barry, Texas
Bonnie Battles
Jean Beall, Michigan
Pat Best, Colorado
Edith Anne Blood, Tennessee
Judy Boegler, Texas
Jeannine Bowles, Washington
Jackie Brandmiller, Wisconsin
Kathy Bratton, Texas
Josie Brummet, Kentucky
Nancy Nichols Bryan, Arizona
Beth Burt, Texas
Marian Butcher, Pennsylvania
Sue Cardinal, Minnesota
Ghita Carter, Texas
Keith Carter, Texas
JoAnn Christal, Texas
Yvonne Constantino, Texas
Judy Cormany, Texas
Eleanor Cowan, Texas
Joyce Crane, Texas
Judy Dashiell, Minnesota
Darlene Davasligil, Wisconsin
Jane Davidson, Texas
Chuck Dawson, Michigan
Laverne Dawson, Kansas
Nancy DeVries, Illinois
Anna Laura Doane, Indiana
Bunny Doucet, New Jersey
Betty Dougherty, Texas
Grace Arledge DuBose, Texas
Myrna DuFord, Texas

Doris Emmert, Nevada
Marilyn Erlandson, Pennsylvania
Sue Everett, Texas
Elaine Fawcett, Texas
Doris Feldman, Arizona
Pat Fenno, Iowa
Lorraine Franklin, Texas
Ruth Frederickson, Wisconsin
Mary Genenwein, Texas
Lyn Gogis, California
Henry Graalfs, Iowa
Zina Versaggi Graalfs, Florida
Nila Griffin, Texas
Marilyn Hamner, Texas
Beverly Harrison, Texas
Bob Heitzman, Iowa
Jim Hester, Texas
Myra Hill, Texas
Donna Hixon, Indiana
Liz Hobbs, California
Dean Ingram
Judy Ingram
June Isgitt, Texas
Hal Jones
Ruth Jones, Kentucky
Cindy Kelly, Texas
Phyllis Kelso, Minnesota
Barbara Konetchy, Massachusetts
Janice Konetchy, Massachusetts
Jean Krest, Colorado
Judy Krohn, Texas
Betty Kuckes, Wisconsin
Janet LaCava, New York
Bill LaFrance, Louisiana
Emily LaFrance, Louisiana
Barbara Langford, Washington and Texas
Joyce Latta , Texas
Peggy Laverentz, Texas
Carol Lazarus, Connecticut
Gerry Lessups, California
Sandy Lester, Ohio
Bernadine Levy, Colorado

Aline Babb Lewis, Texas
Bob Lilly, Texas
Sally Loder, Ohio
Faith Love
Suzanne Lukens, Washington
Fay Luker, Washington
Lou Magel, Michigan
Juanita Magnuson, Alabama
Andrea Martin, Texas
Brenda Martinez, Alabama
Addalie McMinn, Texas
Elizabeth Miller, Louisiana
Elizabeth Miller, New Jersey
Joan Miller, Texas
Joe Miller, New York
Wanda Mueller, Texas
Sharon Odom, Texas
Liz Offord, Texas
Betty Lou O'Rourke, Michigan
Adrienne Padfield, Texas
Lois Patterson, Wisconsin
Armeda Pauken, Ohio
Arlene Perkins, Illinois
Bunny Petty, Texas
Karen Peveto, Texas
Margaret Purkey, Texas
Phyllis Rademacher, Iowa
Jim Ralston, Illinois
Mary Ralston, Illinois
Cordelia Razek, Louisiana
Pam Redus, Texas
Leona Resteiner, Michigan
Barbara Rhoades, Texas
Ruth Rice, Texas
Robbin Roberts, Texas
Jocelyn Rogers, Texas
Lynda Rowan, Texas
Millie Royer, Texas
Lola Russell
Carol Ryan, Kansas
Pat Sampson, Iowa

Jeri Lynn Sandusky, Utah
Cheryl Schmidt, Texas
Jan Schmidt, Texas
Joann Schoen, California
Jeanne Schroeder, Michigan
Betty Sellers, Texas
Betty Ann Sheffloe, Nebraska
Marilyn Sietsema, Illinois
Christine Smart, Texas
Mary Q. Smith, Texas
Pat Steige, Arkansas
Shirley Sterling, Texas
Betty Stockman, North Dakota
Bev Tackett, Missouri
Nancy Tarvin, Texas
Shirley Thomas, Texas
Perry Thomas, Texas
Connie Timko, Illinois
Perry Thompson, Texas
Ase Touba, Minnesota
Martha Trowbridge, Illinois
Gene Uselton, Colorado
Peggy Uselton, Colorado
Jim Van Artsdalen, Missouri
Winola Van Artsdalen, Kansas
Becky Van Vranken, Washington, DC
Maureen Vogl, Kansas
Liv Volland, Wisconsin
Cook Voltz, Ohio
Diane Watkins, Wisconsin
Jan Watson, Illinois
Mary Lee Whipple, Texas
Jan Whittaker, California
Betty Wilkins, California
Cheryl Wills, South Carolina
Nancy Wright, Arizona
Leny Young, Ohio

INDEX

Please send the following:

_____ copies of *Kickin' Back in the Kitchen* @ $19.95 (U.S.) each $_____

Postage and handling $3.50 for first book $_____

Postage and handling $1.00 for each additional book $_____

Texas residents $1.93 sales tax per book $_____

TOTAL $_____

Check or Credit Card (U.S. funds only)

Charge to my ☐ Master Card ☐ Visa Card

account# _____

expiration date _____

signature _____

MAIL TO:
P&P Publishing
3802 Antelope Trail
Temple, TX 76504

Name _____

Address _____

City _____ State _____ Zip _____

Phone _____ Email _____

ORDER ON LINE: www.pandppublishing.com   TOLL FREE: 888-458-1229

— —

Please send the following:

_____ copies of *Kickin' Back in the Kitchen* @ $19.95 (U.S.) each $_____

Postage and handling $3.50 for first book $_____

Postage and handling $1.00 for each additional book $_____

Texas residents $1.93 sales tax per book $_____

TOTAL $_____

Check or Credit Card (U.S. funds only)

Charge to my ☐ Master Card ☐ Visa Card

account# _____

expiration date _____

signature _____

MAIL TO:
P&P Publishing
3802 Antelope Trail
Temple, TX 76504

Name _____

Address _____

City _____ State _____ Zip _____

Phone _____ Email _____

ORDER ON LINE: www.pandppublishing.com   TOLL FREE: 888-458-1229

Please send the following:

_____ copies of *Kickin' Back in the Kitchen* @ $19.95 (U.S.) each $_____

Postage and handling $3.50 for first book $_____

Postage and handling $1.00 for each additional book $_____

Texas residents $1.93 sales tax per book $_____

TOTAL $_____

Check or Credit Card (U.S. funds only)

Charge to my ☐ Master Card ☐ Visa Card

account# _____

expiration date _____

signature _____

> **MAIL TO:**
> **P&P Publishing**
> **3802 Antelope Trail**
> **Temple, TX 76504**

Name _____

Address _____

City _____ State _____ Zip _____

Phone _____ Email _____

ORDER ON LINE: www.pandppublishing.com   TOLL FREE: 888-458-1229

- -

Please send the following:

_____ copies of *Kickin' Back in the Kitchen* @ $19.95 (U.S.) each $_____

Postage and handling $3.50 for first book $_____

Postage and handling $1.00 for each additional book $_____

Texas residents $1.93 sales tax per book $_____

TOTAL $_____

Check or Credit Card (U.S. funds only)

Charge to my ☐ Master Card ☐ Visa Card

account# _____

expiration date _____

signature _____

> **MAIL TO:**
> **P&P Publishing**
> **3802 Antelope Trail**
> **Temple, TX 76504**

Name _____

Address _____

City _____ State _____ Zip _____

Phone _____ Email _____

ORDER ON LINE: www.pandppublishing.com   TOLL FREE: 888-458-1229

Please send the following:

_____ copies of *Kickin' Back in the Kitchen* @ $19.95 (U.S.) each $_____

Postage and handling $3.50 for first book $_____

Postage and handling $1.00 for each additional book $_____

Texas residents $1.93 sales tax per book $_____

TOTAL $_____

Check or Credit Card (U.S. funds only)

Charge to my ☐ Master Card ☐ Visa Card

account# _____

expiration date _____

signature _____

MAIL TO:
P&P Publishing
3802 Antelope Trail
Temple, TX 76504

Name _____

Address _____

City _____ State _____ Zip _____

Phone _____ Email _____

ORDER ON LINE: www.pandppublishing.com   TOLL FREE: 888-458-1229

— —

Please send the following:

_____ copies of *Kickin' Back in the Kitchen* @ $19.95 (U.S.) each $_____

Postage and handling $3.50 for first book $_____

Postage and handling $1.00 for each additional book $_____

Texas residents $1.93 sales tax per book $_____

TOTAL $_____

Check or Credit Card (U.S. funds only)

Charge to my ☐ Master Card ☐ Visa Card

account# _____

expiration date _____

signature _____

MAIL TO:
P&P Publishing
3802 Antelope Trail
Temple, TX 76504

Name _____

Address _____

City _____ State _____ Zip _____

Phone _____ Email _____

ORDER ON LINE: www.pandppublishing.com   TOLL FREE: 888-458-1229

Please send the following:

_____ copies of *Kickin' Back in the Kitchen* @ $19.95 (U.S.) each $_____

Postage and handling $3.50 for first book $_____

Postage and handling $1.00 for each additional book $_____

Texas residents $1.93 sales tax per book $_____

TOTAL $_____

Check or Credit Card (U.S. funds only)

Charge to my ☐ Master Card   ☐ Visa Card

account# _____

expiration date _____

signature _____

> **MAIL TO:**
> **P&P Publishing**
> **3802 Antelope Trail**
> **Temple, TX 76504**

Name _____

Address _____

City _____ State _____ Zip _____

Phone _____ Email _____

ORDER ON LINE: www.pandppublishing.com   **TOLL FREE: 888-458-1229**

- -

Please send the following:

_____ copies of *Kickin' Back in the Kitchen* @ $19.95 (U.S.) each $_____

Postage and handling $3.50 for first book $_____

Postage and handling $1.00 for each additional book $_____

Texas residents $1.93 sales tax per book $_____

TOTAL $_____

Check or Credit Card (U.S. funds only)

Charge to my ☐ Master Card   ☐ Visa Card

account# _____

expiration date _____

signature _____

> **MAIL TO:**
> **P&P Publishing**
> **3802 Antelope Trail**
> **Temple, TX 76504**

Name _____

Address _____

City _____ State _____ Zip _____

Phone _____ Email _____

ORDER ON LINE: www.pandppublishing.com   **TOLL FREE: 888-458-1229**

Please send the following:

_____ copies of *Kickin' Back in the Kitchen* @ $19.95 (U.S.) each $_____

Postage and handling $3.50 for first book $_____

Postage and handling $1.00 for each additional book $_____

Texas residents $1.93 sales tax per book $_____

TOTAL $_____

Check or Credit Card (U.S. funds only)

Charge to my ☐ Master Card ☐ Visa Card

account# _____

expiration date _____

signature _____

> **MAIL TO:**
> **P&P Publishing**
> **3802 Antelope Trail**
> **Temple, TX 76504**

Name _____

Address _____

City _____ State _____ Zip _____

Phone _____ Email _____

ORDER ON LINE: www.pandppublishing.com   **TOLL FREE: 888-458-1229**

— —

Please send the following:

_____ copies of *Kickin' Back in the Kitchen* @ $19.95 (U.S.) each $_____

Postage and handling $3.50 for first book $_____

Postage and handling $1.00 for each additional book $_____

Texas residents $1.93 sales tax per book $_____

TOTAL $_____

Check or Credit Card (U.S. funds only)

Charge to my ☐ Master Card ☐ Visa Card

account# _____

expiration date _____

signature _____

> **MAIL TO:**
> **P&P Publishing**
> **3802 Antelope Trail**
> **Temple, TX 76504**

Name _____

Address _____

City _____ State _____ Zip _____

Phone _____ Email _____

ORDER ON LINE: www.pandppublishing.com   **TOLL FREE: 888-458-1229**

YA'LL COME BACK NOW!